THE THINGS THAT ARE UNSEEN

THE AUTOBIOGRAPHY OF AN AVIATOR

TREVOR VELLACOTT

For the things that are seen are Temporal
But the things that are unseen are Eternal

St Paul the Apostle

Cover picture. Virgin Atlantic 747-400
Sunrise landing London Gatwick
Courtesy Ryan Hemmings

First published 2012

Published for Trevor Vellacott by Verité CM Ltd.

ISBN No: 978-1-907636-42-4

Cover design, Print and production management by Verité CM Ltd, Worthing, West Sussex BN12 4HJ. UK.
www.veritecm.com

FOREWORD

BY CAPTAIN GEORGE NEWBY

I am honoured to have been asked to write this foreword to a superb autobiography.

I have known the author as a colleague and friend for many years. Over this time I had no idea about the unusual and fascinating achievements of his earlier life both under on and over the ground, as recorded in this comprehensive history. The memory and attention to detail are truly remarkable.

Trevor's strong and consistent religious convictions are also much to be admired.

As a fellow retired airline pilot I have to raise my hat in celebration of what you are about to read.

George Newby.
December 2011

ACKNOWLEDGEMENTS

This is a heartfelt thank you to all those who have made contributions and suggestions in the writing of this volume.

To John Manning who read the initial efforts and suggested a complete change of format. He then re-read the entire script, editing errors (many!) and suggesting various textual changes.

To Wendy Baye (USA) who also very kindly read the text, translated it into 'American' and corrected many errors, technical, grammatical and in the punctuation. I have yet to use the American version but it remains on hold should there ever be a demand.

To Robert Stockwell who very kindly proof read the entire script and for his subsequent comments and suggestions.

To Captain Ray Smith whose contribution is fascinating to those in 'the trade' and again much appreciated.

To Captain George Newby who has kindly written an over generous Foreword despite suffering ill health

To the many others who have assisted in various ways, too many to mention.

Finally, my wife Diane has patiently suffered many 'silent evenings' while I wrote the script. She has been a continuous supporter and encourager.

Thank you again, one and all.

CONTENTS

Section III Airlines

Section IV Arabia

Section V Atlantic Airlines

PROLOGUE

An uneventful daylight, thirteen hour flight from Shanghai to London Heathrow. After landing I park the A340-600 on the allotted stand, shut down the engines and together with my two co-pilots, complete the post flight procedures. With the passengers disembarked I say goodbye to the crew. The two co-pilots know this is my last flight (I have not told them but they know!). The cabin crew do not know so there is no post flight fuss. I just say goodbye to them all and thank them for a good trip in exactly the same way as I have done at the end of every flight for many years. It is time to go home!

So for me ends 42 years of flying commercial aircraft. Initially there was bush flying for a mining and earthmoving company in Western Australia. This was followed by Agricultural Aviation in the UK, flying for a major UK airline, a Middle Eastern Flag carrier and finally 23 years for a slightly curious, almost eccentric UK Long Haul carrier. A month or so later totting up the logbook (a little pointless as it really doesn't matter anymore but I hate loose ends) the final total is 26,011 hours flying time. In this day and age where airlines work their crews to the bone this is probably far from a record for a pilot's career. At age 64 I can carry on for a further year but with the Credit Crunch and the company looking to shed pilots, voluntary redundancy seems to be the right way to go.

In the winter that follows together with my lovely wife we escape the appalling UK weather and take 3 months' retirement vacation in Australia and New Zealand. It seems a good time to commence writing down some of the aviation experiences although a few of the incidents were recorded in earlier years shortly after they occurred. Some of what has been written has nothing to do with aviation whatsoever!

As an instructor I used to tell trainees, especially trainee captains, always to tell passengers the truth but not necessarily the whole truth. To give an actual example. At the top of descent into London Gatwick in an ancient 747-200 at 3am on a winter's morning sometime in the late nineteen eighties. We are running many hours late on a flight from Tokyo. An engine threatens an imminent mandatory shut down due to the fact there is an oil leak. The surface wind is blowing from the South West at 50kts (60 miles per hour) generating a cross wind close to the limits allowable for this aircraft type. I apologise to the passengers for the fact that we are running late and advise that it is 'a bit blowy on the ground' so the approach will be slightly uncomfortable.

This is the truth but far from the whole truth but it is all that the passengers need to know. In the same way I omit details in this record for various reasons where appropriate and many names are changed. Where and when is left to the imagination of the reader!

As an avid reader myself I am always curious to know what makes the writer 'tick'. Autobiographies should give the answer but the problem is that such writings tend to vanity. I would suggest that to discover more about an author, you need to read his published fiction which is far more likely to provide a window into his mind. I will never write any fiction so regrettably in the following meanderings the reader will have to sort the wood from the chaff himself.

SECTION I

AUSTRALIA

1. Meekatherra

Professor Stephen Hawking excelled in his complex and semi incomprehensible '*Brief History of Time*'. Should persistence, patience, time and longevity endure, it would be a most pleasurable exercise to compile a similarly complex and equally incomprehensible 'Brief history of alarm clocks'.

These fiendish devices appear in a variety of shapes, sizes and disguises; issue an infinite variety of noises and their effects on the human soul can be compared to the Richter scale in inverse proportion to the hour at which they are set to perform their programmed duty. Their sonic attributes vary from the simple ring to the outrageous discordant buzzer or radio channel, as decided by the manufacturer or programmed by the user. In a lifetime of transiting hotels I have learned that the priority on entering yet another room for the first time is not to check the fire escape as the health and safety gurus advise, but for the sake of personal equanimity to check the alarm device. It is necessary to ensure that the previous occupant has not programmed some outrageous request, whether for the perverted pleasure of destroying the peaceful sleep of the next occupant or, because they genuinely need awakening at such an ungodly hour.

This procedure in itself can be a tiresome exercise as the variety and complexity can test the fatigued brain to the uttermost in determining how to mute the offending device. Since many also double as a luminous bedside clock the ultimate solution of unplugging from the mains is not satisfactory. Even this desperate measure is thwarted by the more perverted manufacturers who add a back-up battery to ensure maximum annoyance to the hapless user.

And so it was that I awoke at 12.30am, something like 8.7 on the Richter scale, to the painful ring/rattle of the alarm clock. This was early in my aviation career and the bedside device was a simple clock that emitted a soporific tick-tock. It was adorned with a bell and on the face it said 'Westclox' and 'Scotland'. (This was before the days when everything said 'Made in China'.)

After a hurried shower, a scalding cup of over-hot coffee and a fifteen minute drive through the deserted streets I arrived at the light aircraft parking area at Perth International airport. I walked over to the Flight planning office in the Department of Civil Aviation office building and began the pre-flight paperwork. Submitting the required flight plan after about fifteen minutes of careful preparation was not the usual pleasure as the flight service officer on duty happened to be a particularly moody character whose inherent sour disposition was no doubt exacerbated by having to work at this hour of the morning. He questioned every detail of the plan before grudgingly adding his signature.

Arriving back at the aircraft parking area I was greeted by the company dispatcher, a delightful character by the name of Kevin who invariably managed a cheerful smile regardless of the hour, day or night. Kevin produced the manifest of passengers, baggage and freight and as usual there was far too much to be fitted into the tiny Beech B58 Baron. After some fifteen minutes of careful organisation, all five passengers were seated and the baggage and freight was installed in the nose compartment with extra items behind the rear seats. Kevin looked with dismay at the quantity of freight left behind and muttered something about there being no room on the next flight before loading it back into his truck and with a cheerful wave, driving off.

Walking slowly around the aeroplane with my torch I inspected the control surfaces, landing gear and tyres, checked the oil level in each engine and examined the propeller blades and a host of other details watchful for anything which could cause trouble later on. Finally satisfied, I climbed onto the wing and stepped across the semi-comatose passenger in the other front seat, closed the door and began the start-up procedure. Number one engine burst into life after turning over briefly on the starter followed by number two, the radios crackled on the loudspeaker as they were turned on and after two minutes of checking instruments and switches Perth tower responded to my request for taxi clearance with the reply,

"Echo Zulu Alpha cleared to taxi and hold short of runway 20."

Echo Zulu Alpha was the aircraft registration which is a shortened version of the Australian registration letters VH-EZA.

Engines at 1000rpm to warm up and brakes released I taxied the few hundred metres to the holding point for runway 20. Running up each engine in turn I checked the magnetos for excessive rpm drop and exercised the propeller pitch and feathering mechanism. With all pre-flight checks completed I asked for take-off clearance.

"Echo Zulu Alpha, cleared for take-off, runway two zero, wind south westerly at less than five" came the response.

I lined up on the centreline, pushed both throttles steadily forward to the quadrant stops and the aeroplane began to roll. The time was 2:05am.

With steadily increasing speed the runway lights began

to flash by until at 90 knots[1], gently lifting the nose, I took the machine into the air. Entering a shallow climb I raised the landing gear and switched off the landing lights. The speed increased to 120 knots and I eased the nose up a little further to commence a normal climb. At 400 feet I reduced to climb power and then patiently synchronised the engines until they ran sweetly and in tune with each other. A gentle left turn brought the aircraft back onto a Northerly heading to intercept a magnetic track of 030° from Perth which was the first leg into the vast empty interior of this the world's second most under-populated continent

Perth tower cleared the aeroplane to the next en-route frequency and with probably no other aircraft in the skies over Western Australia at that time of the morning the clearance to the final cruising altitude was quickly issued.

Fifteen minutes later at 9000 feet I levelled off and reduced to cruise power. With the auto pilot engaged I adjusted it to a suitable heading and settled back for the long duty period ahead.

Turning the instrument lights down to the dimmest setting possible, I reclined my seat as far as was diplomatic in the cramped cabin and commenced the paperwork by the diminutive glow of the map light. I completed the flight plan, filling in the ETA (Estimated time of arrival) at each reporting point based on the departure time from Perth ending up with the expected time of arrival at the first stop for refuelling at Meekatharra.

I worked out a PNR which was a company requirement. PNR stands for 'Point of no return' and is a little mathematical exercise to determine the last point at which the aeroplane can return to its point of departure or other suitable airfield with the fuel available on board. Since

1 Knots. Nautical miles per hour. Distance and Speed used in aviation. 1 nautical mile = 15% more than a statute mile. See glossary for expanded description.

Meekatharra was the only airfield with lighting available and there was no alternate this was a vital piece of information. I completed some of the company paperwork with names of passengers, the freight and its sundry destinations and made some fuel computations to decide how much would be required at Meekatharra for the next leg to Dampier. The wheat-belt was invisible with no moon and shortly after passing the first reporting point at Ballidu I established communications with Perth using the HF radio which was for long range communications.

The stars were brilliant as always in this part of the world. There was little pollution with the prevailing Westerlies bringing clear Indian Ocean air across the continent and after the wheat-belt no lights at all on the ground from horizon to horizon. Mount Singleton, unseen but estimated by a combination of radio beacons and dead reckoning came and went and I duly called Perth and Meekatharra giving the position, altitude and estimate for Mount Magnet, the next reporting point.

I had made this particular trip many times over the previous three years while working for the large mining and earth moving company who were my employers. Apart from the daytime summer trips when there was the drudgery of the thermal turbulence and circumnavigation of the odd thunderstorm there was rarely any variation of the routine although the job could never be described as boring. More eventful were the shorter hops around the various bases and camps in the Pilbara area of the North West as this was 1970 and the mineral boom was in full swing. Mountains of iron ore had been discovered inland and huge railway building projects had been undertaken to take this ore to ports on the coast from Mount Newman, 250 miles inland and others such as Parapardoo, Goldsworthy and Mount Tom Price. In addition to this there were the company's own wide range of projects amongst which were a Solar Salt project near

Dampier, a Manganese mine at a curious place on the edge of the Great Sandy Desert known simply by its mining claim number, 'Camp 487', a copper mine at Thaduna and oil rig supply work in the Great Sandy Desert proper.

"Echo Zulu Alpha, this is Perth!"

The call came through crackling a little with normal HF static. This was unusual between reporting points but there was also a sense of urgency in the tone which encouraged instant attention.

"Perth, this is Echo Zulu Alpha, go ahead."

"Meekatharra is reporting 200 meters in fog, suggest you return to Perth, advise intentions."

The peace and routine of the flight was instantly over. A quick check of the Point of No Return revealed that it had been passed 10 minutes before.

Should a professional aviator read these lines his immediate question would be;

"How can you dispatch an instrument rules flight without fuel on board for an alternate airport?"

The answer lies in the peculiarities of the Australian situation. Due to the vast distances not only light aircraft but also the airlines are permitted dispatch to a destination without carrying alternate fuel provided the weather at the destination is forecast to be above certain very strictly defined minima. On this particular night the forecaster was terribly in error.

With rising alarm I considered options finding very quickly that there were none. Return to Perth was impossible with the fuel remaining. Mount Magnet ahead was possessed of a dirt airstrip but no lighting and getting anybody out at that time of the night to rig up some lights was fanciful to say the least... a great pity as by this time the lights of the township of Mount Magnet were clearly visible ahead. First things first, I reduced power on the engines and twiddling the little fuel computer (actually a sophisticated slide rule and long before the days of portable electronic calculators), worked out the engine settings for minimum fuel flow. The engines ground down to a very unfamiliar 1800 revs and the manifold pressure to 20 inches all of which was not at all good for them but the low fuel flows were marginally gratifying. By now both Perth and Meekatharra were demanding my attention on the HF radio. As politely as the circumstances warranted I told them to standby while trying desperately to formulate a viable plan. Fear paralyses the brain and the awakening interest of the passengers, who had heard far too much on the loudspeaker, did not ease the situation. Carnarvon on the coast was an all-night airfield but was only slightly closer than Perth and in the time available a positive calculation was not possible.

"Perth/Meekatharra, this is Echo Zulu Alpha"

"Echo Zulu Alpha, this is Perth, go ahead."

"Echo Zulu Alpha, have reduced power for maximum endurance. Intentions are to proceed to Meekatharra for one approach followed by diversion to Carnarvon if unsuccessful... calculated fuel remaining on arrival Carnarvon 10 minutes."

This was largely guesswork but it was gratifying to hear that this decision was not questioned. An argument or any further hassle was not going to be of any benefit at this stage. Meanwhile the airspeed had dropped by some 30 knots with the reduced power settings giving a true airspeed, taking into account altitude and temperature, of 160 knots. Meekatharra by now was audible on the short range (VHF) radio as the aircraft passed over Mount Magnet and it was at least comforting to hear the clear voice of the flight service officer. I passed the revised estimated arrival time and the radio operator confirmed that the weather situation was light and variable wind, with visibility 200 meters in fog.

As carefully as possible in the deepening crisis I made some simple decisions. Meekatharra had only very basic facilities for an instrument approach. (For the aeronautically minded, this consisted of an NDB[1] and a DME[2]). A procedural approach taking up to ten minutes, normally a mandatory requirement in the circumstances, would use far too much fuel. I decided to descend direct to a point about one mile short of the centre of the airfield using the official minimum instrument approach height which was 550ft above the ground. If the runway wasn't in sight at that point I would descend to 300ft above the ground which was totally illegal but desperate situations call for desperate measures. Fortunately I knew the airfield very well from three years of regular operation in and out and was aware of the position of the radio masts and other obstructions.

Leaving cruising altitude, as calmly as possible, I began the approach preparations and was able to see in the starlight that the fog was in waves across the ground. Praying silently that the runway would be between waves I gradually descended into the top of the fog which was about 1200 feet above ground level. The light from the aircraft's rotating beacon bounced back defiantly from the enveloping mist as an insolent reminder that all was far from well. The official minimum height of 550 feet above the ground came and went but suddenly at about half a mile out and 300 feet above the ground there were the runway lights dimly visible from left to right across the nose. I turned parallel to the runway lights keeping them firmly in sight and then, grossly out of order in a professional sense, steep turned in the darkness on to a very short final approach. Sweetly and suddenly with utter relief the runway lights were straight ahead and in a few seconds the wheels were on the ground. Closing the throttles and gently braking I made the turn off to the building that served as an excuse for a terminal at Meekatharra.

---

1 & 2 NDB and DME. See glossary for expanded description.

Seriously shaken, even with the advantage of young years and displaying as little emotion as possible to the passengers I taxied up to the refuelling area. The cheerful greeting of the Mobil refueller who suddenly seemed to have an even friendlier face than his usual happy disposition broke the silence which followed cutting the engines.

Leaving the passengers to have a smoke and a little exercise I wandered over to the flight service centre. The radio operator with no traffic other than the recent arrival emerged from the lighted doorway to have a chat in the damp night air.

"Cleared up a little in the last few minutes" he said giving no indication that he had any grasp of the enormity of what had just occurred.

Those 'few minutes' could easily have resulted in the deaths of six people in a fuel starvation accident while attempting the last desperate option of trying to reach Carnarvon. The radio operator was not responsible for the meteorological debacle so there was not much to be said, however he seemed a little uneasy and his remark confirmed my suspicions.

"Are you going to file an incident report?" he enquired slightly too casually.

Filing an incident report was serious business and by the relatively inflexible nature of the authorities there would be trouble for someone. During my first year working for the company I had suffered an engine failure on a single engine aeroplane. An incident report was mandatory in this instance and I had written up the required documentation in great detail embellishing in my favour all the things that went right and playing down all the things I had mis-managed. I was about to hand it in at the local aviation authority office when a friendly flying doctor pilot of advancing years asked if he could have a look. He was aghast.

"If you write all that they will hang you on at least three counts!"

He pointed out in detail the potential offences the chair bound wise men could construct. The report was re-written and reduced to a very few totally pertinent phrases. The response was similarly minimal. On this morning, after a little interval to assess the advisability of taking this step I said simply,

"No, it's just not worth the hassle, but compliments to the forecaster and would you suggest he check the weather properly once in a while rather than just guessing."

The operator's obvious relief suggested that the melancholic dispatcher in Perth had already been on the telephone lest he have to protect his own backside and that of the forecaster.

2. Beginnings

Where did the aviation enthusiasm originate? Childhood influences obviously form the basis of the entire life of the typical member of the species Homo Sapiens but where the attraction came from or why it has been so intense throughout my life is undeterminable. A model aeroplane built at the tender age of seven won me a prize and probably a lot of conceit as well! I read aviation books endlessly and the exploits of World War ll aviators were very much being publicised in the early 1950's while I was at a very impressionable age, but the origins of this interest remain a mystery.

Father was a farmer and I lived and grew up on farms in the South East of England near Worthing in West Sussex. Father felt that if his sons remained on the farm and went to local schools they would come out as young men with "The order of the Dung Fork!" To avoid this he sent us to boarding school which he couldn't really afford and I remember a childhood of family strain due to debt. However, despite this there remains a deep thankfulness for the broad horizons opened up by this education even though neither I nor my brothers reached anywhere near the brilliant university scholars Mother obviously had decided each of us would become.

Leaving school at seventeen I entered an apprenticeship with the Vickers Armstrong Aircraft Company at Weybridge, Surrey. In the naivety of my farming upbringing I expected that everybody in the factory would enjoy their work and would be heart and soul for the good of the company's endeavours. At the time Vickers, later to become BAC, were engaged in building VC10's as well as BAC1-11's and military projects such as the long defunct TSR2. With gradually dawning and somewhat shocked surprise I was to find in the course of four long and unhappy years that in general the work force lived to fiddle the bonus system, knock off (steal) everything and anything that was useful (or of no use) and live for the next Friday.

Along with this I went to the local flying club at Shoreham and learned to fly. In retrospect it is difficult to understand the passionate motivation. Apprentice wages amounted to the princely sum of four pounds, eight shillings and eleven pence per week and flying lessons cost five pounds per hour. So by scrimping and saving it was just possible to have half an hour's instruction per week. The aeroplanes consisted of two ancient DH82A's (Tiger Moths) and were run by an irascible old man (71 at the time) by the name of Cyril Pashley. 'Pash' had 22,000 hours of instructing time, first taught himself to fly using the aeroplane he and his brother built in 1910 and instructed continuously, including through both World Wars from thenceforward.

The demeanour of this antiquity of aviation was enough to sour the enthusiasm of any young aeronautical aspirant. Many years later I could still recollect the military command "Use your rudder !" bawled through the Gosport speaking tube on a freezing winter's day when the instructor should have been comfortably wrapped up in blankets in the local OAP's rest home and definitely not in the open cockpit of an ancient biplane. The weather was a great help when it came to the final check flight for the issue of a private pilot's licence. It was a particularly freezing February day in the early Sixties and after 20 minutes 'Pash', who was authorised to test for the issue of a licence, had had enough. He instructed me to land and taxi to the clubhouse whereupon he climbed out of the front cockpit. By now I had learned to detest that leather coated head in the front cockpit despite his comparatively reasonable behaviour on the ground. With a wave of the hand he bawled,

"Go away and practice your steep turns!".

A little later when I returned 'Pash' was sitting almost on top of the club house fire, signing the papers for the issue of my private pilot's licence.

Eventually it dawned in the simple agricultural mind that there were better things to be had in life than working in an aircraft factory despite previous longings to be an aircraft designer. It also grated that I was not very good at the block release college training that ran alongside the apprenticeship and also that just a few of my colleagues were very much smarter at the job than I would ever be. To be constantly struggling to keep up is not nice in the long term and so gradually, professional aviation became the goal. The ambition strengthened when, despite indifferent eyesight, the commercial pilot medical examination, then far stricter than now, was successfully passed.

The first problem was money. At the time the commercial licence training cost about £4000. An impossible sum let alone on apprentice wages. To give a comparison, brand new houses on the outskirts of the local town in West Sussex also cost £4000. To Mother's extreme anguish I quit the apprenticeship (no good changing horses in mid-stream was her sage advice) and obtained a job as a mechanic working for an Eastern European of dubious origin and descent who ran an aerial crop spraying business. Apparently, during the course of the all too recent Second World War, he was a spy and nobody seemed to know for whom he practised this unhealthy calling. For me, the job as a mechanic was far more lucrative than the apprenticeship and thereby I hoped to finance the training for a Commercial Pilot Licence and embark on a career as a pilot.

3. The Sudan

The crop spraying company was based in Essex and as an un-licensed mechanic working on crop spraying aircraft the work was varied and interesting. It was also agricultural in nature which had formed the basis of my up-bringing. In addition there was a measure of enthusiasm amongst the other employees to get the job done so the environment was a great improvement on the previous four years. The few aircraft based in East Anglia worked flat out through the summer months and much of my time was spent at an outstation in Norfolk where I was very much left to myself keeping three aircraft operational with daily maintenance and routine repairs. Back at the base, work was primarily major maintenance in preparation for the winter season in The Sudan, for which the machines would be ferried to Khartoum. This also involved converting the chemical tank on each aircraft to a temporary additional fuel tank to enable the required endurance for the ferry flight and involved some careful work with improvised fuel lines and transfer pumps.

At the appointed time the four mechanics boarded a scheduled BOAC VC10 flight at Heathrow and headed off to Khartoum. Shortly after arrival the ferried aircraft arrived containing their very bored pilots (crop spraying aircraft do not travel very fast and Essex to Khartoum is a very long way) and the mechanics set about preparing the machines and equipment for the spraying season. The heat at that time of the year was in the high 40's centigrade and was a character building shock to a young 'green' Englishman. About a week later the operation moved South to the cotton growing area set between the Blue and the White tributaries of the Nile. Two mechanics manned one base in the Northern area of the 'Gezira' while the other two went to another base about 50 miles further South.

Work began in earnest and was very demanding. Frequent bird strikes were the biggest problem and the damage caused to the leading edges of the wings needed constant repair. Along with this there was the usual run of regular aircraft checks, semi-major maintenance in terms of engine 'top' overhauls and some particularly difficult problems with the fuel system on the star of the fleet, a Pilatus Turbo Porter. While an excellent machine with a huge load carrying capacity compared to the bulk of the fleet which was made up of PA25 Piper Pawnees, the very fine settings of the fuel control unit did not take kindly to the poor fuel that was supplied. The chief engineer, a German universally known by the name of Charlie and very expert was left scratching his head. Eventually an engineer from the manufacturer was summoned. The fuel control unit was stripped, cleaned and re-assembled and all was well except that a massive micronic fuel filter arrived on the scene and each 40 gallon drum of Kerosene was laboriously hand pumped through the filter prior to entering the aircraft fuel tank.

Accommodation was very basic. Both pilots and mechanics slept under mosquito nets on the veranda of a long defunct British Club. The food was adequate even if not particularly appetising and in the evening the alcohol flowed freely. Most of the pilots were New Zealanders and a very mixed bunch they were, varying from the totally sane and normal through the entire human spectrum to the bottom end of the scale where one was probably mentally certifiable should the relevant authorities ever catch up with him.

As the autumn progressed the weather cooled a little and Christmas approached. The not so highly esteemed employer arrived at base on the 21st of December in his brand new Piper Twin Comanche. To ameliorate the festive season on behalf of his workforce he deposited a very large quantity of cheap French wine and purchased a live pig locally, obviously considering that food as well as booze was needed to keep the workforce content until his return. He then departed for Khartoum and, we later heard, to the UK by airline to spend Christmas with his family.

Christmas duly arrived and operations were suspended for two days. Christmas Eve saw me and one of the saner New Zealand pilots who also had an agricultural background slaughtering and butchering the pig, which was a particularly gory and unprofessional exercise, memories of which were to haunt me for many years to come. At lunchtime on Christmas day there was the sound of multiple aero engines from the South and the Southern based Pawnees arrived with the two mechanics squashed in beside the pilots in two of the aircraft. The Pawnee is a single seat machine and 'two up' is manageable provided both occupants are reasonably slim but it is neither a comfortable nor a particularly safe exercise.

About four hours later with the sun going down and enough alcohol and poor quality pig having been consumed to lighten any sense of responsibility a general move was made towards the airstrip. The Southern group took up their previous contorted positions in their cockpits and proceeded to start engines. Charlie managed an attempt at a protest but by this time he was used to the wilder nature of some of the Kiwis and with a helpless shrug of his shoulders he manifestly decided to do nothing to prevent the inevitable.

One of the pilots, a diminutive Englishman, so small that he always worked sitting on a cushion to enable him to see over the coaming, was unable to start his engine. I walked over and after a quick look around the cockpit pointed out that the fuel mixture lever was set to idle cut off and it needed moving fully forward before anything would work. After proffering profuse thanks in slurred speech, the little man pushed the lever forward and the engine fired up immediately. Worse was to follow. Each machine became shakily airborne and instead of proceeding immediately to their base, which was becoming urgent in view of the gathering darkness and lack of any runway lighting at either end, they proceeded to beat up the airstrip.

This was not an unusual event. Something similar happened every evening as the pilots cleaned out the spray booms and nozzles with a run up and down the field using plain water to rinse out any remaining chemical, but this was very different.

The multiple machines roared up and down the airstrip erratically weaving their way around each other performing what appeared to be attempts at aerobatics (full aerobatics are not a forte of this type of aircraft at the best of times) before finally setting off towards the South, quickly lost to view in the darkness. There was no contact whatsoever with the Southern base other than a very long and most inadvisable night drive so it wasn't until the following day that information was received that they had all arrived and landed safely.

The season came to an end, the Kiwis headed back to New Zealand after ferrying their machines as near to the UK as they could in the appalling European winter, and the remainder returned to the UK.

A most beneficial legacy remained in terms of the advice given by the Kiwi pilots. They suggested that I was wasting my time trying to save the money for a UK Commercial pilot's licence and it would be much simpler and cheaper to go to New Zealand and obtain a New Zealand licence.

4. New Zealand, Wanganui

I awoke after the long sleep of total exhaustion coupled with jet lag and gazed from the window at the cloud shadows far below playing on the surface of the South Pacific. While something of a novelty, the 12 hour flight in economy class from London to Los Angeles on a PAN AM first generation Boeing 707, a five hour technical delay courtesy of Air New Zealand and finally setting off across the Pacific for Auckland on a DC8 had taken its inevitable toll. Two eventful months had elapsed since arriving back in the UK after the hectic months in the Sudan.

Firstly, a life changing event had taken place, the subject of a later discourse. Secondly, I had been paid off by the dubious owner of the crop spraying company who manifested his Eastern European origins by underpaying the hard earned and promised Sudan bonus by some £250, a not inconsiderable sum in those days. In later years, completely by chance, I was to bump into the same slightly shifty gentleman in the lobby of the Heliopolis Hilton in Cairo but having matured and mellowed somewhat it did not seem right to challenge the non-payment. In the Sudan I had headed up a complaint about various unfulfilled contractual promises which, although not without good reason, was unwise to the point of foolishness. In retrospect it became clear that I had been used by my older and wiser colleagues as the 'Fall Guy'. The result was that conditions improved for all, but half of my promised bonus failed to materialise.

It is hard to imagine the whole picture in this day and age. Setting off for New Zealand, the other side of the world, on my own, at the age of 21. At that time folk emigrated and never expected to come home. The distance was huge, the expense for a normal citizen was enormous and communications were extremely limited and where available, impossibly expensive. The very rich would consider an occasional phone call, normal folk used air-letters, surface mail or a cable (telegram) for special occasions.

There had been letters to three flying schools in New Zealand of whom only one had deigned to reply. What amounted to an offer by the New Zealand Embassy in London which would have cost £10 for an assisted passage to emigrate had been turned down as the conditions would have seriously inhibited my ambition to obtain a commercial pilot's licence. The sum total of my savings was £1250 of which £250 went on the airfare. Astonishingly, the remainder kept me for the next six months and was sufficient to obtain my Commercial Pilot's licence with the princely sum of £6 to spare.

Wanganui Flying School in the North Island was the first port of call. It was they who had replied to the correspondence and I was expecting to remain with them for the duration. In actual fact, as the money dwindled alarmingly plans were modified. There were twenty aspirants on the ground school course. One older student dropped out almost immediately with eyesight problems as he tried to master the books. His eyes, used to the outdoors as he was essentially a farmer, couldn't manage the intense regime of studying. Another by the name of Ted, who lived in Nelson in the South Island, I remain in contact with to this day. Of the remainder probably none ended up flying for airlines and probably very few continued as commercial pilots. One was subsequently killed in a flying accident. The ground school lasted some six weeks and all the remaining students passed. Then came my first experience of a real Kiwi party.

It began at the flying school early one evening and as the alcohol intake progressed, became wilder and wilder.

The piano went over on its back, one particularly evil character broke a leg off an upturned table and started swinging it menacingly around over his head while everybody dived for cover until he could be placated. At some stage later in the evening some of the students adjourned to the communal lodgings and I drove the car. Practising total abstention from alcohol at the time was the forerunner of many future events where I was to be designated the driver.

Many of the flying school students stayed in a boarding house run by a delightful single mum known universally as Mrs G. Discipline was not her strongest point and she ruled her establishment gently and by appeal rather than any attempt at regulation. The party continued in one of the bedrooms which contained about four beds and more alcohol flowed.

A trainee helicopter pilot, not on the course and somewhat older than most, began to bounce up and down on his bed. The ceilings were quite low and on one particularly energetic bounce his head hit the ceiling with a loud crash making a large dent in the plasterboard. In the boarding house there were residents other than the flying folk, one of whom was a universally disliked Pom (Englishman) called George. Awoken from his slumbers which he had previously advised to all and sundry were essential to maintain his wellbeing, George, a self-confessed Karate expert, arrived on the scene stark naked and in a distinctly threatening oriental pose. He was quickly followed by Mrs G hastily donning her bathrobe evidently fearful at the destruction of her establishment.

Dear Mrs G had no doubt seen it all before and with a withering glance at the disgusting effigy presented by the naked George she asked if everybody was alright and then quietly retired to her room. George was told in no uncertain terms to go and do something impossible to himself and appeared to decide that this was a better option than trying to sort everybody out despite his accomplishments as a 'Grand Master'.

While at Wanganui I had managed a few hours flying and obtained a New Zealand Private Pilot Licence based on my UK licence. Prices for flying at Wanganui were comparatively high and through a contact from the Sudan days I was put in touch with the Aero Club at Rotorua. At this stage I was seriously short of the requisite two hundred hours for the Commercial Pilot Licence and Rotorua would let me use their 90hp Piper Cub for two pounds and ten shillings per hour provided it was hired for at least 100 hours flying. Since this was the hours shortfall almost exactly before intensive training for the licence test began it seemed the logical way forward. Packing the small holdall containing my very minimal worldly possessions it was off to Rotorua.

5. New Zealand, Rotorua

A month was to elapse based in Rotorua and some most interesting aviating ensued which taught many long lasting lessons. It is said that "There is no better way of learning than by mistakes" and plenty were made. In later years as an airline training captain this evidenced itself as by far the best method. Allow the student as much rein as possible and he/she will learn very fast. This means watching and interfering as little as possible, the primary means of teaching being by de-briefing. Obviously for a new trainee there needs to be more instruction but as they become competent it pays to keep quiet unless things are going really wrong. I was to remain extremely thankful to those instructors who used this policy during my training on various aircraft type courses in the following years.

The self-generated task was to fly to as many of New Zealand's airfields as practicable in the time available for the purposes of gaining both flying hours and experience. Days would be pre-planned with circular routes to include as many landings as possible. In this way most of the airfields in the North Island were visited, from Kaitaia in the extreme North to New Plymouth in the West, Napier in the East and Wellington in the South. A couple of times I became lost especially when the cloud base was low and the weather poor. In this instance with the mountains of New Zealand it would have been very easy to terminate the human existence by colliding with high ground. The guardian angels worked overtime during those days. After about two weeks, the course was set for Nelson in the South Island and I puttered across the Cook Strait in the diminutive Cub, meeting a pal from Wanganui, Ted Priest, in Nelson. Staying the night with him a proposition was put forward. The go ahead owner/operator of the Nelson Aero Club, a gentleman of Dutch descent who rejoiced in the glorious name of Wally Wagtendonk, was keen to establish his own flying school. To set the ball rolling he was offering some good introductory flying rates if Ted and I would complete our training at his school. There were also two other potential candidates in the wings, so with four embarking on final flight training for a commercial licence things would get under way. There was also the mutual advantage of safety pilots being on hand for all the instrument flying training required. The arguments were good. With little persuasion a date three weeks hence was set for commencement of the final stage. By this time all the necessary hours on the Rotorua Cub would have been flown.

Meanwhile, Ted and I proceeded South East to Christchurch, Ted in a similar aircraft hired from the Nelson Aero Club. We flew in loose formation from thence until several days later when we returned to Nelson. This was very useful in another respect in that the radio on the Rotorua Cub was very poor (you pay for what you get!). This was an embarrassment at larger airfields with control towers. Ted in his aircraft was able to communicate for both of us. From Christchurch we headed South to Dunedin and enjoyed some glorious low flying down the beaches in the vicinity of Oamaru and Timaru. At Dunedin we met up with Dave, yet another of the students from Wanganui, stayed the night with him and then proceeded through the valleys to Queenstown and Te Anu, landing at other airfields en-route as a threesome. Dave was possessed of a more powerful Piper Cub, a 150hp PA18A and took pleasure in demonstrating the superiority of his machine.

Landing in Queenstown on what was then a dirt airstrip with the breath-taking view of the snow covered aptly named Remarkable Range of mountains in the background was an unforgettable experience. On a 2010 visit to the same place I was appalled by the commercialisation and ravages of the tourist industry, both virtually non-existent in 1967.

Continuing on to Te Anu we spent the night in the one and only hotel and I recollect being dismayed by the 36/- (£1.80!) accommodation fee which was way above the normal budget for the night. The following day the weather had closed in to the West so the anticipated venture over to Fjordland was cancelled and we headed for Invercargill, refuelled and on to Dunedin for another night. The following day we left Dave behind and set direct course for Franz Joseph on the West coast in near perfect weather. The route took us directly over the top of Mount Cook, at 12,000 feet the highest mountain in New Zealand. The little 90hp Piper Cubs were not happy at that altitude. There followed a glorious descent down the Franz Joseph Glacier to land at the bottom on the ill-defined dirt airstrip. After this it was a straightforward cruise up the sparsely populated West Coast arriving back at Nelson in the evening.

The next day I returned to Rotorua on my own and shortly afterwards, once again set course for Nelson with another 'hours builder' on board to fly the aircraft back. With bad weather in the Cook Strait this flight was terminated at Paraparamu and the aircraft returned to Rotorua. I was forced to take the train into Wellington and then catch the evening NAC flight to Nelson which was another serious dent in the budget.

6. New Zealand, Nelson

So a new phase began. The ground exams had been completed at Wanganui, the hours had been built up to just over 150 with the flying from Rotorua and the final leg was to train to the required standard to pass the Department of Civil Aviation flight test. This was to take a further 6 weeks during which precise manoeuvres of all description needed brushing up to a high standard and instrument flying was perfected. In addition a minimum number of hours night flying were required and the ultimate objective was to achieve the licence with the exact minimum of 200 flying hours in order to keep the costs within budget.

One evening three of us trainees were left on our own to complete the night flying. The airfield at Nelson was very provincial and of the very few regular airline flights in and out there was little if any traffic during the evenings. We had access to the control tower and airfield lighting, indeed one of the students was an active Air Traffic Controller. Since for the night flying there was no additional training required, just an hours requirement, we set ourselves a little competition.

Using a PA 18A Super Cub with its more powerful engine the objective was to see how high it would climb. The first went up and on his return some 30 minutes later announced he had reached 12000 feet. Ted went next and achieved 15000 feet. Finally, it was my turn and I was not going to be outdone. I managed to coax the machine up to 20,000 feet. In actual fact this was complete foolishness as without oxygen anoxia and unconsciousness quickly ensue. Being young and healthy I survived the exercise in fine fettle and the thought occurred long after that the Wellington Radar controllers must have been scratching their heads at this unidentified blip on their radar screens and probably logged it as a UFO.

The day came for the flight test. A Department of Civil Aviation examiner arrived from Christchurch. Ted went first and passed. Meanwhile the weather was closing in and the examiner was short of time. I was next and also passed. The examiner announced that the weather was too bad to do any more examinations and anyway, he had run out of time so the other two tests were cancelled. This was terribly hard on the students involved. We were all on a shoestring budget and fine-tuned to take the test. Ted was to tell me many years later that after the examiner had returned to Christchurch he was due for his bi-annual medical examination. This he failed and he was never to fly as an examiner again.

Ted, being a local man, picked up casual flying work almost immediately and subsequently went to work whole time for an aerial survey company. I was not so fortunate and was unable to find employment as a pilot despite trying all the avenues I could think of and writing many letters. I needed money to live. New Zealand was transiting to the decimal currency and with my engineering background and the kind offices of one of the Nelson Aero Club members I was given short term work in a business machines repair workshop in Nelson modifying cash registers. This quickly came to an end and then I was given work in a hangar at the airfield on general maintenance. So money for board and lodging was there and as I used to tell my children in later years, if you have a roof over your head, food to eat and clothes to wear you are better off than a great many other folk in this world.

It was always an advantage to have specialised in electrical work during my apprenticeship back at Vickers as most engineers, automotive or aeronautical are wary of the mysteries of this discipline. One day a top dresser DC3 which was working out of Nelson taxied over to the hangar with a serious electrical problem. Peter, my employer, assigned me to the job and almost immediately a simple broken bus bar was located. This was fixed very quickly by the simple expedient of bolting a short length of copper across the break and the delighted pilot invited me to go along for the ride on his next load. Peter agreed and so it was away for a quick flight down the valley South of Nelson to spread 7 tons of superphosphate on a property some 10 miles away. These machines are not used for this type of work anymore but the experience was fascinating and just emphasised all my frustrations of having a commercial pilot licence but being unable to use it.

It became obvious that there wasn't going to be a flying job in New Zealand for the foreseeable future. All doors had been knocked on and while there might have been the odd job for an experienced man there was nothing for a new licence holder. I decided that it was time to move on and with limited funds the nearest country to pursue my aspirations was Australia.

7. Australia, Sydney

The evening departure from Wellington on an Air New Zealand Lockheed Electra was interesting from an aeronautical point of view. The Electra was one of the last of the long-haul turbo props and had gigantic broad bladed propellers. Climbing the air-stairs to board this huge machine I wondered whether I would ever get far enough up the aviation ladder to fly anything approaching such manifest immensity.

Sydney was reached four and a half hours later and the customs officer followed by the taxi driver into town were such wonderful optimists that I was already beginning to feel at home in Australia. After a night in a cheap hotel it was out by suburban train to the general aviation airfield that was and still is the centre of light aircraft activity for Eastern Australia at Bankstown. There was approximately $30 in the kitty after the expense of the trip so accommodation and work were essential and needed very quickly. I wandered around the airfield and enquired for work at a likely looking busy hangar and was directed to a neighbouring enterprise. The lessee, one Bill Smith, asked a few questions which were apparently answered satisfactorily. Producing the letter containing an open reference regarding my apprenticeship from Vickers/BAC there was an immediate job offer. After a few more enquiries accommodation was arranged in a fairly standard boarding house local to the airfield so things were looking up.

The optimism was short lived. 'Joi de vivre' gradually disappeared over the coming months. Bill Smith was a visionary and very clever man at modifying light aircraft to suit the eccentricities of his clients but he appeared to be a hopeless businessman and I was to find the work as depressing as my apprenticeship, or in fact worse. I took responsibility for far more than my abilities allowed. Various aircraft were in various stages of modification. Amongst several other projects, a Piper PA25 Pawnee crop-sprayer was being modified to the requirements of a New South Wales top-dressing company from a single seat to a two seat side by side arrangement to be used for training new pilots into the arts of agricultural flying. This involved major re-design of the tubular steel structure and while Bill managed the design expertly, the work, primarily welding, needed a licensed aircraft welder and Bill seemed to be too broke to pay someone to come in and do this work. I could weld adequately but did not have the requisite licence as an aircraft welder so the work ground to a halt.

Another project, in retrospect, defies the imagination. A wealthy Queensland cattle station proprietor had spotted a Fletcher crop duster while on vacation in New Zealand. He ordered a brand new machine from the manufacturers and it was flown across the Tasman. Bill was given the job of turning this into a multi-purpose utility aircraft. There were at the time several aircraft available on the open market superbly suited to a general utility role so the owner either had some ulterior motive in this expensive modification or he had more money than he knew what to do with.

In normal circumstances the job would have been very satisfying. The spray tank area was converted to a general purpose cabin with a strong floor. Control runs were re-routed along the inside structure of the fuselage where in the original design they ran through the normally unoccupied centre of the rear fuselage. A large hole for the cargo door was cut in the side behind the port wing and the skin was reinforced around this opening. A door and suitable opening and closing mechanism were designed and constructed. Thankfully, one way and another, this project was completed and the machine was successfully test flown.

The work force consisted of an elderly licensed ground engineer called Clive who was seriously alcoholic, a young apprentice who should have been with a more viable organisation to learn his trade, and me. At one stage I found quite by accident that Clive had been evicted from his lodgings and was sleeping in his antique Holden motor car. I was able to get him installed in the boarding house I was using and the owners were most kind in accommodating him despite age and obvious alcoholism.

The one plus of this period was that I successfully sat for and passed the Australian Aviation Law exam, did a little flying to satisfy local licensing requirements and obtained an Australian Commercial Pilot Licence. There was even a little semi-remunerative flying available, the most memorable of which was taking a Cessna 177 from Bankstown to Bathurst at the request of the owner. I had gained the mistaken impression that mountains were not a problem in Australia (which would be true compared to New Zealand) and I headed West one Saturday morning in indifferent weather with low cloud base and pouring rain. Suddenly and fortunately seeing it in time, I arrived at a wall of rock which was definitely impassable without trying to climb into the cloud and fly over the mountain range on instruments. This was a machine which lacked even the basics for blind flying so I turned around and held off for a while until the cloud lifted and was then able to climb high enough to proceed to Bathurst by climbing over the Blue Mountains in the clear.

Once again, with Christmas approaching, all efforts to find a flying job had failed. Even the wealthy cattle station owner from Queensland did not want a pilot for his extraordinary machine presumably because he intended to fly it himself. It was time to move on and I decided the next move should be Western Australia. I gave the required one week's notice to Bill, who manifestly failed to understand that I was seriously going to leave, and the following Saturday went down to Sydney railway station intending to get on a train to Perth. Things were not so simple. The next available seat on a transcontinental train was on the following Friday.

8. Hill 50 Goldmine

After a week kicking my heels in Sydney I boarded the train for Perth. In the 1960's this was a five day journey with several train changes as the track gauge in each state was different. More recently the line has been upgraded to standard gauge throughout and the journey time is now reputed to be about 3½ days. The class was of course second, the cheapest available, and it was hard to get any sleep at night in the packed compartments.

The load did reduce for the crossing of the Nullabor plain as passengers disembarked en-route and few had boarded. More space made it easier to sleep. Christmas Day passed on the longest piece of straight rail track in the world running for hundreds of miles from South Australia to Kalgoorlie in Western Australia. The scenery was open bush and not far short of monotonous but the company in view of the festive season was pleasant and convivial.

Kalgoorlie arrived in the early morning on the fifth day and the change was made to a delightful air-conditioned carriage on the narrow gauge West Australian railway. A huge nutritious cooked breakfast was served as the little train wound its way down the valleys to Perth which inestimably raised the spirits.

Finding economic accommodation on Boxing Day was a primary objective and this was in scant supply. A job could wait as there was a little money in the bank left over from the job in Sydney. Eventually I found a downmarket doss house at the West end of Hay Street which was very different then from the relatively salubrious area it has since become. This was not a nice place. In those days you didn't see many street dwellers such as are common all over the world today and those who would have been in this position were apparently accommodated in the likes of that which I now found myself. The inmates slept in large dormitories. The odd one or two of the more dissolute variety would arrive 'home' around 3am seriously drunk, fall asleep immediately indicated by loud snoring and then wet the bed. Initially there would be the ominous unattractive sounds associated, shortly followed by the even less attractive splashing as the urine seeped through the mattress onto the floor below. Naturally the place stank and it is difficult to understand how the owners were able to cope with this kind of behaviour.

The foolishness of youth! Even though there was no wife or family to support, no mortgage to pay and my entire worldly possessions in a small holdall, the stupidity of arriving in a strange city, unemployed and homeless between Christmas and New Year when most of the sane world ceases to operate simply had not registered.

About three days later when the world half awoke for a couple of days before plunging into the New Year long weekend (does anything ever change!?) an advertisement appeared in 'The West Australian' jobs vacant column for qualified tradesmen of all descriptions and also unqualified labourers. The company advertising went by the delightfully descriptive name of "Hill 50 Goldmine NL". I was later to discover that 'NL' stood for 'No Liability' which presumably was a corporate threat rather than a personal one but it did increase my misgivings about the whole scenario, and anyway, what had become of all the other hills before hill 50, like Hill 49 for example or even Hill 27!? It didn't sound too re-assuring. However, anything was better than the doss house. I phoned the mine from a public call box and was told to board a train to Mount Magnet at which place I would be able to sign on. Mount Magnet is a town in central Western Australia some 400 miles North East of Perth.

So, it was back to Perth railway station and yet another train. This was not air-conditioned and the journey was to take 24 hours. There were not many passengers and I found myself in a compartment with a chatty little man aged about 35 who introduced himself as 'Les Ferris'. Les along with most of the occupants of the train was also bound for the Mount Magnet gold mine.

Some characters stick in the memory for ever and Les was one of these. Twenty four hours allows a long time to talk and we became well acquainted. He had spent many years travelling Australia and in that time had worked in some 50 different jobs. His alleged exploits, sacred and profane, more the latter than the former, were extraordinary. He was an expert at playing cards and seemed to have a pack constantly in his hands shuffling them in the slick manner I had only ever seen in the movies. He knew any number of tricks and it soon became obvious that if you ever played the likes of Les for money you could never win. He seemed to know the position of each card in the pack at any one time which sounds impossible but he was an impresario in his trade.

The train clattered along endlessly and incredibly slowly. It seemed that once away from the metropolitan area it would stop unscheduled for anyone who hailed it regardless of whether there was a station or not. It became hotter and hotter as we moved away from the coast and further northward. Finally, mid-morning on the second day we reached the township of Mount Magnet which on first sight ominously lacked the attraction its name implied. A large coach pulled up which most of the travellers boarded and it was off to Hill 50.

A long queue formed outside the mine office in the hot sun, which gradually reduced as folk signed on. Les was immediately in front of me and when his turn arrived he announced his name as 'Les Claridge'. In my unbelievable Pommie naivety and genuinely puzzled I said,

"That's not your na..."

There was a sharp backwards kick on the shin from Les

and I stopped in mid-sentence.

After I had signed on, been allocated a bunk hut followed by a brief job description and work schedule I was sent to the equipment shed to draw a battery belt, miners lamp/helmet and all the other necessary paraphernalia associated with my latest profession. Here I ran in to Les,

"Sorry about that old man, not good to use the same name too often!'

No reply was invited and I realised the matter was closed. Shortly afterwards it became apparent that Les and I had been allocated the same hut. This was one of many in long lines, each being about eight feet square with a bed each side leaving a small floor space between. There was a louvered glass window in the back and the door at the front remained open all day and night because of the heat, unless both occupants were on shift at the same time.

There were three eight hour shifts in each working day and these rotated every week. Initially the mine was very interesting as was the work. The cage full of miners, labourers etc. descended incredibly rapidly to the allocated level, the deepest in this particular mine being around 4000ft. I was to find myself working mainly around the 2000ft level.

At each level tunnels went out into the surrounding rock to the work face and small gauge rail tracks had been laid on the floor. There were no pit props as the type of strata was of sufficient integrity to make the tunnel roofs self-supporting. The gold bearing rock was blasted out by professional miners on a previous shift. A small team, one of which I was attached to, would load a small truck using a miniature mechanical loader whose motive power was water pressure. Two of us would then push the full truck back to the shaft. A tipping mechanism allowed the contents of the truck to be jettisoned onto a large metal grid and any rocks too large to fall through the grid were broken up using a sledge hammer. The ore was then collected from a hopper at the next level down and raised up the shaft to the surface.

It was the breaking up of rocks while standing on the grid and pushing of trucks to and from the face that was my primary duty and I rapidly became very fit. Eight hours of fairly continuous sledge hammer work interspersed with pushing empty trucks up to the face and pushing full ones back was muscle building and even character building. The track was superbly graded which made the task of pushing the empty truck to the face and the full one back to the shaft very similar in effort and was easily within the capability of two reasonably fit workers.

Occasionally a rock in the pile at the face which had been expertly blasted out by the miners would be too large to load. This was when things became really interesting. A few sticks of gelignite, the number of sticks being decided by the estimated obduracy of the rock, would be slapped onto the offending obstacle using a wet clay mix. A fused detonator was inserted into one of the sticks and lit and the team would retire to a safe distance and block their ears for the anticipated explosion. The team leader was very experienced and usually the number of sticks and their positioning on the offending obstacle were precision personified for the desired fragmentation.

At some time during this period, possessed of an inveterate curiosity by nature, I requested and was allowed a conducted tour of the surface works. It seems that with this type of ore bearing rock, many tons are brought to the surface, crushed, followed by treatment with a chemical process. The final production is of the order of two or three ounces of gold extracted from each ton of ore.

All of this was not helping me attain my objective which was to fly aircraft commercially. The irony of working several thousand feet underground rather than a similar distance above ground was not lost. Filling in time to enable a reasonable bank balance was an interim goal and the ideas and dreams were not suppressed. Hearing that there was work available on the surface as a 'Greaser' in the powerhouse at a better hourly rate than labouring underground, I applied for and was gratified to be awarded the 'promotion'.

The extra pay was not without reason. Underground the temperature was a steady 20-25ºC but in the powerhouse with the midday heat at around 40ºC, on top of which was the heat generated by the engines, things were definitely 'character building'. There was also the noise and this was before the days of 'Health and Safety' such as we see today. Under modern regulations doubtless the entire mine would be shut down overnight.

The power house contained 16 large diesel engines coupled to generators, mostly completely different by design and manufacture and mostly acquired second hand from various sources. On each 8 hour shift there was a 'Driver' whose job was to match the supply of electricity to the demand by stopping and starting engines as required and who generally oversaw the whole operation, and a 'greaser' who did exactly what his name implied. Such was the variety of machines that a measure of intelligence was required to match up the various lubrication products with their respective engines, gearboxes and bearings.

The drivers were fascinating characters and there was a fair amount of time to talk between duties and during brief times of refuge away from the noise. They carried much responsibility as this power house not only supplied the large amounts of electricity required by the mine itself and the processing of the ore on the surface but also all the domestic needs of the township of Mount Magnet. There was no other supplier.

Occasionally at the shift change the relief would fail to arrive. In this case a double shift was required and I was to work several of these. The worst was when the 8am relief didn't show. Midnight through to 4pm was a long time to stay awake and try to operate coherently.

Les meanwhile had progressed from mainstream labouring and was working at a pioneer shaft which sounded far less mundane than the early work. He arrived back at about 5am from one particular shift in a state of complete and total exhaustion. The winding gear had failed and he and a few others had elected to climb to the surface using the emergency ladder system which was adjacent to the shaft. Apparently this was a system of short ladders and small platforms which were designed and used purely for emergency. The old timers had simply resigned themselves to waiting at their work level until the gear was fixed but Les and a few other new-comers had elected to climb. It had taken him the entire 5 hours from the shift ending at midnight to reach the surface.

There was little social life for the casual workforce. The mine was several miles from the town and the permanent workers who were mainly tradesman or possessed of some qualifications associated with mining maintained a more normal existence, many having their families living in the town. The one 'party' I observed was sponsored by the four occupants of the adjacent two huts. A small keg of beer was delivered on Friday evening and was consumed in its entirety by shift start on Monday morning. The four fellows drank steadily, slept little and occasionally arose to slug each other over some trivial disagreement, whereupon honour would be satisfied and drinking would resume. For the following week, nursing black eyes and swollen faces, they could be heard congratulating each other on what a great weekend it had been. Les was not given to much alcohol which was fine as far as I was concerned and discussions sacred and general continued for long hours when we happened to be off shift at the same time.

Religion of course arose frequently and Les was

fascinated by my recent conversion. Being very new to faith myself I failed to realise, and this was true for many years to come, that it is a waste of time to argue intellectually about these things. Some few weeks later I left the Gold Mine and headed North to the Pilbara where by all accounts the 'big money' was to be earned on the new iron ore projects and the parting shot from Les, whom I was never to meet again, was inestimably profound,

"You've either got it or you haven't got it!"

This is amazingly in accord with Holy Scripture, John 3v8, so it is probably time to say some more of these things.

9. Faith

My parents were loving, possessed of great personal integrity and devout Christians. I was brought up with church as the norm on Sundays and retained a modicum of the faith I was taught until mid-teen years.

While the early attachment to aeroplanes grew, my childhood Christian Faith diminished to the extent that I became essentially an Atheist. Simplistically, with scientific advances, the theory of evolution and the general prevailing philosophy of the early nineteen sixties how could anybody believe the fairy tale God of the Bible? At the same time the early space exploration was in full swing which seemed to further deny the existence of any Superior Being.

During my agnostic/atheistic teens, my Father enthusiastically took me along to a local Gospel Chapel on a weekday evening to see a Billy Graham movie called "Shadow of the Boomerang!" In recent years I have come to respect the work of Billy Graham probably far more than any other 20th Century evangelist but at that particular time it heightened my unbelief. I simply didn't want to know the rather 'wet' profession of faith of the key characters under obviously rigged circumstances but was totally captivated by the glorious scenes of the Australian outback. One of many proofs to me not only of God's love and patience but also of His sense of humour came in the subsequent baptism into commercial aviation that was to occur during my years in Australia.

Returning from the contract as a mechanic in the Sudan I had spent a few weeks living at my parent's home before achieving my resolve to go to New Zealand to obtain a Commercial Pilot's licence. Since it was normal in the family to go to Church on a Sunday I went along simply to avoid offending anyone. Thus, one Sunday evening, sitting in the pews listening to the usual, to me, boring platitudes issuing from the pulpit I began to think.

"What are all these folk doing sitting listening to these old wives' tales in this day and age when the real world knows it's just stuff and nonsense?"

It was a packed Church and I had known most of the people there since childhood and indeed had grown up with all those of a similar age to myself. After the service was over I hastened home. The house was empty as my brothers and parents had remained to chat for a while. Still totally confused in my thoughts I said to nobody in particular,

"God, if you're really there what's this all about?"

All I can say to this day is that is when IT happened. I just simply had sudden and total conviction that God was there and all I had been brought up to was not 'Old Wives' Tales' but the real and complete Truth.

In retrospect I was to spend most of the next twenty years or so examining everything from obscure philosophy to alternative religions and there was simply nothing to compare even remotely with what I had received. This was assisted by the fact that I was and still am an inveterate reader and devour anything and everything that comes my way including the Christian Bible from cover to cover. Incidentally, if the reader should want to know about a religion, he must check out the founder. There are four biographies of Jesus, these being Matthew, Mark, Luke and John in the New Testament section of the Christian Bible. Compare these with Biographies of Confucius, Buddha, Charles Russell (Jehovah's Witnesses), Joseph Fielding Smith (Mormons), Mohammed (Islam) and any others and the evidence speaks for itself. Even so, Belief does not come by intellect. It is a gift from God, far more precious than anything else this world has to offer and it is 'The Pearl of Great Price', to be sought after. As Les said to me in the Gold Mine,

"You've either got it or you haven't got it!"

There is an important codicil to this as Jesus said,

"He who comes to Me I will not cast out."

(John ch3 vv1-21 New Testament, Christian Bible)

10. A Long bus ride

I made my way to one of the few vacant seats on the long range bus at the Mt Magnet bus station. The service had commenced in Perth and was bound for Port Hedland on the North West coast. It contained 40-50 seats and was almost full. There was a driver, a relief driver and a stewardess. There was a very small toilet cubicle, equally small galley and there was air-conditioning.

In the hot sun the bus proceeded North and arrived at Mount Newman in the early afternoon for a brief stop. At this time Mount Newman, or rather Mt Whaleback to give it the correct title, was a recently discovered mountain of iron ore. A development camp had been established by the mining company and a railway line to transport the ore to Port Hedland some 250 miles away was just moving forward from the survey stage.

Heavy summer thunderstorms had caused some problems with the un-sealed road but so far the bus had encountered no difficulty negotiating the occasional soft spots. Leaving Mount Newman there were increasing problems related to the unstable road surface and finally we came to a complete halt, bogged in the mud.

All the passengers disembarked and many put their shoulders to the bus. Eventually, shunting backwards and forwards a hard surface was reached and it was all aboard and on our way again. Even at this early stage I conjectured that things were not looking good. The situation was repeated several times and a rapport developed amongst the passengers in the midst of these difficulties.

Seated close to me were a German and an Austrian, both young men like me and headed for the North West mining projects to find work. The sum total of their collective understanding of the English tongue seemed to be,

"Shut up Grandma and keep pushing!"

The context and the connotations were unfathomable and presumably the expression related to an obscure Mid European fairy tale but for some reason it was incredibly funny. There was no two way radio on the bus and there had been no traffic or signs of humanity. About 25 miles North of Mount Newman the end came. On yet another wet stretch the driver in his efforts to keep moving fast to avoid getting bogged, lost control and the bus slipped sideways into the shallow graded ditch from which no amount of man-power was ever going to extract it.

A conference was held and it was eventually decided that the slightly older relief driver and the stewardess would stay with the passengers and the bus. Meanwhile the driver would walk back to Mount Newman to get help. Having not lost a youthful sense of adventure I volunteered to accompany him. The driver seemed to be used to problems of this nature and I didn't question the fact that bottles of water, available on the bus, were not taken with us but a backpack, containing some cans of beer, was.

It was very hot and there was no wind. The driver and I began walking. The open bush was totally silent and occasional emus could be seen striding away in their awkward gait as we approached. The pace appeared to be lethargic and somewhat to my astonishment I realised the driver was barefoot.

"Shouldn't we go back and get your shoes?" I asked innocently.

"I'm a Queenslander," was the confident reply, the implication being that shoes were for weaklings and an unnecessary impediment. After about an hour it was obvious that Queenslander was in some distress with his feet but I judged it unwise to say anything. Shortly after this Queenslander announced that he needed a rest and promptly sat down under a small gum tree which afforded the barest minimum of shade. He opened a can of beer. Some twenty minutes later he opened a second can and I felt that this was an unspoken announcement that he was not going any further.

"Do you think we should carry on and try to get to Mount Newman before dark?" I suggested.

Queenslander said,

"Tell you what, you carry on. I'll sit here for a while and catch you up later!"

He was to keep his promise.

Unshackled from Queenslander, I set off at a fast pace towards the south. Flies were a continuous problem. Australia seems to breed a particularly large and virulent variety of these insects and anywhere outside metropolitan areas they abound in gross profusion.

Some four hours later after sunset and with the lights of Mount Newman in the distance there was the sound of an approaching vehicle from behind. A four wheel drive utility (ute) with two surveyors in the cab appeared. In the back was Queenslander sitting on a heap of equipment. There was a large grin on his face and he was barely perceptibly hiccupping. He had kept to his word to catch up but his condition suggested that he hadn't moved from the gum tree until the vehicle had arrived and that all the beer had been consumed.

The ute took both of us on to Newman and, as seemed normal in the Pilbara and probably anywhere in the Australian outback, folk in any sort of difficulty couldn't be helped enough. Queenslander and I were offered a shower and towels were produced. Emerging from the morale boosting cleansing we were sat down at an outside table and provided with a huge meal. Only then was the bus situation addressed although the travellers were aware that help was on the way. The surveyors had stopped by the stranded vehicle and assessed the situation before collecting

Queenslander and subsequently, me.

We were soon on our way back to the bus in another four wheel drive vehicle with a large road grader following. On arrival I took no further interest in the proceedings except to note that the grader was hitched onto the front of the bus using a steel hawser and while I fell asleep in my seat with total exhaustion I was sub-consciously aware that the grader towed the bus through most of the night, departing back to Mount Newman in the early hours of the next day when solid road was reached to the South of Nullagine. I was half awake for the stop at Marble Bar and later awoke fully to realise we had stopped and to observe a haggard looking Queenslander emptying the toilet tank into the bush immediately outside my window. From then good speed was made to Port Hedland and we arrived in the early afternoon some 28 hours after leaving Mount Magnet.

There was absolutely no accommodation available and it soon became evident that while the town was furiously busy there were no job vacancies either. Every enquiry ended up with the rebuttal,

"We only employ through the Perth Office."

11. Port Hedland

Being in a mining boom town even though the mineral was iron ore, the situation was similar to that which must occur with a gold strike. There were simply no beds available in any kind of public accommodation with which Port Hedland was markedly un-endowed anyway.

Sleeping on the beach was not desperately uncomfortable. It was a matter of digging one hole for the shoulder, another for the hip and using a shirt as a pillow. There were, of course, sundry creepy crawlies but they tended not to bother another of the terrestrial species. Anyway, youth tends to sleep through most disturbances so there was no problem.

Semi-vagrancy is easily learned and thankfully it was midsummer with intense heat in the day and not cold at night. The really miserable aspect to the whole situation was utter depression. The glorious promises that seemed to lie ahead on achieving my Commercial Pilot's licence had long disappeared and once again I was assessing the options. I decided that the next move would be to try South Africa for a flying job and wearily set my sights in that direction.

It is a fact that qualifications *per se* do not guarantee a job except in an employee's market. Pilot recruitment tends to be cyclical worldwide and it just happened that I had qualified right at the bottom of the cycle. Things were not looking good. It was 6 months since I had obtained the licence and all avenues for pilot employment appeared to have reached a dead end as far as New Zealand and Australia were concerned.

One day, I found myself on my own having dropped the two mid-Europeans of the bus trip as they had decided to go into town and organise some affairs of their own. I had not realised that attempts to get work were probably inhibited by the fact that the spoken English of my two companions was negligible.

The first solo attempt at knocking on doors bore fruit. It was at a camp on the outskirts of town which appeared very busy with many large trucks, road trains and several huge earthmoving machines in the yard. There was general frenetic activity. I proceeded to the sign marked 'office' dressed in the grubby T shirt, shorts and flip-flops which were *de rigueur* for the status. Sleeping on the beach and trying to clean myself up in Port Hedland's one public toilet had not enhanced the appearance. I enquired at the desk for a job in the wonderfully cool air-conditioned unit.

The friendly clerk was impeccably dressed in a spotless white T shirt, dark shorts and long white socks beneath which were perfectly polished leather shoes. He gave no indication of revulsion at the hobo figure in front of him and advised that there were only jobs as kitchen hands available and this would likely be at one of the outstation camps. Certainly no pride left and actually intense with anticipation, the job was instantly accepted.

"When can I start?"

"Well we need somebody right now!"

Forms were filled in and feeling slightly foolish, as an aside, I said,

"Incidentally, I have a Commercial Pilot licence!"

Smartly dressed clerk rapidly raised his head from filling in forms and shot a glance of unexpected interest. Was there was more to this vagrant than met the eye?

"Hang on a minute". He disappeared into an inner office.

Returning shortly,

"The manager would like to see you."

Without more ado I was shown into the site manager's office.

Harry was a dark haired slim man in his mid-thirties

with a face that suggested long exposure to the Australian outdoors. Looking slightly harassed he invited me to sit down and said,

"I understand you have a commercial pilot's licence?"

"Yes!"

"Do you have any papers for this?"

Back to smartly dressed clerk's office I eventually found buried under my scant possessions in the grubby holdall my flying log book and Australian licence and took them back to the manager. Harry examined them with an increasing frown and eventually said,

"I don't know much about this, but can I send them to head office in Perth?"

"Of course" was the immediate response (they weren't going to be a lot of use in the kitchen!).

Harry had a word with the clerk and I realised that I was going to be assigned to the kitchen at the Port Hedland base and some other hapless character was going to be transferred to one of the outlying camps.

My performance in the kitchen, then (and to this day in a domestic sense), was distinctly lacking in charisma. There were immediate problems in that I was doubled up in one of the air-conditioned twin bunk units with the chief cook.

Gerry was of florid, alcoholic countenance, obese appropriate to his profession, very outspoken, and didn't like kitchen hands especially one who purported to be a pilot in disguise. Wake up was 5am and rapid ablutions in the communal washhouse were followed by preparing breakfast.

It was in complete ignorance of the dissolute habits of West Australian insects that two days later I followed Gerry to the ablution block and left the light on in the bunkroom and, worse, left the door open. Gerry was back first and found the room matted from floor to ceiling with flying ants. A swarm was passing and were attracted to the light.

There was much abuse in almost incoherent colloquialisms which were impossible to follow but the mood was unmistakeable. A low profile was called for.

Most of the workforce in this, the North West Base camp, were friendly enough but one Sunday evening after the fellows had consumed a few beers one of them taking a dislike to the new kitchen hand, grabbed me by the collar across the counter behind which I was serving Gerry's indifferent cuisine and threatened to modify my face. The offence was not clear. In his right hand were firmly clenched a knife and fork and I realised that this could cause serious damage should the seemingly inevitable punch eventuate. Several quite large genial fellow workers were on the scene in the nick of time and hauled away the aggressor with deep apologies for his behaviour.

After about 10 days during which my lack of any culinary common sense was causing deepening problems there came a call to go to the office.

Company chief pilot, Captain Keith, had just arrived from Perth. He was known by everybody in the company and was highly regarded for his renowned aviating ability and by default for the fact that as with the other pilots he was the man who took them home for leave and kept them supplied with essentials when they were away from base. He was fortyish, about five feet seven inches in height, dark haired, bronzed with droopy, almost spaniel eyes. He looked me up and down with critical, even mournful appraisal and said slowly and thoughtfully,

"Come with me son!"

We proceeded to the local airport and an introduction was made to the aircraft that was based at Port Hedland. It was a Cessna 205. This is not a large machine, a high wing monoplane with a Continental 260hp engine and capable of carrying 5 passengers, 6 persons including the pilot, and a tricycle undercarriage. It was an earlier version of the more powerful Cessna 206, also used by the company which was a workhorse world-wide and is much better known. Unfortunately, most of my flying to this time had been on 'tail-draggers' and the only aircraft anything like the machine in front of me that I had flown before and that for a minimal amount of time was the much smaller tail wheel Cessna 180.

Keith sat in the right hand seat, started the engine and told me, positioned in the left seat, to taxi out and fly a circuit of the airfield at 1000 feet followed by a full stop landing. The machine was fitted with dual controls. Desperately trying to master an unfamiliar aircraft in the alien environment of an unfamiliar airfield, quite out of my depth and out of practice I shakily attempted to do as I was told. I took off, flew a conventional left hand circuit at 1000 feet, managed a reasonable landing and taxied back to the hangar. Captain Keith shut down the engine. He raised his hooded eyebrows and slowly turned to face his kitchen hand applicant. With gentle accusation he said,

"You're not very good Son, are you?" This was a rhetorical question.

Clouds of gloom and visions of long service under Gerry in the misery of the kitchen descended upon my mind. In addition was the fact that all the time and expense pursuing a career in aviation had been a waste of time and money and I was probably never going to get a flying job.

"But... I told you to fly a circuit at 1000 feet and you flew a circuit at exactly 1000 feet, I'm giving you a job!"

Flying the circuit at exactly 1000 feet was probably the one and only section of the brief that I had achieved with some measure of professional accuracy.

Things happened quickly. I bade farewell to Gerry. There was a predictable response which, sprinkled with a few coarse epithets and a barely perceptible wink, ran something like:-

"If your performance in the kitchen is any indication of

your ability to fly an aircraft then Heaven help us all!"

Within the hour I was on my way direct to Perth in the right seat of the company twin-engine Cessna 411 with Captain Keith.

The next few days were a whirl of aircraft familiarisation, getting the Cessna 205/6 on my licence, and purchasing aeronautical charts to cover the whole of Western Australia. Within a week I was assigned a trip back to Port Hedland via points en route with another of the pilots based in Perth to accompany me for the first few days. On arrival at Port Hedland I found myself sitting at the managers' table in the company mess and receiving some ribald comments from the folk I had been serving from behind the counter only one week previously. There followed another three days of familiarisation on local routes and from then on I was the resident pilot and was left very much on my own to satisfy the aviation needs of the Port Hedland base.

Over the coming months, getting to know the company and the staff, the possible reason for the hasty recruitment became clear. While I had been toiling at Hill 50 I had answered an advertisement for a pilot in the local newspaper, the 'West Australian'. This was with the company I was later to work for. Predictably there had been no reply to my application. A man from Perth had been taken on and plainly his heart was not in the job. Port Hedland was not a suitable place for wives and he had recently married. Accommodation, even if it could be found, was extremely expensive and the primary work force of single males was generally accommodated in company quarters. In addition, apparently new wife wasn't interested in going to such an outlandish place, full stop.

The day prior to my knocking on the door at the Port Hedland office and beginning work in the kitchen, the new resident pilot had scared harassed Harry out of his wits. Apparently they had nearly collided with the windsock on take-off at one of the company quarry airstrips. The pilot had then expressed the fact that the whole business was not his scene. The full story can only be guessed at but it was possible to surmise that Harry was far keener to have someone who could demonstrably cope with Port Hedland and put up with Gerry and the kitchen with all its problems than any blue eyed boy from down South.

12. Bush Flying

The first morning on my own I checked in at the office after breakfast and was presented with my first unassisted assignment. Three workers were standing around with their personal baggage dressed in typical mining camp casual gear. This consisted of shorts, blue singlets and flip flops. Harry said, with a lack of confidence that implied that he wasn't really sure of the abilities of his new pilot,

"I want you to take these fellas to Horseshoe."

With carefully staged confidence which I didn't feel I responded,

"Fine, when do we go?"

"Well, now."

"Okay, should be back about lunchtime, any return load?"

"No."

I loaded the fellas and their gear into the company car and we proceeded to the airport. Leaving them by the hangar I went off to the flight service office to file a fight plan. Returning twenty minutes later, it was all aboard and we departed Southbound.

Horseshoe was a manganese mine about three hours flying South of Port Hedland and in the middle of nowhere. It was also reputed to be difficult to pick out of the surrounding terrain and was best located by the nearby DC3 size airfield known as Peak Hill. I had gained enough confidence in the actual flying of the unfamiliar aircraft type in the preceding few days but finding my way around these vast unpopulated areas was another matter.

All navigation was visual and the pilot I had been with for the previous few days had given a few good pointers. The main thing was to identify each of the many creek beds which were displayed reasonably accurately on the maps.

These were relatively well defined even though by definition they rarely contained any water. Other than that, good planning and rigorous adoption of standard navigation procedures were called for in terms of time, heading and forecast winds. The simple bubble compass was the only viable navigation instrument available; however, there were serious magnetic anomalies because of mineral deposits in various parts of North Western Australia where the magnetic compass could be very inaccurate. I was to become familiar with the worst of these areas over the coming months.

The aircraft was not fitted with a directional gyro. There was an ancient ADF set fitted which had a tendency to point at thunderstorms when they were active and it could even point at an NDB occasionally (it was supposed to point at NDB's when tuned correctly but there were scant few of these anyway). To all intents and purposes it was completely useless. Such delights as Satnav or GPS were of course purely in the realms of science fiction in those days. I was probably over anxious and the flight proceeded according to plan. Horseshoe appeared in the expected place and at the time estimated on the flight plan. Returning was easy as the coast defined the place to stop and look for the destination of Port Hedland but with the anxiety of the outbound trip behind I was much more relaxed.

It is worth noting that there were, even in 1968, serious deficiencies in the topographical charts which were the only viable means of navigation. In my first few months flying in the area I noted that a mountain of estimated height in excess of 4000' was reported in the notams (notices to airmen) based on a range and bearing from Mount Tom Price. This was subsequently confirmed in terms of position and height and eventually was acknowledged to be the previously undiscovered highest mountain in Western Australia. (Mount Meharry).

And so the work continued. My enthusiasm was not lacking and I worked hard as there was in fact far more work available than could possibly be completed by a single pilot and single aircraft. There was a difficulty in that Harry wanted the aircraft full time for his work and a newly hired quarry manager similarly needed an aircraft full time.

The quarry manager was a well built, delightfully laid back character with a happy disposition called Ron. In the manner of many companies Ron had been hired on some promises which were unfulfilled, one of which was that he would 'Have his own aeroplane'. He was a licensed private pilot and his previous employer had allocated him an aircraft for the work he was involved in South Australia where he was managing several projects in different parts of the State. What his new employers did not say was that Ron would be flown around by a 'green' Pommie commercial pilot rather than flying himself and that he would not have sole use of the aircraft. After some difficulties a compromise was reached and Ron had the aircraft in the morning and Harry was able to assign it for his own purposes in the afternoons. The down side to this was that most of the time I was flying excessive hours and the Australian Department of Civil Aviation were very strict about such matters.

Another problem also manifested itself very early on. Captain Keith ran a tight ship and insisted on strict procedures being followed. These were very necessary but keeping to the rules was not easy. There was a company requirement for full position reporting. This is an international standard procedure and requires that pilots report at certain pre-defined positions on their routes to the appropriate controlling authority in terms of position, time at that position, flight level (or height) and estimated time at the next position. This is based on a paper flight plan filed before departure. The procedure can be ignored for visual flying which was the norm for the daylight operations in the North West but was not acceptable by the standards laid down in the approved company operations manual.

With the requirements of the delightful Ron full reporting was impossible. His main work was centred on the quarries where rock was blasted, crushed and delivered as ballast for the construction of the Mount Newman railway line. The company operated three such quarries and had sub contracts at some of the others which were spaced at intervals down the entire length of the 250 mile railway under construction. I would start the day by taking Ron accompanied by spare parts, workers, mail and a host of other bits and pieces to a particular quarry with a schedule worked out for various other destinations. For all sorts of reasons the requirements would change as the morning progressed and a scheme worked out first thing and presented to the DCA on a written flight plan fell to pieces.

Re-filing a flight plan on HF[1] radio on a regular basis was hopelessly lugubrious. It is hard to imagine how things were before the days of mobile phones although I doubt even now that there is sufficient network coverage to make these devices viable in the outback!

This problem was overcome by a private arrangement with the local DCA flight service station manager who appreciated the difficulties. A compromise was reached. I would file an open flight plan before the start of each day's work which gave all the basic required information but the route section would simply say "Route and destinations to be advised by VHF[2]/HF radio as required". On each departure I would simply advise on the HF radio my departure point, expected destination and ETA. On arriving at that destination I would advise that I was in the circuit and cancel the safety watch until advising the next departure. This did mean that the approximate position of the aircraft was known at all times and satisfied Captain Keith's very wise procedural requirement which was in essence a safety issue.

1 HF radio. See glossary for expanded description.

2 See glossary

I was to remain with the company for over four years. The first year was based in Port Hedland and subsequent years based in Perth. The pay was derisory and initially worse than the pay as a kitchen hand but the professional experience gained and the sheer pleasure of the kind of work in which I was engaged was most gratifying. There were numerous incidents and many, many problems and curious situations, ranging from the hilarious to the unresolved and occasionally very sad.

13. Of Highways etc

Marble Bar, some 120 miles South East of Port Hedland, is reputed to be the hottest place in Australia and is an interesting little town with much history in Australian terms. The place was named after the 'bar' or 'reef' of multi-coloured marble that runs through the adjacent creek. The latter normally contains water in pools and the bar itself is fascinating to walk all over and one can marvel at its beauty. There is some very interesting geology associated with the area and a history of gold mining.

For reasons beyond recall writing this some 40 years after the event, I was flying Ron North West out of Marble Bar. This was unusual territory for Ron as it was well away from the quarries he managed. Ron insisted we follow the dirt surfaced highway at low level and he was peering forward at the road below with unusual intensity. A cloud of dust behind a moving vehicle appeared ahead and Ron made motions in the noisy cabin that he wanted to go lower. Easing down to about 1000 feet above the ground a 'ute' in the distinctive red and white company colours could be seen preceding a cloud of dust like a ship at sea with a wake behind it. After a minute or so during which Ron's gaze at the moving object intensified he said,

"I want to talk to him."

"Okay", I said, thinking that the nearest viable airstrip was at a station some twenty miles ahead. There was never a problem with the owners using these strips unannounced. I added power and put the machine into a shallow climb,

Ron said firmly with an edge of hostility,

"I want to talk to him now!"

With a premonition of what was to follow I feigned lack of understanding. Somewhere, probably during my labours in the kitchen, I had heard that Captain Keith had been known to land on roads when the occasion demanded but it would be severely out of order for me to do so. Anyway it was not approved by any officialdom. Not only that, this was the public highway, unsealed but still for the use of the general public and maintained by the governmental Main Roads Department. Finally, ground vehicles used roads, ships used the sea, aeroplanes used airports or even water if it was a floatplane but aeroplanes did not use roads. Sensing my procrastination bordering on obduracy Ron said,

"Tell you what, I'll do it and then you'll be in the clear!"

This was definitely not the case. The specific brief from the transport manager in Perth was that Ron was only permitted to fly the aircraft should there be a direct instruction from head office. It was a difficult situation especially as Ron was such a pleasant character. He had apparently already decided he was going to land the machine and was adjusting his seat to a position such that he could fly from the right seat. I had previously observed Ron's aeronautical performance and while completely safe it was similar to the way one presumably handled a Caterpillar D8 bulldozer. His huge hand would grab the centre of the control wheel and the performance could be likened to a bull in a china shop. With deep unease I said reluctantly,

"Okay, if that's what you want I'll do it this time but in future I need to find out how I stand with the company".

The Cessna was well equipped for bush work with balloon tyres and high wings so there was no danger, it was just completely out of order as far as my experience and job description was concerned. I chose a straight piece of the highway about a mile ahead of the speeding vehicle and flew low along it to make sure there were no obstacles. Carrying out a low circuit and assessing the wind direction from the dust cloud of the speeding ute I applied full flaps reducing to the slowest safe approach speed and landed to the West. The corrugations associated with dirt roads were not too severe and the landing was completely normal.

There was no point in turning the machine around which would have been difficult given the width of the road as there was plenty of clear-way ahead for our departure. Ron climbed out of the aircraft and shortly after, the ute pulled up. The driver showed no surprise at the aircraft standing in the middle of the road and he and Ron engaged in 5 minutes or so of deep conversation. Waving a friendly goodbye Ron returned to the aircraft and we were quickly airborne heading back to Port Hedland. Nothing more was said and I presumed that in his South Australia job Ron was used to landing on roads to talk to vehicle drivers as a matter of course.

I said little to anyone about the unusual incident but did make a few discreet enquiries amongst the four other pilots employed by the company who were all based in Perth but regularly over-nighted in Port Hedland. Opinions varied. The 'bottom line' seemed to be, do it if deemed really necessary and completely safe but don't make a habit of it. A deliberately vague enquiry to Captain Keith was received with a sharp raising of the hooded eyebrows and that was the end of the conversation. The impression given was that the honourable Captain knew exactly what had happened and neither approved nor disapproved but the message was,

"I don't want to hear anymore but be careful."

A couple of months later there was a late afternoon telephone call to the Port Hedland base office from the Post Office Department. A small truck of theirs had gone missing on the Port Hedland to Wittenoom road. There had been no contact for two days, the weather was bad and the road had become impassable. They were concerned for the safety of their two employees known to be in the truck. Harry explained the situation and I agreed to go and look for them despite the marginal weather. I set off to the South with two Post Office office employees on board as observers. They carried a small bag of well wrapped provisions in the hope that they could drop some food and water should the truck be found stuck somewhere on the road.

The weather worsened and it was impossible to continue legally as the low cloud base and heavy rain meant following the road at a maximum height of some 200 feet. I was aware of all the potential obstacles on the first part of the route as this followed the Mount Newman railway line with which I was intimately familiar. Declaring a "Mercy Flight" to the Port Hedland Flight service centre I pushed on for a few more miles. (A 'Mercy flight' is a little used Australian device which allows all the normal rules to be broken when lives are at stake. A well-documented example occurred many years later with the rescue of the inhabitants of Darwin after a severe cyclone sometime in the 1990's when apparently some 800 passengers were crammed into a Qantas Boeing 747.)

There was no sign of the truck and in the gathering darkness I decided enough was enough and reluctantly turned around and went back to base.

First light the following morning saw us airborne again and the weather was fine. About 40 miles North of Wittenoom we found the truck lying on its side in a creek bed. The two occupants were standing alongside and one had his arm in a makeshift sling. The two Post Office employees on the aircraft were immensely relieved and asked if I could suitably position the aircraft for throwing the package containing provisions out of the window. Assessing the situation and surrounding terrain I said,

"Hang on a minute; I might be able to do better than that."

I found a straight flat piece of road about 300 metres away from the creek and did a low pass to check it out. Although only just long enough it was suitable and with the passengers going distinctly pale, carried out a slow approach and landed safely with plenty of room to spare. The immense relief of the marooned drivers made it all worthwhile.

To keep the aircraft load to a minimum the un-injured driver was left with the truck, well supplied with the package brought from Hedland and a promise that surface help would arrive as soon as possible. The rest of the party re-embarked taking the injured man who obviously had a broken arm.

Turning the aircraft around a little carelessly, bearing in mind that the road was quite narrow, we quickly became airborne. Setting course back to Hedland I advised the flight service centre of my intentions on the HF radio. At this point there was a tap on the shoulder and one of the passengers pointed back to the tail plane. There was a large piece of Spinifex firmly lodged in the elevator horn which had obviously been collected when the tail went out over the bush as we turned around. This was not good news. Port Hedland was a major Flight Service centre and there were many aircraft based there. To arrive with this appendage would be noted in the wrong sense and reports and explanations would be demanded. I turned back South heading for Wittenoom and advised the flight service centre of the change of plan. Wittenoom was always nearly deserted so there would be no unwelcome attention. Soon after landing the Mobil re-fueller appeared and as I removed the prickly piece of local flora he said,

"Been doing a spot of low flying then?"

I smiled in reply but judged it better not to say anything. The re-fueller was a happy character with whom I was well acquainted from previous visits and would be unlikely to mention the misdemeanour to anyone other than as a joke.

There were other very occasional landings on roads but more often on those constructed by the company for their own operations than official highways. There was in fact little difference between a designated airstrip constructed by the company for that purpose and a road except that the airstrip was usually wider. There was one more noteworthy event of this nature which will be recorded in a later chapter.

14. Peter and the propeller

One of the Perth based pilots was a Dutchman by the name of Peter. He was in his early forties, blonde headed and moustachioed. He always appeared immaculately dressed in a khaki drill shirt with long trousers to match and polished brown shoes one of which was specially designed to assist with a foot damaged in an aerial crop spraying accident some years before. This resulted in him walking with a pronounced limp. He had seen much in his life, especially in Holland at the end of the war followed by military service in Indonesia and I was to find that he was a man of few words and stood no nonsense from anyone. He always had a smile on his face which didn't necessarily betray his true feelings in any given situation.

Early one morning I was engaged on the quarry run when a call came unexpectedly from the Hedland flight service centre on HF advising that my company required me to go to Wittenoom. This was most unusual. The company simply didn't use the Department of Civil Aviation to pass instructions to its aircraft, besides which, the DCA frowned on such use of their facilities. Without questioning the reason, especially as the radio communication was unusually poor, I proceeded as instructed and gave a provisional ETA to flight service.

On arrival at Wittenoom I observed the company Cessna 411 parked in the small dirt surfaced parking area adjacent to the miniscule terminal shed. There was a huddle of passengers nearby and Peter was standing, leaning on the port engine, arms folded. Drawing closer and shutting down alongside it could be seen that the port propeller of the 411 had been removed. Completely misunderstanding the situation I surmised that Peter was multi-talented and had removed the propeller himself for some obscure mechanical reason. That things were seriously awry was not immediately obvious but walking over to Peter with the question in my mind as to why I should have been diverted and what did the company require, it became evident that the 411 was not only afflicted with an instantly removed propeller but also that there was serious damage to the fuselage above the cockpit, the fin and one side of the tail-plane. The HF aerial which normally ran from the port wingtip to the top of the fin was missing. Peter was wearing his statutory grin, but his eyes and utterance were a mixture of fright and fury.

"B..... propeller came off in flight and I need you to take some of my passengers over to Camp 171, come back here and take the rest on to Port Hedland."

The clipped Dutch accent was more pronounced than usual and further conversation was not invited. It became obvious subsequently that it was a miracle that the aircraft and all its occupants had not been destroyed. Some of the story came out as I flew three of the passengers over to Camp 171 on the Mount Tom Price railway line. The latter was a company camp which had started as a line camp for construction workers when the Mount Tom Price railway line was under construction two or three years before. It had become semi-permanent as a base for various road building and other operations in the area.

After what had occurred the passengers were understandably nervous about any more flying especially as my machine had only one propeller! I dropped the three at Camp 171, some 30 minutes flying away, returned to Wittenoom, collected the rest and took them on to Port Hedland.

Piecing things together from things said by the passengers and subsequent chats with Peter it was possible to get a rough idea of the events of that morning.

Peter had departed Perth at about 2am and proceeded uneventfully to Meekatherra. After re-fuelling he was bound for Camp 171 to arrive at first light as this was a dirt airstrip with no facilities for a night arrival. Shortly before top of descent the port propeller separated and in the manner of its function disappeared rapidly forwards into the dawn and Peter quickly shut down the engine. In the middle of this procedure the rogue propeller reappeared straight ahead still turning but having rotated into a horizontal plane and Peter pushed forwards on the control column in a desperate reflex generated manoeuvre to avoid it. In this he was only partially successful as the boss hit the cockpit roof causing a pronounced indentation, the inside of which hit Peter on the head, fortunately not too severely. It then took away the HF aerial and caused some damage to the left tail-plane and the top of the fin.

Peter was forced to remain in Wittenoom for several days, much of it spent in a DCA helicopter looking for the lost propeller. This was not for any intrinsic value of the article in question but for metallurgical examination to determine the cause of the failure. It was not found, which is hardly surprising in view of the fact that the separation occurred over the Hammersley ranges which were rugged, bush covered and un-populated. It is probably still there.

15. The Great Sandy Desert

There was a surge of work out in the Great Sandy Desert around this time. Interest in the possibility of there being oil in the area revived after falling dormant for several years following initial exploration. The primary company involved was Ampol Exploration but my employers were heavily involved in supply and transportation. The first destination was a company built airstrip at Willara which was about 20 miles inland from the South West end of the Eighty Mile Beach.

My first arrival was nearly a disaster. The strip was up to standard on the Western end which was the touch down area with the Easterly winds on this particular day but thereafter degenerated into soft sand referred to locally as 'Bulldust'.

There was no way of seeing this anomaly from the air. The Cessna 205 slowed rapidly then finally very abruptly as the nose-wheel dug into the sand. The local manager, a tall fair headed South African apologised for the poor surface and we then proceeded to extract the machine from the sand. With some difficulty it was turned around manually then with four fellas pushing on the lift struts and much engine power which generated huge amounts of dust the aircraft was extracted successfully to solid ground. I calculated that I could get off again on the small amount of hard surface available provided the 205 was empty and this was successful. Before departing I was assured the strip would be upgraded before there was a requirement for another visit.

The next occasion a few days later went without incident as South African had found some gravel locally and had graded and rolled this into a passable surface. With various road building machinery on hand this was a comparatively trivial achievement. About a week later there was another call to go to Willara with some workers and bring others back to Port Hedland. Arriving overhead I observed that the adjacent camp had completely disappeared and there was a dirt road proceeding Eastwards into the desert between the sand ridges. Somewhere the already poor communications had completely broken down and it was difficult to decide what to do.

The Great Sandy Desert is an amazing sight with sand ridges stretching East/West for hundreds of miles, each being two or three hundred feet in height and spaced several hundred metres apart. Temporary roads East West were no problem for the constructors provided gravel could be found but any attempt at North South traverses was fraught with problems. Bulldozers would heave a way through the ridges but the gap would fill up very quickly with any wind as the sand was very unstable.

I followed the road Eastwards for about forty five minutes and it seemed to go on for ever. There were occasional traverses to the South through ridges which could be seen to be filling rapidly with sand. Eventually I sighted a company four wheel drive vehicle and flew low over it with lack of purpose as at that time there was no company radio in the aircraft and the frantic waving of the occupant meant absolutely nothing. There was no doubt at all that trying to land on these roads, given my earlier near disaster at Willara, was asking for trouble. Reluctantly I turned back and proceeded to home base, by this time some two hours away to the West.

The following day I was off again in the same direction. South African had been in contact with base overnight and advised that if I had continued for another 5 minutes to the East I would have found the new airstrip. Pilots are not generally psychic and on arrival at the new camp, at which an up to standard strip had been constructed, there was a minor altercation with South African who seemed to think that I should have known that Willara was no longer used and that the new camp was 110 miles to the East.

During the Antipodean autumn of 1968 there was unusual rainfall over the North West and the Great Sandy Desert assumed a green tinge as long dormant seeds germinated and quickly flourished. Ampol produced an oil rig which was erected alongside a large and very excellent DC3 airstrip that had been constructed for the initial work some years before at a location in the Desert some distance to the South of Broome known as McLarty Hills.

There were regular supply trips to and from civilisation and the whole operation was very interesting as the well was drilled deeper and deeper eventually reaching 11,000 feet with only the barest traces of oil being found. Although nothing was officially announced presumably the entire enterprise was a waste of shareholders' money but such is probably the nature of oil exploration.

Wandering round the original campsite one afternoon, waiting for passengers, I happened upon what had obviously been the old camp dump. With the recent rains there was an abundance of huge water melons produced from the dormant discarded seeds of the previous occupants. After loading the passengers I added as many of these luxuriant green spheres as would fit in to the space available and took them back to Port Hedland. They were a very welcome addition to the mundane fare normally available and a rare word of thanks emerged from Gerry's unsmiling visage. Despite this he couldn't resist some muttered innuendo about light fingered Pommie ex-kitchen hands.

Another incident occurred around this time when some transfer of personnel was required between McLarty Hills and Broome. Landing at Broome for the last transfer before heading home there was a message from the company advising me stay overnight for a charter flight the following day.

The Broome hotel to which I retired was the only public accommodation available. It was a typical outback establishment constructed of wood, corrugated iron roof, high ceilings and of course, no air conditioning. Worse, it was plagued by gigantic but fortunately non-malarial mosquitoes which emanated from the local mangrove swamp. I was used to the luxury of mosquito nets from the Sudan days but enquiries revealed that such things were not available and very few had even heard of such decadent colonial devices. There were also some unhelpful derogatory remarks about thin skinned Poms.

Sleep proved impossible with the constant buzz and bites of aggressive mosquitoes around my head. I eventually decided that there was only one option. This was to pursue and destroy each and every one of the voracious insects which had so un-thoughtfully decided to share my room. I rolled up a copy of "The West Australian" and, despite the height of the ceiling, by standing on the rickety chest of drawers I was able to achieve total extermination. The final headcount was fifteen. The demoralising codicil was that with each victory a large blob of blood stained the ceiling or wall and it was not hard to figure from whence this had been extracted.

Relief came with the dawn. Checking out of the hotel I facetiously advised the hotelier that his resident mossies' were a threat to the lifeblood of the British Empire. Such deliberately confrontational remarks frequently provoked wonderful adjective filled responses and the reply on this particular occasion was well up to expectation. Out at the airfield, a police vehicle arrived and I was informed that I was to fly a convicted murderer to Port Hedland accompanied by a member of the local constabulary. Both the officer and the murderer were of similar build, large and muscular, there were no handcuffs and the situation wasn't appealing. I sat the two together in the centre seats. To have used the back seats, more distant from myself and the controls, would have meant a centre of gravity problem.

The operation was treated as so routine that I could only think that the transportation of large passive convicted murderers was a commonplace event. Anyway, I reasoned, being the Antipodes there was plenty of good historical precedent and experience. A strong medical smell pervaded and a quiet enquiry revealed that the convict had been sedated. The sedation was of a very curious specification as en-route an intelligent conversation took place during which the malefactor asked many questions about the aircraft, the maps and charts and the route flown. After landing at Port Hedland there was a very polite thank-you for services rendered. This was not accompanied by a tip.

After I returned from annual leave, which was unusually prolonged due to having accumulated excessive flying hours for the year, I heard another story about Willara.

Apparently it was still in use as a staging post for desert operations but was un-manned. The resident Port Hedland pilot dropped off a crane driver to do some heavy load transfers from regular road trucks to the huge 'Peterbilt' rig trucks in use in the desert. All the trucks departed following the transfer and the crane driver was due to be picked up in the late afternoon on the return flight to Port Hedland. The weather turned bad and it began to rain quite heavily. With Willara's reputation the pilot decided that it was not circumspect to land and left the crane driver there. The strip was wet for three weeks and the roads were also impassable. The pilot dropped food every few days to keep the poor fellow alive and he was eventually rescued by road apparently far from good humoured and looking like a modern effigy of Robinson Crusoe.

16. A bad day

The months moved on, the afternoon thunderstorms became relatively insignificant or disappeared completely. The thermal turbulence which rose as high as 18,000 feet during the summer months began to calm down and even disappear. Temperatures during the daytime became pleasant and at night could even be considered to be cool, especially inland.

One fine morning in April I took off out of Port Hedland in the Cessna 205, the destination being one of the desert airstrips. There were no passengers, I had removed all the rear seats and there was just a mound of freight amongst which was a large reel of nylon rope. The sun rose straight ahead as I climbed East in perfect weather, the air was crystal clear and perfectly still. I reflected on the hectic months since the job had started with some satisfaction. This was a job I loved with a good solvent company and well maintained aircraft. The pay was derisory but the experience gained was invaluable and the months of frustration had been broken with the advent of the all-important first job.

The North West coast, with the brilliant azure blue of the Indian Ocean, stretched abeam on the left hand side. The desolation of the 80 mile beach was just beginning. Ahead and to the right stretched mundane bush, punctured with sparsely scattered outcrops of rock. The odd white clay-pan made a sharp contrast to the dun, almost red coloured landscape. Levelling off at 9000 feet I settled into the cruise which would last about one hour and thirty minutes to the first destination.

Nearly an hour out of Hedland, deep in my own thoughts and with little to do for a while except keep the aircraft on the calculated compass course (there was no autopilot on this machine) I noted idly that the engine revolutions were increasing. This was strange and I checked the throttle lever finding that it was acceptably tight and should not have permitted any unscheduled engine changes. Coming fully awake I realised that the engine revolutions had now increased rapidly to maximum, about 2800 whereas I had set them at 2300 for normal cruise power.

"Port Hedland, this is Bravo Bravo Alpha" I called on the VHF radio which was still usable with the relatively short distance from base.

"Bravo Bravo Alpha go ahead" was the immediate response."

"I seem to have an engine problem will advise intentions."

"Bravo Bravo Alpha. What is the nature of the engine problem?"

By now the engine revolutions were decreasing, not only so but I tried to compensate by moving the throttle lever fully open, they were reducing rapidly through the pre-set 2300rpm and passing 1800 with an unpleasant vibration associated. At this stage I checked the rest of the instruments and immediately all became clear. There was no oil pressure. The needle was pegged out at the bottom end of the scale indicating zero.

Oil pressure on this type of engine not only lubricates the engine bearings but also operates the pitch mechanism on the constant speed propeller so when the oil pressure fell to zero there was no control of the propeller pitch and it had defaulted to full fine giving the increase in revolutions. The other immediate facet of the situation was that the engine was not going to run without oil pressure and would shortly fail completely.

"Bravo Bravo Alpha, I say again, what is the nature of your engine problem?"

"No oil pressure and the engine is quitting completely. Shutting it down to avoid further damage and will be making a forced landing."

"Bravo Bravo Alpha, that's copied, what is your position?"

The dedicated radio man was simply doing his job but I had plenty to think about and needed a little peace and quiet. Looking at the map there was only one feature which stood out and that was a large clay-pan which even had a name...

"Claypan Well, but will probably land on the highway, estimated about 30miles East of Pardoo station, will call on HF shortly."

The latter was necessary as I had commenced a descent by default with no engine power and would be out of VHF range almost immediately.

There was no panic as the North West Coastal Highway was alongside stretching from horizon to horizon and there was no sign of road traffic which would have been indicated by dust kicked up by any vehicles. 9000 feet is a long way to glide down and I had some 10 minutes before the inevitable forced landing. After selecting a piece of road where there was a minimum of surrounding bush and which looked suitable I called Port Hedland on HF with confirmation of the position and advised that I didn't think the forced landing would present any problems.

As I was to find over many years of sporadic real aviation problems there was little drama. Drama appears with monotonous regularity in simulators, check flights and man devised situations but when a real emergency occurs it is rarely dramatic and the procedures to be followed seem to be orderly and logical. Often they are so unlike those anticipated by routine training that the solutions are modified to suit what is actually going on and the emergency procedures laid down in the various operations manuals and so precious to training departments are totally irrelevant. All the forced landing training of my commercial licence instruction from the previous year had little relevance to what I was actually experiencing. There was an obvious first choice of where to land, there was absolutely no hurry and I could select the stretch of road to be used, in a leisurely fashion.

The aircraft electrics were still active on battery power so I was able to lower the flaps and carry out an orderly approach and gentle landing followed by light braking to bring the aircraft to a halt. The dramatic difference between this situation and a normal landing was the complete, almost accusing silence. No engine idling with associated vibration and no movement, just the remnants of the dust kicked up by landing on the unsealed road settling slowly after the wheels ceased rotating. I set the parking brake and surveyed the situation.

The area chosen was on a slight embankment about 3 feet above the level of the surrounding bush so there was going to be a problem as soon as any vehicles arrived as the machine was blocking the road. I felt that to try and manoeuvre off the road needed more than my strength alone. The aircraft might gather a little speed rolling off the embankment and do itself some damage as it hit the fairly substantial surrounding bush. Before long a utility appeared and thankfully there were two strong male occupants. They seemed little surprised at the situation and even less surprised when I explained what had happened and asked them if they would help me get the machine off the road. In actual fact they had little option but help out although they could have manoeuvred their vehicle around off the road and continued on their way but it seems everybody helps everybody else in the Outback and such was the case this time. The machine was soon parked off to one side in a natural indentation in the bush at right angles to the road and clear of any passing vehicles.

The next occurrence was quite heart-warming. Even though I had called Hedland flight service on HF after landing to advise that all was okay an MMA[1] DC3 appeared overhead having diverted from its route to check for sure that everything was in order. I had a brief conversation with the pilots on VHF and assured them that all was well and after wishing me luck the big machine lumbered off with a throaty roar on its scheduled business.

Sometime later I called Hedland again just to ask if any plans had been made to recover the aircraft (not to mention myself!) and was assured that the resident ground engineer in Hedland was on his way by road.

Seven or eight vehicles per hour passed by and some stopped for the occupants to say 'Hello' and ask if help was needed but most slowed down, presumably decided nothing unusual was going on and sped off on their way. The really curious event was when a whole convoy of vehicles from my own company passed heading in the direction of Broome and didn't stop. A cheery comment in the Hedland mess about two weeks later defined the thinking.

"Saw you stopped for a cuppa on the way to Broome a while back. Would have joined you but we were running late and had to get on!"

It was nearly midday when the engineer finally arrived in his large Ford station wagon. There had obviously been a mis-communication as Carl had been told to bring cans of oil.

Pilots or engineers check engine oil daily or after each flight and there had been plenty of oil in the engine before I departed that morning. I explained the progression of the engine failure. Carl still checked the oil dip stick and found there was adequate in the engine. He then removed the engine oil screen and found it to be full of ground metal. This machine was going nowhere under its own power.

The Cessna could not be left by the roadside. While crime was rare there was always the possibility of cattle using

1 MacRobertson Miller Airlines known affectionately at the time as Mickey Mouse Airlines

it as a rubbing post or similar misadventure or misuse by wild creatures. It was simply too much of a risk to leave unattended and it would be at least the next day before a team could be assembled to take the wings off and truck it to Hedland.

Between us we came up with a solution. We cut off a length of the rope that was being carried as freight and using it as a tow rope, attached it to the back of the station wagon and the other end to the nose-wheel leg of the Cessna. So began a long gruelling tow with Carl driving his station wagon and me sitting in the aircraft, steering with the rudder pedals and applying the brakes when necessary.

Pardoo station, which had an airstrip and was some thirty-five miles back down the road towards Hedland, was the nearest point of civilisation and this was the chosen destination. Every few minutes a vehicle would appear and the machine would have to be manoeuvred off the road to enable it to pass. Sometimes this was easy but other times where the roadside was thick bush or the vehicle was a large truck it was heavy going and exhausting work manually manipulating the aircraft such that the vehicle could get by.

There was never a word of protest from any of the travellers whose journey was thus disrupted but merely a keenness to help. The sun was going down as we pulled in to Pardoo station.

The station manager was quite happy to look after the stricken machine and with great relief we left it parked and tied down on the side of the airstrip and departed for Port Hedland.

Both completely exhausted, covered in red dust grime and sweat, I volunteered to drive for the first half of the trip. This was my first serious mistake of the day. We made good speed for an hour or so until accelerating out of a dip where the road went through a creek bed we observed in the half dark a herd of cattle on the roadside. I should have slowed down, knowing from my agricultural upbringing the capricious nature of young beef, but this I failed to do.

One of the playful young animals darted out into the headlights and there was no avoiding it. We finished in a heap of buckled bonnet, radiator steam and mortally wounded bullock.

Life is full of surprises both pleasant and unpleasant. The next on this increasingly tiresome day was the arrival of a stockman in a utility shortly after the collision. He was on his way to Port Hedland. He had a rifle and dispatched the groaning bullock to put it out of its misery. Amazingly Carl had thrown the tow rope into the back of the station-wagon instead of leaving it with the aircraft and thus it was that about two hours later we arrived back at Hedland under tow courtesy of the helpful stockman who seemed to regard this misfortune as nothing out of the ordinary.

I walked wearily into the base office. Harry and some of the staff were still there even though it was about 10pm. Harry grinned,

"You need to have a look at yourself in the mirror!"

Subsequently, when the engine had been stripped down, the cause of the failure was found to have been due to the break-up of a crankshaft bearing. This was not a common fault and was probably due to a manufacturing flaw. I was allowed a few days off in Perth and then embarked at 2am with Peter the Dutchman in the Cessna 411 with a replacement engine in the back.

We arrived at Pardoo via Meekatharra at first light, Carl arriving by road soon after. It took most of the day to replace the engine and the aircraft was pronounced fit to fly by late afternoon. Thereupon it became necessary to give all the station staff, including the manager, a joy ride as a measure of good will and Carl was a little unhappy at the strain on a recently re-conditioned engine. Heeding this very sensible warning I was as gentle as possible with use of power.

Towards sunset I set course alone back to Hedland and operations were back to normal.

17. This and that

The company employed many hundreds of people in the various operations scattered all over Western Australia and on occasion into the Northern Territory. In this as in many other organisations, various folk would re-appear regularly like bad pennies or, more commonly, as welcome faces. Others once seen would never be seen again.

One morning, departing Perth at 6am after a maintenance trip with the Cessna 205, amongst the passengers was Gerry the cook. A few uncalled-for comments were made to the effect that Gerry had taught me all he knew (which in culinary terms could not be disputed) but there were a few worried expressions on the faces of some of the other passengers who naturally misinterpreted in exactly the manner Gerry intended. The trip proceeded smoothly as far as the inevitable re-fuelling stop planned at Meekatharra.

Taxiing for departure from that most curious of outback towns there was an ominous grinding sound from the left main wheel coupled with a severe tendency to pull to the left. I shut down the engine, set the parking brake and climbed out to examine the cause. For reasons undetermined and never explained the alloy cast wheel had cracked and the tyre was pushing the rim out to contact with the brake assembly. I unloaded the passengers and with the joint effort of all concerned the machine was pushed back to the ramp.

Communication was made with head office in Perth and an arrangement made to dispatch a new wheel/tyre assembly to Meekatharra on another flight the following morning. With the help of a local mechanic I was able to jack the aircraft up and remove the wheel before retiring to a hotel.

Meekatharra was nothing special. A dying Gold-mining town whose prosperity was a distant memory, it boasted 4 pubs in various stages of decline, a general store, a few other tumbledown establishments and sundry buildings aligning the lone unsealed main street. There was little else other than a general air of fading glory and advanced decay. The chosen hostelry was the Railway Hotel which was named after the fact that this was the end of the railway line from Perth. It was a typical two storey outback pub with full length verandah, balconies supported on pillars and a standard corrugated iron roof. There was no shortage of vacant rooms.

The first surprise was when, having coaxed a welcome shower from the antiquated plumbing, I dressed, ventured downstairs and entered the deserted lounge. The closed shutters allowed little light and a disembodied voice began pouring abuse in my direction in a wide range of fluent full blooded Aussie vernacular.

At a loss as to what, if anything, I had done to cause such a tirade and with a measure of umbrage at insinuations as to my lineage and descent, I found a light-switch. It worked! In the un-shaded pathetic illumination provided by a low wattage bulb I made out a dishevelled parrot in a cage hanging from the ceiling. Having been 'found out' and probably having exhausted his one track vocabulary the profane avian relapsed into sullen silence.

Getting the message that my presence was neither required nor welcome, I ventured out onto the stoop shading my eyes against the brilliant sunshine. Gerry was leaning on the rail, puffing on the inevitable cigarette, gazing at nothing in particular and obviously bored. Seeing me approaching he took a long deep drag on the carcinogenic weed and battle commenced.

"Didn't expect to see you flying the plane this morning... thought by now they'd have sent you back to the kitchen with me!"

"And why might that be?" I asked innocently.

"Well, rumour has it that you broke a company aircraft and wrecked a car all in the same day. Surprised they didn't give you the old 'heave ho' let alone allow you to keep on flying."

"The aircraft had an engine failure which was not my fault and was un-damaged in the subsequent forced landing. The car belonged to the engineer and it wasn't entirely my fault that a bullock jumped out in front of us in the half dark and anyway, the car wasn't wrecked, only damaged... talking of getting the sack, rumour has it that the fella I took down to Perth last week in a coffin died as a result of food poisoning. There was even a suggestion that his last meal was in the Company mess in Port Hedland so it was a surprise to me to see you on your way back North this morning!"

This accusation was a gross distortion of the truth but I had learned that to respond to abuse from Gerry with both barrels was the only way to keep on top in these situations. There was no chance of a response as our mutually outrageous repartee was interrupted by the roar of an approaching motorcade of six or seven vehicles proceeding at some speed down the un-sealed main street generating a huge cloud of dust. The individual cars then turned off in formation to park line abreast in front of the Railway Hotel.

This had the suggestion of an auspicious occasion. The occupants disgorged noisily onto the street and stomped into the bar. They were led by a formidable looking female dressed from head to foot in ceremonial black. Loud orders for drinks could be heard and then the shrill voice of the leader protesting,

"It's all off! B..... funeral's all off! B..... b.....s frozen to the block and they can't get him off!"

The rail began to shake and I realised that the carefully staged taciturn image that Gerry always tried to cultivate couldn't be controlled any longer. A casual enquiry to the barman that evening suggested that the vocal female was the widow of the recently deceased.

A miserable night in the non air-conditioned hotel ensued and to the great relief of all, an assembled wheel and tyre arrived on schedule the following morning, was quickly fitted and we were on our way.

18. Harry and the starter motor

For reasons long forgotten the Cessna 206 was in Port Hedland for a short period. While not such a pleasant aircraft as the 205 to fly, it did carry a heavier load and had the same balloon tyres for the various sub-standard airstrips in use. What was not fine was that when the Perth based pilot handed the aircraft over, there was a comment about the starter motor being dodgy. This proved to be the case and after a morning's work it died completely. Harry, the base manager, had an urgent appointment that afternoon at a Cattle station some 40 minutes flying to the South East of Hedland and there was only one possible way to fulfil this engagement.

Hand starting aircraft by propeller swinging was nothing new in my experience. Since Tiger Moth days at Shoreham it had become a regular practice and provided certain rules were strictly adhered to it was no problem. Charlie, the German engineer of the Sudan, had also imparted useful tips. Amongst these was the necessity to use chocks as well as the brakes and having a competent pilot or engineer operating the cockpit controls and switches. The technique of swinging the prop with both hands while moving slightly backwards as each swing was executed was clearly defined, as was the need to hold a healthy respect for this potentially lethal piece of rotating machinery. Regrettably familiarity breeds contempt and I had become markedly slapdash especially as my services had been called upon to start aircraft with flat batteries many times in the interim.

I asked Harry if he was prepared to handle the engine controls while I swung the prop.

"Yes, should be no problem as long as you show me what to do."

No problem at Hedland as the engine was cold and I didn't need any help. Setting the parking brake as firmly as possible and with chocks in front of the wheels, I primed the fuel system with the boost pump, set the fuel control to full rich, propeller pitch control to full fine and throttle to about one quarter inch open. One pull on the propeller and it started. I removed the chocks, installed Harry and myself, being particularly careful to keep Harry well clear of the spinning propeller and we were away.

The problem was at the other end. Harry concluded his business in about 20 minutes and then it was a case of waiting another hour for the engine to cool or trying to start it hot.

Starting a Continental 285hp 6 cylinder horizontally opposed fuel injected engine when hot, exacerbated by a tropical climate, is a clearly defined procedure. It is necessary to set the throttle fully open and the fuel flow control to idle cut-off. Following this the engine must be turned over a number of times on the starter before it will fire up. This is a somewhat laborious procedure even with a serviceable starter motor. Once the engine fires it is necessary with reasonable rapidity to set the fuel control to full rich (fully forward) and then to pull the throttle back to just above the idle setting. If there is any delay in pulling the throttle back the engine will rapidly accelerate to full power. For this reason alone, hand starting a hot engine is an ill-advised procedure.

The chocks had carelessly been left behind (they were not normally taken anyway) and there was no experienced pilot or mechanic to help. Harry was installed in the pilot's seat. The motor was primed, pitch fine, throttle fully open, fuel control to idle cut off, park brake firmly set. Harry was looking worried.

"It's very simple", I explained,

"When the motor fires, which will take about ten swings, you push the red knob fully forward and immediately pull the throttle back to about half an inch from the back stop." I pointed to one of the two adjacent white knobs indicating which was the throttle. With lack of conviction Harry replied,

"Okay, got that" and carried out a dummy run through the procedure.

Just when I was about to forget the whole exercise having become very hot after many swings on the prop, the engine fired. Harry achieved the first instruction impeccably. He pushed the fuel control fully forward. Meanwhile I had come around to the left hand door with the engine rapidly accelerating to full throttle to see that Harry had 'frozen' over the issue of which of the two white knobs he was required to pull back. The Machine leaped forwards with the power too much for the brakes and made about twenty metres rapidly accelerating down the airstrip leaving me standing helpless to intervene. It was several traumatic seconds before Harry, hair standing vertical, realised things were going seriously awry, unfroze and pulled the throttle fully closed.

Fortunately the engine didn't cut out and I was able to catch up and adjust the throttle to a sensible idle power. Harry, looking slightly sheepish, apologised but with no reason as the whole exercise was caused by my stupidity. I should have declined to fly until a new starter motor had been fitted. We departed for base.

A few minutes later, cooling off in the breeze from the air-vents at a suitable altitude, Harry was back to his normal self and commenced to relate a tale from his large store of jokes. These were usually about Sydney and he seemed to have an inexhaustible store of hilarious tales about that unfortunate city. Arriving at Hedland I suggested that it would be wiser to cease flying until the machine was fixed. Harry's grin indicated that there was wholehearted support. A spare starter motor arrived on a flight from Perth the following morning and things were back to normal.

19. Refrigeration and Radios

There were two essential types of tradesmen required for the day to day survival of the enormous numbers of men associated with the mineral boom in the Pilbara region. One was the Fridge Mechanic and the other the Radio Mechanic. As resident pilot there were frequent trips with experts in either of these two disciplines to resolve various outstation faults. I used to joke that the Fridge Mechanic was the backbone of the society as it was in his power to keep the beer cool or otherwise and the Radio Mechanic was equally essential as he kept the communication lines open such that more beer could be ordered. (Possibly the pilot made up the trio as without him there would be no transport, especially in the wet season, to bring either of the above to complete their urgent duties let alone transportation of the beer).

The most regularly used Radio Mechanic, Jim, was a small chatty little man who seemed to have the ability to scale aerials with primate ease and solve all the problems presented to him with the simplicity of peeling a banana. Problems usually seemed to be with aerials rather than the two way radio sets he was called upon to repair and I was never to return to base with Jim having been unable to fix the problem assigned.

The company used the services of two Fridge Mechanics, the first by the name of Bill, tall, well built, urbane, cool, calculating and always about to clinch some deal which would enable him to retire early. An incident bears relating which had nothing to do with his profession.

Bill seemed to fancy himself as a prospector and on one occasion talked the co-founder of the company, Dave Bell, into some interest in mineral deposits near a station called Pannawonica. I flew the two from Hedland to

Pannawonica early one morning which was about one hour and thirty minutes flying time from base. Having not been to this particular station previously I examined the area before landing, noting that there was a short airstrip right next to the Station itself and a much larger strip some 4 or 5 miles away. For the Cessna 205 the small strip was adequate and after landing we were met by the inevitable red and white ute which spirited Bill and old man Dave away with the promise that they would only be gone an hour or so. Good as their word they were back on time and while chatting briefly to the ute driver I noticed with a little sub-conscious concern that Big Bill was loading some sacks into the back of the aircraft. We all boarded and while concentrating on starting the engine, without turning round, I said,

"What was in those sacks I saw you loading?"

In the manner of a man who really wanted to say

"None of your business", but didn't have the gall, Bill said casually,

"Oh, just a few mineral samples."

Regrettably, I gave the matter no further thought.

I warmed up the engine for a few brief minutes and taxied to the North end of the strip to take advantage of the slight Southerly breeze to assist the take-off. The strip was probably not much longer than a mere 1500 feet which, three up should have been no problem for the 205. Acceleration was sluggish and sufficient airspeed for flight was only gained as the crude boundary markers flashed by and the machine was entering the fortunately sparse bush native to the area. Finally airborne Old man Dave said,

"We only just made it then!"

He was not in the least perturbed and appeared to regard the take-off as nothing more than a curious exercise but I was not so happy. Thinking it all through as we climbed up to cruising altitude the reason for the sluggish take-off could only have one explanation. Turning to Big

Bill, who despite his endemic sunburn was a serious shade of white, my worst suspicions were concerned.

"Just what is in those bags?" I demanded.

Barely audible above the noise of the engine Bill muttered,

"Lead ore samples!"

It was impossible to be angry as this was purely and simply my own fault. The pilot is responsible for the loading of any aircraft and while with larger machines this is often delegated it is still the pilot who checks and signs for the load.

"It would have been no problem to move the aircraft to the longer strip. You could have brought the samples over and we could have loaded them there. Why didn't you tell me?"

There was no reply.

Reaching base I unloaded the bags myself and estimated the lead bearing rock in the sacks was well over 300kg and probably nearer 500. The machine was close to its maximum certified load and well overloaded for the short station airstrip.

The other Fridge Mechanic was an old drunkard called Jack. By reason of his lack of personal hygiene one of our fastidious, impeccably dressed office clerks referred to him by the slightly puerile nickname 'Smelly Jack' although never to his face of course. Jack was a totally delightful character, well-built but not tall, overweight, dirty clothing confirming his alcoholic lifestyle, crinkled face with a profusion of blackheads on his nose which was crowned with thick dirty spectacles. Added to all this was the fact that he was totally disorganised. Possibly because Jack, as an independent tradesman, charged less for his services than Bill I was to encounter him far more regularly. There was no doubt that Jack was also an expert at his profession as we never once set off back to base without the fridge or freezer problem assigned having been fixed.

On the morning of the incident about to be related, Jack reversed his battered old utility up to the aeroplane at Port Hedland Airport and proceeded to unload his astonishing collection of equipment into the vacant space where I had removed the rear two seats. Jack could never manage the organisation of Bill who would come with only about six smartly packed toolboxes. He wittered and mumbled as he transferred umpteen tools, bits and pieces of equipment, pipes, gas cylinders etc. etc. as to how I would miss all these little treasures when he was gone. Jack hated flying and to counter this he always had a few tots of spirits for encouragement before he arrived at the airport. A whiff of strong liquor pervaded his labours.

The freezer breakdown on this occasion was at camp 171 on the Dampier to Mount Tom Price railway line. Besides Jack there was another passenger to be dropped off at Dampier and so it was that I set off on the 107nm trip down the coast which would take about 1 hour.

I have always felt that I have been blessed by God with two essentials for an orderly life in aviation. I have little penchant for excess alcohol (quite apart from religious conviction) and have a reasonably strong constitution with respect to potential stomach troubles. The former could cause much distress among colleagues, long or short term and the latter could cause endless difficulties associated with irregular sleep/eat patterns, foreign food etc.

On this particular day increasing stomach cramps on the way to Dampier indicated a rare stomach upset was pending. Looking forward to quick but embarrassing relief behind the corrugated iron shed that served as a terminal building at Dampier I increased to maximum cruise power and broadcast on the local chat frequency that I would be making a straight in approach to land on the Westerly runway. To my dismay as I slowed and turned off to the parking area there was a small crowd awaiting the arrival of the local airline scheduled F27 and the planned activity was definitely due for postponement.

I dropped the passenger off and departed rapidly for camp 171 a full hour and twenty minutes to the South knowing in my heart of hearts that it was fanciful to expect to last that long. In desperation, soon after departure I spotted the long abandoned construction camp airstrip at the 34th mile on the Tom Price railway and advised a slightly astonished Port Hedland radio operator on HF that I would be making a brief stop there. I did not give reasons. Even Jack's alcoholic geography had made him aware that something was wrong as power was reduced and a descent commenced while only just out of Dampier. I muttered,

"When you gotta go you gotta go!"

Jack sat, wide eyed, as the machine touched down on what was really a grossly unserviceable airstrip. Negotiating my way around, and when unavoidable through, spinifex clumps up to 4 feet high, I brought the aircraft to a rapid stop. Setting the parking brake and leaving the engine idling, I heaved the door open grabbing a toilet roll kept for just such emergencies (usually passengers) from the rear of the aeroplane. Hotfooting into the bush there was a brief glimpse of a statuesque, white faced, totally bemused Jack.

With intense relief taking precedence over embarrassment I emerged from the bush a few minutes later to find Jack still sitting in his seat, his face a picture of delight and amusement and seeing me he broke into uncontrolled laughter. This deepened the embarrassment. There was little doubt this incident would become the talk of the mining camps for days but he simply said,

"If you can land an aeroplane just for that, I'll never be scared of flying again!"

(His actual language was much more descriptive but, regrettably, un-repeatable). Jack never was scared of flying again, at least, not when I was his aeronautical chauffeur.

20. Beech 36

Time went by and with two of the more experienced company pilots moving to airline jobs, I found myself based in Perth. The company very occasionally had a quantum shift around of aircraft types. This appeared to coincide with the end of the tax year and/or the number and size of the anticipated projects forecast or contracted for. Such an event had just occurred. The Cessna 205 was sold, the Cessna 206 was sent to the Port Hedland base and a new Beech 36 took over to supplement a newly acquired Cessna 401 for the longer Perth to North West trips. I was instructed to co-ordinate with Captain Keith at the Guildford (Perth) airport for type rating on the Beech 36.

At the appointed hour I met the captain and exchanged pleasantries for a few minutes alongside the brand new aircraft and was handed a key for my personal use. (Yes, just like a car, a key(!) which opened the cabin door and also functioned to turn on both magnetos and operate the starter motor). Captain Keith made a move towards the door and then stopped and said,

"You know how to fly this thing, son, let's go and have a cup of coffee!"

Taken aback, I felt the need to protest.

"But I've never flown anything with retractable gear before and anyway it is a completely different machine to the Cessna."

Feigning great reluctance the Captain agreed to fly a circuit and we climbed on board. Temporary dual controls had been fitted. There was no difficulty with the basics as the engine and controls were very similar to the Cessna. Clearance was received from the tower and we taxied out and took off.

Captain Keith was quite correct, it really was very

simple to fly and the only extra was to remember to retract the wheels when airborne and more importantly to extend them for landing. I speculated over whether the worthy Captain himself had flown the aircraft before as he seemed to be as much at sea as I was. We landed, taxied to the ramp and shut down the engine. The necessary papers were signed over the promised cup of coffee. I submitted the forms to the local DCA office and came away with the Beech35/36 added to the type rating page of my licence.

The real learning began the following morning when I set off for the North West with a full load. Having devoured the contents of the aircraft manuals overnight there were some good clues as to cruising speed, engine settings for the various phases of flight and all the other bits and pieces needed to handle the machine as per the manufacturer's recommendations.

This was probably the most remarkable light aircraft I was ever to fly for several reasons. It carried 6 people including the pilot and you could cram most of their baggage in one way or another although this could make life quite uncomfortable. It cruised at 160 knots (184mph) and used 11 gallons per hour giving an astonishing 16 miles per gallon. There was an infallible visual fuel measuring system which was simply a metal extrusion from the filler caps down in to the tanks giving a precise indication of the permitted fuel load with a full payload. The loading envelope was such that within reason you could place passengers and baggage at your convenience as the centre of gravity range was huge compared to the Cessna which became very limited with a heavy load. With respect to loading there was one vice which could be highly embarrassing. We quickly learned to load the largest of the passengers into the centre two seats, followed by the next largest into the front passenger seat and finally the rear two passengers. The pilot would then climb over the front seat passenger to his own seat. If this procedure was not followed the machine could ignominiously tip on its tail which was no problem but could cause much mirth from onlookers. As to the passengers, the prospect of flying was not loved by many of them anyway and to feel the machine sink and sit up on its tail like a dog before even starting the engine did not inspire much confidence.

I was to operate this machine for some 1500 hours and enjoyed every minute of it. I figured that sooner or later there was bound to be a distraction and I would forget to lower the landing gear. There is a warning horn fitted on all light aircraft[1] such that if the throttle is closed and the wheels are not down a horn sounds. This is fine but allows little time to realise the error of one's ways and discontinue the landing. Landing with the wheels retracted with the inevitable damage to the airframe, the engine and one's pride, not to mention the possibility of losing one's job, is bad news.

Aviation is a disciplined profession and little rules are enforced or constructed personally to enhance the possibility of dying at a good age rather than prematurely. Racking my brains over the possibility of inadvertently failing to lower the gear a simple solution was devised. As almost all of the airstrips this machine was used for were more than adequate in length, if the approach was made 10kts faster than the approved approach speed, it would give time and airspeed to 'go around' if the horn sounded when the throttle was closed.

This was retrogressive on the one occasion I felt the need to land on a road but did save the day when once, and only once, there was a distraction, long forgotten, and I

1 Large Airliners are fitted with far more sophisticated systems with typically three different and independent devices to warn the pilot that he is trying to land with the wheels up. These have been known to have been switched off, usually on training flights, with inevitably sad results.

didn't complete the landing check approaching Paraburdoo in the Pilbara. The horn went off and more than red faced I rapidly applied power and went round for another landing, this time with the wheels down.

Two or three years had gone by and I was well entrenched at the Perth base flying the Beech 58 (see later chapter). I was still flying to the Pilbara area on a regular basis but had lost the familiarity with the local operations and integration with the folk involved. This was sad as those had been good days.

The Cessna 205 was long gone and the Beech 36 which had been Perth based was now the resident machine. Being a much faster single engine low wing monoplane with retractable undercarriage and small wheels, it was definitely not a bush aircraft. Most of the time this was of little concern as the airstrips used by the company were generally very adequate for this type of machine.

Occasionally one of the Perth pilots would work for a week or so based at Port Hedland to enable the incumbent pilot to take leave. I was operating such a week. Ron had moved on and Harry had sole control of the locally based aircraft and things were well organised. Each day's work was carefully planned and the schedule was usually straightforward. Single side-band surface to surface radio had improved so that most of the time the various camps had been advised when the flight would arrive and they would have a 'ute' out at the airstrip at the appointed time.

One day, at a recently constructed strip South of Dampier that I had never visited before, I arrived and landed but there was no sign of anyone. There were no passengers on board, merely an instruction to collect two and move them to another destination. I waited a while then took off again and 'buzzed' the camp which was situated some 3 miles away. In my Port Hedland based days this was normal procedure, you flew low over the camp and this was the message for them to get transport out to the strip. Landing back at the airfield I waited awhile and still nothing happened.

This was going to throw the whole day's schedule out of kilter and the situation was becoming irritating so something had to be done. I took off again and looked for signs of life in the area. There was a huge quarry size dumper truck in company colours traversing slowly down a dirt road two or three miles away and there was a reasonably straight stretch a short way in front of it. Forgetting all the previously hard earned lessons I put the aircraft down on the road facing the direction of the on-coming dumper. Several things were out of order and I realised too late that this was not good. The approach speed of the Beech was much faster than that of the Cessna. Anyway, I hadn't bothered to use short landing techniques. As a result there was a serious mis-judgement of the landing distance required.

The road surface was stony and the undercarriage communicated its displeasure with severe vibrations. The diminutive wheels, when braked, had little stopping effect on the gravelly surface. As the machine slowed it was rapidly approaching a corner and I could see the dust cloud raised by the oncoming dump truck which was still out of sight obscured by an outcrop of rock. All too slowly the aircraft came to a halt as the dumper rounded the corner and the huge machine, towering above the aircraft stopped about 20 metres in front. As the dust settled the bulky form of the driver could be seen wearing only a pair of filthy black shorts and sockless boots extricating himself from the cab. He manoeuvred himself backwards down the ladder to the ground, turned around and walked slowly over to stand, hands on hips in front of the wing alongside the now stationary propeller.

Expecting a dose of serious Australian vernacular, it was a huge relief to see a familiar face set in an enormous fair haired Englishman wearing grimy glasses. He was instantly recognisable as Peter 'O' who I had known well in Port Hedland based days.

Peter with a friendly grin said,

"It had to be you, didn't it?!"

Peter agreed to drive to the camp in his bulky mount and find out what was going on. I flew back to the airstrip and shortly after the two passengers appeared and we were on our way. This was to be the last time I was ever to land on a road.

21. Coffins, etc

Orders came direct from the transport manager to my home telephone usually in the late afternoon or early evening on the day before an assignment. The overall schedule seemed to work out at one or two days off between trips and the trips themselves progressed over two days or occasionally longer. Very occasionally they were out and back in the same day.

Instructions usually consisted of the number of passengers and details of the freight to be delivered to and/or collected from the various destinations. I would then sit down and figure out how to execute the sometimes very complex requirements outlined by the transport manager as efficiently as possible. Before departure the following day I would leave a written programme with the dispatcher outlining the destinations and approximate arrival/departure times. The various bases concerned would be advised of the schedule by SSB radio from head office if they could be contacted. The system worked well albeit there were frustrations and problems usually associated with poor communication and the odd misunderstanding.

An unusual instruction was received late one afternoon during the period in which I was flying the Beech 36 based in Perth. There was a list of northbound requirements for the following day with about four bases to be visited and an overnight stop scheduled at Port Hedland. For the return there was a requirement to take one passenger back to Perth with a stop at Marble Bar to collect a coffin. The manager advised briefly that a plastic body bag with sealing tape would be supplied by the Perth dispatcher and I was to take these northbound and present them to the local police officer at Marble Bar the following morning. Being aeronautically aware himself the manager also advised that it would be inadvisable to climb more than the minimum required for terrain purposes en-route to avoid the possibility of surface atmospheric pressure in the sealed bag causing it to explode with unmentionable results. The officer would provide a coffin to enable the corpse to be transported back to Perth.

The body was that of a truck driver who had been involved in a tragic and avoidable accident involving two trucks parked on a slope while the drivers inspected their loads on the main road South of Nullagine. For indeterminate reasons the front truck had slipped back and crushed one of the drivers between the two vehicles while he was inspecting the load.

All went well northbound. Leaving Port Hedland for Marble Bar the following morning calculations indicated that with the prevailing winds and topping up the fuel from 40 gallon drums available at Marble Bar, the trip to Perth could be flown with no re-fuelling required en-route. The next leg would be just under five hours which was the limit for this machine with the required minimum reserves.

Landing at Marble Bar the officer was waiting. He was typical of those found in the North West. A tall broad shouldered man with a pleasant demeanour who had no doubt seen much in his profession. He looked into the now stationary aircraft and said with a deep sigh of disappointment,

"You didn't think to bring a coffin then?"

"No but I've brought you this!" was my response, producing the body bag and reel of tape.

'This' failed to impress the officer who shrugged his shoulders and said,

"Well, I guess I'll have to go and dig one up from somewhere then!"

Australian humour is of a type and variety found nowhere else in the world. Statements made with a deceptively bland expression have to be interpreted by the listener to determine whether the perpetrator is joking or not. Sometimes the joker actually has no idea whether he/she meant it as a joke and the subsequent response frequently decides the matter. Such was the case on this occasion and my reply was cautiously ambivalent but I noticed that the surveyor, who was my sole passenger, had decided it was a joke and was having difficulty keeping a straight face. Surveyor and I were then invited to go with the officer to help put the body in the coffin when one had been 'dug up'. We obviously made simultaneous decisions that such duties were not part of our respective contracts of employment and politely declined in unison.

The officer was gone a long time and, after filling the fuel tanks from a forty gallon drum with a wobble pump, we grew steadily more uncomfortable as the sun rose and the flies commenced their statutory onslaught. There was neither building nor shade at the Marble Bar airfield.

After about two hours a cloud of dust appeared from which emerged the constabulary ute with a large black coffin bouncing about in the rear. Police officers the world over, going about their bounden business, seem to sound exactly the same regardless of whether they are arresting a murderer or cautioning a 10 year old. The laconic voice said,

"Sorry to be so long. Couldn't find a coffin big enough and he was frozen solid so had to cut him up a bit to get 'im in."

With the hint of a smile but the same dispassionate countenance as before, we had no idea whether what was said had any other meaning than the words conveyed.

At this stage the problems really began. The officer had said the coffin wasn't large enough. For the little Beech 36 it was too large. The ute had been backed up to the double doors and the four rear seats had been removed from the aircraft. It was heavy. I pushed the pilot's and front passenger seat as far forward as they would go and with a struggle (pall bearers are rarely a threesome) we managed to get the box inside and pushed it back against the rear bulkhead. Squashing myself into the pilot's seat I pushed it back hard against the coffin. There was just enough room to fly the aircraft albeit when pulling the control column back as far as possible, full rear elevator was un-achievable but since this should never be required, I adjudged the flight could be carried out safely.

The whole performance had taken another half-hour so, while previously hot, all were now sweating profusely.

Waving goodbye to the officer who was rubbing his hands together and exhibiting some self-satisfaction at the completion of his macabre duty we took off and set course for Perth.

An hour or so later passing Mount Newman things were becoming miserable due to the thermal turbulence and the heat, both associated with flying much lower than normal.

Then the corpse began to smell. Obviously this was as a result of the predictable unfreezing of the corpse. The surveyor and I held an emergency conference which centred on schoolboy physics. There were vague recollections of the laws of Messrs Boyle and Charles. They ran something like this,

"If we can smell the corpse the bag can't be properly sealed?"

"I have to agree in which case if we climb to a sensible altitude the bag is not going to explode as the pressure inside can't increase since it's leaking already."

The vote was taken and it was unanimous albeit the 'bottom line' was that the responsibility would land squarely my shoulders should the unmentionable occur.

Contacting the Meekatharra flight service centre I climbed to 10,000 feet, the maximum legal height without oxygen and the correct level for the direction of flight.

The result was a much needed cooling off, loss of the thermal turbulence and while the smell was noticeable it did not worsen. Needless to say, the correct interpretation of Boyle's law must have been achieved as the unmentionable did not occur.

A hearse was awaiting the arrival on the tarmac at Perth and we were able to leave the extraction of the box from the machine to professionals.

A further two similarly macabre stories (chosen from many!) are outlined but neither affected me personally.

One of the Perth based pilots was a very fastidious gentleman and a delightful character along with it. He mournfully described how he was sent to Dampier with the twin-engined Cessna 401 to collect two bodies and on this occasion he did have coffins and body bags on board to collect his sad cargo. Unfortunately, he was presented with the subjects laid out in the back of a ute and he and two others had to do all the encasement and handling themselves.

Another of the Perth based pilots was a bit of a law unto himself. He would head for the nearest available airfield and land at the first sign of bad weather. Some even said that he would land as soon as the first cloud appeared in the generally clear skies over Western Australia.

In earlier days he was heading for Perth in the Cessna 206 with one passenger and a coffin containing a body on board. The passenger was the manager of the company manganese mine at a place universally called Camp 487 which was the mining claim number but which can be identified these days on the edge of the Great Sandy Desert as Woody-Woody. The manager, who I knew well, related the story some time later.

Apparently they were about 100 miles North of Perth when the pilot decided that the weather was getting bad and the operation should be terminated. He promptly landed at

Wongan Hills and phoned the local funeral home to explain that he had a coffin that should be delivered to Perth. The hearse duly arrived manned by the local one-man undertaker with eyes looking like dollar signs at the prospect of hearse-per-mile charges and the coffin was loaded.

This left the manager at a loose end. Should he spend the night in a local hotel with the pilot, for which the company would pay or hire a taxi to Perth at his own expense? The problem was that he had only a limited time off duty anyway and his intractable wife was not going to take kindly to the delay.

He casually asked the undertaker if he would mind an extra passenger. There was instant agreement and so several hours later the manager arrived at his home in the suburbs of Perth in a hearse complete with coffin. After a few cryptic comments at the manner of his delivery the wife gave way to her statutory outburst and after the minimum time possible the manager fled back to his comparatively serene existence at camp 487.

22. Beech 58

During financially good times there had been another shift around with the aircraft and a twin engine Beech Baron (B58) had appeared which was the mainstay of the fleet and was operated on a 24/7 basis.

An HS125 executive jet, purchased new from Hatfield UK, also arrived on the scene. The Beech 36 was sent to Hedland on a permanent basis but was never a good bush aeroplane although its higher speed was very satisfying compared to the Cessna. I was mainly to fly the Beech 58 but occasionally was assigned to operate co-pilot on the HS125.

The Beech 58 was a good machine and being a twin was much more versatile for the company's operations, especially the ability to operate through the night. I was sent for a few days to Jandakot (the light aircraft airfield for Perth) to obtain a twin and instrument rating and during the course of this I was able to get my pilot licence upgraded to a Senior Commercial licence which was the same as an airline transport licence except that I didn't work for an airline. This had involved months of study in a correspondence course in my own time for the theoretical subjects but the simulator training in an antiquated Link Trainer and the few hours flying training required was all paid for by the company.

The Beech 58 was not flawless. There were problems which were only partially resolved. Heavy interference on the HF radios was eventually supressed but was initially very frustrating. The biggest problem was the fuel loading.

The company operated with full commercial loads most of the time and this meant that full fuel could rarely be taken as that would result in the machine being outside legal weight limits. For reasons never determined the Beech 58 had adequate fuel capacity but only one fuel tank in each wing. Its fore-runner, the Beech 55, which I occasionally flew when a replacement was hired while the company machine was on maintenance, was possessed of a much more versatile fuel tank design. There were two tanks in each wing which were simply designed such that full inners and empty outers meant that maximum payload could be taken without overload.

Use of the fuel gauges was not a cast iron measurement of the fuel on board. Fuel gauges in light aircraft (and cars!) are poor at the best of times (this is not true for larger airliners).

A method was even experimented with where the fuel drains under the tanks were extended and a clear plastic tube was attached during refuelling. Marks were calibrated up the adjacent fuselage to show the fuel loading but these were found to be hopelessly inaccurate unless the machine was stood on completely level tarmac. Tarmac is never completely level by definition to allow for rain run-off so this device proved to be useless.

Thus, a measure of anxiety was associated with the operation due to simple bad design. The eventual, not fully satisfactory solution was careful completion of company paperwork in terms of flight time and fuel used based on learned actual fuel consumption figures. Coupled with the readings of the fuel gauges the fuel loaded was probably fairly accurate as a result and the ultimate test, an engine failure on take-off with a full load, did not occur during the company's operation of this type.

Peter the Dutchman, always a law unto himself, simply gave up and with his immaculate attire and ever-present grin announced that he would always put in full fuel as he felt that the risks of an engine failure while overloaded and at a critical stage of the flight were less than those incurred should he run short of fuel. There was some logic in this argument, however, I used to maintain that to overload a single engine aircraft was a sin but not criminal as if the engine stopped there was only one route and that was downwards. A twin or multi engine aircraft was certified to remain airborne in the event of an engine failure at the most critical stage of flight, usually take off. Therefore, to overload was criminal as should such a disaster occur and the aeroplane was overloaded it would not remain airborne and was most unlikely to have the performance to return to the airstrip before crashing.

Notwithstanding these vexations, life was straightforward and pleasant. The 24 hour operation did not bother me and I was quite happy to do the first trip of the day which usually commenced at 2am. The auto-pilot, after some initial problems were resolved, was superb and with the greater cruising speed of 190kts navigation was simple even on the routes with few ground based navigation aids. Frequently it was possible to go Dampier direct to Perth or Port Hedland direct to Perth on the return trips as there was usually a lower South-bound load. While Hedland to Perth had the DME and NDB at Meekatherra en-route, Dampier to Perth had nothing. By laying off drift based on forecast winds and going direct the machine was never far off course even after 4 hours flying with little, if anything, recognisable en-route in the darkness. As a general rule there were no other light aircraft flying at night and I became very familiar with the friendly voices of the flight service personnel, communicating at each reporting point every 30 minutes or so.

Other than one incident as recorded in the opening chapter, which could have resulted in the untimely termination of my career, there was another which is worth mentioning if only as personal condemnation of myself. It may serve as a warning to any light aircraft aspirant pilots who might one day read these lines.

As has been said, the weather in Western Australia is generally very good in aviation terms. This was to cause complacency which is an unhealthy state of mind in the aeronautical profession.

One day I was headed direct from Perth to Paraburdoo in daylight. There was a rare meteorological event in progress in the form of an upper air depression over the North West. About two hours out of Perth the sky was overcast well above the cruising altitude of an unpressurised aircraft and it was pouring with rain.

Approaching destination the cloud thickened and lowered until I was flying fully IFR (Instrument Flight Rules) with no external visibility and no ground in sight. This was so unusual that I was confident there would be an adequate cloud base underneath and it would be practicable to land at the destination especially as a new airstrip had recently opened which had a sealed runway and an NDB. There was as yet no official chart for the NDB approach but this had been written down in terms of tracks, heights and timing in the DCA notams and I had taken the trouble to draw my own approach chart based on this information. It should also be mentioned that weather reports at these remote places were to some extent guesswork as the only meteorological officers and flight service personnel were based at Meekatharra, Port Hedland and Carnarvon each of these places being more than 200 miles away.

Arriving overhead the NDB there was no let-up in the cloud. With little concern, I descended as per my approach chart and arrived at the DCA specified minimum altitude to find that there was no view of the runway or the ground whatsoever. Gear up, flaps up, go-around power and I climbed back to the approach commencement height over the NDB. I reported the conditions to the Hedland flight service centre on HF and re-assured the passengers that all was well except that we might have to go and land somewhere else until the weather cleared. With adequate fuel it was worth another try.

Down through the laborious procedure once again which took a full 7 or 8 minutes and still nothing. Gear up, flaps up, go-around power and back to the NDB. Dallying overhead, considering the options for an alternate, there was a tap on the shoulder from the passenger seated next to me. He was pointing ahead and to the right. Dipping the right wing there was a glimpse of the piano bars at the runway threshold through a hole in the cloud and 1500 feet below.

This was when complete and utter foolishness prevailed and to this day the memory of the event causes a blush at the ensuing appalling airmanship.

An instant decision to go for it! Engines back to idle (never a good practice in the air in this type of machine…they might not pick up again should rapid and immediate power be required), flaps to full, a crazy descent with the vertical speed indicator pegged down to its maximum rate and almost immediately I was touching down on the piano bars and slowing down in visibility which had suddenly deteriorated to about 50 yards. The passengers clapped their approval but taxiing slowly through the murk and eventually finding the brand new bus stop style terminal building I was in a cold sweat of personal recrimination. There was the inevitable red and white utility parked nearby. The driver was astonished at the arrival and remarked that he was on his way back to the camp thinking that he would have to come back later when in disbelief, with the prevailing visibility, he heard the machine land.

To the uninitiated there would seem to be little wrong with this operation. The objective of getting the passengers to their destination had been achieved and surely that was the purpose of the exercise?

Aeronautically there were at least two major transgressions. Firstly, Newton's calculations ending up in the laws of motion define that a body moving at fixed velocity in a fixed direction will continue along the same path unless acted upon by an external force. Descending at a high rate in an aircraft leaves little room for error should there be any mis-judgement when the time comes to stop the descent, in this case, arrival at the runway. The standard approach path of 3° has been devised over a century of aviation as a sensible and completely controllable way to approach a runway. There are exceptions where higher angles are used but never more than 6°. This approach was probably of the order of 40°. Secondly, high powered fuel injected piston engines are not supposed to be descended at idle power. Idle power is for use for landing and taxiing and definitely not for descent. Cooling is excessive over the air-cooled cylinders and there is always the danger that the engines will not pick up quickly if treated in this way should a mis-judgement occur and rapid application of power be required.

23. HS125

The Hawker Siddley 125 executive twin jet was a particularly useless machine for the type of operations assigned to it in Western Australia. It was purchased as a result of the intransigence of the Australian Government who would not permit private companies to run any aircraft which could pose a threat to the monopoly of the two designated internal airlines. This strangulated the needs of larger corporations who ideally needed big machines for their own operations unrestricted by airline schedules.

The company tried all sorts of angles with the government. These included attempts to introduce a DC3, an F27 and even an ageing Bristol Freighter, all of which would have suited the work perfectly although there was some dismay amongst the pilot force when the antiquated Bristol Freighter was suggested. All applications were refused and so the hopelessly uneconomic and unsuitable HS125 arrived on the scene. The fuel consumption and maintenance costs were horrific for the maximum of 10 passengers it could carry, one of whom was assigned to the undignified position of sitting on the modified toilet at the centre rear of the cabin. The machine was supposed to be able to use dirt airstrips which were almost *de rigueur* in Western Australia. However, for this usage the pressure in the tyres needed lowering with the encumbent inconvenience. The practice was discontinued after a compressor blade on one of the engines was found to have been chipped by a stone while operating the machine into and out of an unsealed strip. This threatened extreme expense should it occur on a regular basis.

There was one amusing little incident on this type. I was flying co-pilot for Captain Keith on a trip from Perth to Dampier. Once established in the cruise at an unfamiliar Flight Level 370 (37,000 feet) Captain Keith instructed me to go back and say 'Hello' and pass the time of day for a few minutes with the Chairman of Hamersley Iron who was one of the passengers. Hamersley Iron, a vast wealthy iron ore conglomerate whose power dictated almost everything that occurred in the Mount Tom Price and Paraburdoo area, were key users of the services of the company so politics naturally dictated that their staff and especially the Chairman be treated with great respect.

Captain Keith had failed to describe the Chairman and I surveyed the full cabin attempting to select the most likely subject to fit such an exalted position. Surmising that the personage would not have been subjected to the indignity of the toilet seat there were nine other potential candidates. Right at the front of the cabin there was a gentleman dressed immaculately in a suit and tie who seemed to fit the bill. I tried to engage him in pleasantries. This gradually became embarrassing as while there were nods and smiles there was no reply and I retreated to the cockpit in some confusion not to mention, embarrassment.

Arriving at Dampier a short while later (the trip to the Pilbara which took most of the day in the Cessna 206 amounted to a paltry 2 hours in the HS125) there was an entourage to greet the Chairman. Looking from the cockpit I watched with dismay as a man who had been sitting at the back of the cabin dressed in mundane denims was greeted formally and driven away. It transpired that the smartly dressed gentleman I had been trying to converse with was a Yugoslav labourer, straight off a flight from Europe, who couldn't speak a word of English!

There was a significant bonus to this brief excursion into jet aircraft which was of great benefit when some three years later I decided that the future had to be working for an airline. Although the experience gained was relatively insignificant a few clues had been assimilated with the completely different style of operation involved with jet engines, high speeds, high altitudes and multi-crew.

24. Moving on

All good things have to come to an end and the mining and earth moving organisation had changed significantly over the four years of my employ. Towards the end of this period a personnel manager was hired by the company. This was a curious phenomenon at the time and it is hard to understand it as such in the light of vast "Human Resources" departments seen in 21st century organisations. There he sat in a smart new office at the headquarters building in Perth with many certificates adorning the walls which proudly proclaimed his multitudinous exploits and qualifications. Previous to this, local managers hired and fired and dealt with 'Human problems' in a time honoured manner largely governed by their individual wants and compassion according to each situation.

The eponymous Timothy Burke, new appointee to this exalted position, was a dapper young man, always smartly dressed, extremely offhand to pilots on the rare occasions he deigned to converse with them or when he ventured into the outback in an aeroplane. Worst of all, when he did decide on a 'field trip', he was always late. This could throw carefully worked out schedules into chaos and became an increasing irritation. In retrospect it is possible he detested flying and also wanted to score points with regard to his importance and these two facets exacerbated an increasingly acrimonious relationship.

One morning I was assigned to take Tim to Mount Newman together with other passengers and the usual paraphernalia of parts and supplies. The departure was very early with a refuel stop at Meekatherra and scheduled arrival at Mount Newman at first light. The orders were to drop Tim and proceed on to Camp 487, discharge and collect passengers then return via Newman to collect Tim and bring him back to Perth. Another trip with the Beech 58 was scheduled for the afternoon with one of the other pilots and it was important to get the machine back to Perth on time.

Dropping Tim off at Newman where there was a company vehicle waiting as arranged, it wasn't necessary to stop the engines and I left them at idle as he disembarked. There had been a stern admonition issued en-route to the effect that it would disrupt the entire day's schedule should he be late back. There was a short stop at Camp 487 and a very welcome snack in the mess followed by return to Newman. On arrival there was no Tim and no sign of a company vehicle. I parked and shut down the engines. The passengers welcomed a quick bit of exercise and visit to the toilet (open bush!).

Impishly, I resolved to teach Tim a lesson in punctuality. When a cloud of dust appeared in the distance indicating the imminent arrival of a vehicle I embarked the passengers and started the engines leaving the front seat next to the door vacant. As the vehicle approached I started a slow taxi away and turned around to see Mr Burke sprinting across the tarmac, leap on to the wing walkway and throw himself into the vacant seat in a manner most undignified for his exalted status. Reaching across the breathless Tim, I slammed the cabin door shut, applied the locking mechanism and said,

"Mr Burke, you're late!"

There was no apology and in the coming months there was little doubt that the incident had not been forgotten.

Not long after it became obvious, although there was no official statement, that the transport manager who had handled the aircraft operations from his utilitarian office on one side of the Perth transport workshops and had always been very friendly, had lost control of the aircraft operations. Mr Burke seemed to be taking over. His briefing in matters aeronautical had plainly not been covered in his specialised training and he completely failed to understand the issues involved. He made some really bad changes especially with regard to scheduling which enraged the pilot workforce although to be fair, with no consultation whatsoever, he didn't achieve much co-operation. Even Captain Keith was subjected to the new regime in no uncertain terms and found himself departing at 2am on regular Beech 58 operations and the HS125 gradually became lost to view presumably because of straitened financial circumstances and the enormous expense of its operation.

The co-founder of the company, David Bell, who with his brother had brought the company to its very considerable size from humble beginnings in the 1930's, was in failing health and was to pass away in 1973. Even in the year 2010 he rates well in the information available on the internet. He had been particularly pleasant to me personally and there were good memories of flying him around the Pilbara. It is probable, again with the benefit of hindsight, that as the old man's health faded, others less wise moved the company in an unsustainable direction and soon after I left, the aviation division was closed except for the Port Hedland operation.

Not many years later the company was taken over by a much larger conglomerate.

By now there was a wife and a child. There were a few thousand hours of flying behind me. I asked Captain Keith if he would give me an open written reference. He complied writing a magnanimous and totally undeserved document which I'm fairly certain was of great assistance when produced for various future job applications.

With probably an over-exalted appreciation of my potential worth in the aviation employment market, I decided to head for pastures new and gave in my notice.

SECTION II

AGRICULTURE

1. Pastures New

There was a brief abortive attempt at employment in the Middle East. Back in the UK it became necessary to turn to the "Situations Vacant" at the back of "Flight International". Three of my long term employments have had their origins in this worthy journal and it wasn't until imminent retirement in 2009 that I was to drop the habit of starting to read the magazine from the back. At some time in recent years, in conversation with an unusually honest ecclesiastic, he confessed that he started reading clerical periodicals from the back for exactly the same reasons so there is no shame attached. We are all made from the same dust!

There was a minor advertisement, just three small lines, for an agricultural pilot. There had been no response from pilot recruitment agencies or other leads and it was becoming a case of 'beggars can't be choosers'. I called the number and was astonished to find myself talking to a pilot whom I knew well from the work in East Anglia in 1967.

"Come and see us, have a look and see what you think!"

Arriving at a rusting Nissen hut on the disused wartime airfield at Enstone in Oxfordshire in the miserable weather of an English February, there was little to impress. The company had been newly formed and was entirely owned by the pilot to whom I had been talking on the phone. There were two old Piper PA25 Pawnees and an enthusiastic young operations manager by the name of Martin. They were a breakaway from a long established agricultural aviation company based in Bedfordshire. It wasn't really my desire to go back to agricultural aviation despite the fact that I had never worked in this particular industry as a pilot. I guardedly accepted the job offered on the basis that the family had to be fed and options were running thin.

First things first. I only had an Australian licence. There had been no suitable applicants for the job other than myself. The Department of Trade and Industry who were the reigning UK governmental aviation authority at the time granted a validation to enable me to operate. The encounter at the Flight Crew Licensing office at Shell Mex house in London was unforgettable. The gentleman of distinctly foreign extraction made a provocative statement,

"We can't have all you foreigners coming in here and taking jobs from local pilots!"

Rather than make an issue of it, which would have been justified with my family history being traceable to Doomsday, the circumspect course of action was to remain silent. Australian Nationality had been obtained while working in that country but I had not dropped the Nationality of my birth. The basis on which I was granted a validation was that no suitable UK pilot had applied for the job. I made a promise that the UK licence would be obtained as soon as possible.

Early March 1972 saw me back at Enstone to start work. The PA25 Pawnee was familiar, albeit I had only flown the type ferrying between operating bases in 1966. I had not operated the machine in its designated role of application of chemicals from the air. In terms of engineering I knew it inside out. It was also on my Australian licence having been transferred from the New Zealand equivalent by default.

Jack, my new employer, gave some verbal instruction which lasted all of 10 minutes. This was a little alarming as in the Antipodes, Agricultural aviation was treated with great respect. There were ratings in the application and use of chemicals from the air which were a legal requirement for operating in both Australia and New Zealand. These courses took weeks, if not months and there was considerable expense involved before a pilot was considered fit to exercise the trade. It was, in many ways, bizarre that I was about to be let loose in this complex new environment after a few simple words of semi-anecdotal advice.

The instructions were roughly as follows. Solid fertilisers were to be dropped from about 50 feet to enable a good spread and this would be the primary work through to about June. From June onwards, other than the occasional need to drop granular insecticides, the work would be liquid spraying which was best carried out at about 5 feet above the crop. The fields would be marked. The markers were fluorescent cards attached to the top of sticks which were placed across the fields to be treated. These were placed by a fieldsman at the correct intervals to give guidance to the pilot for an accurate application. They were alternating, 3 yellows followed by 3 reds and I was to find the system very satisfactory. Location of the fields to be treated was by use of 1 inch per mile Ordnance Survey maps.

Jack advised that the best way of turning 180° at the end of each run would be initially downwind as this, followed by a steep turn in the other direction, enabled the accurate positioning of the aircraft for the next run. He also suggested that if a field had to be flown upwind and downwind as opposed to across the wind direction which was the favourite, care was required to pull up over any trees or wires well before it appeared necessary while flying the downwind run. There was also some discussion on application rates. This was to prove the greatest headache as with the wide variety of materials used, the gate settings for solids and spray pressure for liquids were immensely variable and only experience brought some satisfaction of a job well done.

For any pilot readers it might be useful to make a general comment with regard to turning close to the ground in agricultural aviation. Many airline colleagues over the years have suggested that agricultural pilots might use a technique known as stall turning at the end of each run. This is an aerobatic manoeuvre where a machine is placed into a steep climb until the speed reduces to the extent that an aerodynamic stall occurs. The nose is then allowed to drop and recovery occurs as speed increases in the subsequent dive. This is never used in agriculture and indeed, is completely non-viable. To rise into a stall turn, especially when the machine is heavy would inevitably end in disaster while so close to the ground. The technique used may look similar to a stall turn to the ground observer but this is because it is circumspect to climb up to 150ft or so for the turn both to give adequate ground clearance and for a good view of the crop being treated such that the line-up for the next run can be accomplished accurately. The standard technique is simply steep turns, always maintaining adequate flying speed.

The work commenced in earnest. The airstrips in use were mainly farmers' meadows and varied from delightful to just plain awful. In New Zealand I had seen Pawnees modified to the New Zealand standard and had been amazed at the crude additions to Mr Piper's basic factory design.

Firstly, they were equipped with very "Heath Robinson" mudguards. The reason the Kiwis resorted to these crude devices was almost immediately apparent when I commenced using the original unmodified machine in the UK. On take-off in a recently grazed cow paddock, cow pats were picked up by the unguarded wheels, proceeded forwards as if in slow motion then returned increasingly rapidly as the aeroplane accelerated, desiccating into an unhealthy slurry while passing through the propeller finally impacting the windscreen in a filthy green morass, blotting out all forward vision. Sometimes it would slither away leaving enough vision to complete distribution of the load but usually it was a case of putting a hand out into the 100 mph slipstream through the direct vision window (a 6 inch openable panel in the side screen) and attempting to wipe enough space clear with a rag to be able to see ahead, such that the load could be dispersed.

This was a loathsome and quite an un-gentlemanly procedure, not to mention the smell! I quickly learned to avoid cow pats where possible and having marked out a clear run through the meadow with the wheels on take-off, it was circumspect not to deviate one inch from this track for subsequent take-offs and landings.

Secondly, the Kiwi machines had an infallible lever system to open the top of the chemical hopper. On the Pawnee the hopper is directly in front of the cockpit and needs opening to allow reloading after each landing while using any solid materials. The pilot would pull on a lever in the cockpit which mechanically opened the lid to allow the ground equipment operator to place the spout of his machine into the mouth of the hopper for reloading. It was crude and agricultural but strong and reliable. Jack's machines had an automobile choke cable to effect this same task which was subject to frequent breakage. In this case the pilot had to climb out and hold the hopper lid open for each re-loading until a new cable could be fitted. In view of the cold weather and idling propeller this was a most unpleasant task not to mention having one's face in the acrid fertiliser dust. It should also be said that on fast work, ie work near the strip, landing to re-load could occur as often as every 5 minutes.

Thirdly and finally there was the fuel tank. The Kiwis

had removed the fuel tank which Mr Piper had placed in front of the fuselage chemical tank on their Pawnees but which was prone to cause a catastrophic fire in the event of a crash and replaced it with two wing tanks in the out board sections of the wings. Mr Piper eventually incorporated this modification into the design with some grim side effects. More about this in chapter 11 of this section.

I plunged into the work with excessive enthusiasm and rapidly gained experience. Low flying, initially exciting, quickly became the norm and I learned to check carefully for wires and other hazards before starting a field.

Very early on I experienced the reason for Jack's caution with reference to flying up and down wind. It was on a long narrow field which could only be flown lengthwise. On the first downwind run I pulled up in what seemed to be good time to clear a tall tree. The judgement was wrong because the machine and I ploughed through the top of it with a dramatic thump as the propeller chewed its way through, scattering twigs and small branches in all directions. The aircraft was undamaged and the lesson, as with most learned the hard way, was not forgotten.

A major facet of the operation was the change in aircraft performance as the load reduced. Fully loaded it was necessary to 'handle like eggs' to avoid an aerodynamic stall especially when turning. As all aviators know, stalling at low level brings disaster. Most agricultural aircraft have the stall warning device 'nobbled' simply because it will be going off constantly in turns and when the machine is fully loaded. The Pawnee, before fuel tankage was moved to the wings, possessed very straightforward stalling characteristics. You could pull as much 'g' as was comfortable in the turns. If aerodynamic buffet occurred one notch of flap cured the problem. When buffeting occurred with a notch of flap that was the limit and it was necessary to ease off the elevator pressure. I was to find at a future date that this was not the case when the basic design was changed and fuel was carried in the wings.

I was to remain full time in this specialised crevice of aviation for some eighteen months. Incidents, amusing, scary and plain hilarious peppered the experience at regular intervals. The one really dangerous incident involved a near disastrous encounter with electricity wires. This occurred in later years when I was occasionally helping out a different operator during the agricultural peak season while working for an airline.

2. The Cub

The season progressed. Work was hard and for long hours as the evenings lengthened. There were two good rules. We didn't start work until 8.30am and we didn't work on Sundays. This gave the basic necessities for survival. God took six days to create His universe and then he rested on the seventh day. This is a blueprint for the well-being of the human race. With the daylight hours running from 4.30am to 10pm during midsummer, overwork, always threatening when the weather was right, could be a lethal trap. This was exacerbated by the fact that the primary pay was in the form of acreage bonus. The more work completed, the higher the pay and natural human avarice lurks in the minds of most men. I would suggest that there are far more accidents in agricultural aviation caused by over-work and exhaustion leading to fatal mis-judgements than any other cause.

Early on I made a stupid error and tipped a Pawnee on its nose. This meant a new propeller. Fears of engine damage subsequently proved groundless but there is no question that the incident was expensive. The circumstances were unusual. Tail-wheel springs on the Pawnee were not man enough for the poor airstrips in use. They were a regular cause of disruption to the operation as they broke and while it was possible to fly the machine empty, back to base, it was not possible to operate. Exactly this happened but on arriving back at base there appeared to be no one to help me move the machine from the runway back to our Nissen hut base, an impossible task single handed with a broken tail-spring. I attempted a difficult manoeuvre which I had used before.

With full flap and considerable engine power it is possible to taxi the machine with the tail off the ground using brake against engine power. This was going well until

I turned with the tail into wind. A sudden gust and the machine was on its nose, crashing ignominiously back onto the already broken tail spring assembly as natural centre of gravity took over. The boss emerged from the Nissen hut. Apparently he had been on the phone. To say he was not happy would be an understatement. At the time there was a lull in the work load so the demands of the farmers and agencies could be met with the remaining machine. It was about 10 days before the aircraft was back in use.

Whether this had anything to do with subsequent relegation to a smaller machine I will never know. Much money was obviously being made in this the first season for the new company. New cars appeared for The Boss and the manager. The Boss's car was an up market sports model. Major improvements were made to the Nissen hut and we even had a toilet block erected which was an even bigger plus for the lady secretary who previously had to use the facility at a commercial enterprise on the airfield but some 5 minutes' drive away. The other sign of prosperity was the arrival of a PA18A Super Cub. The Boss wanted to use this as a 'run-around' and supplement working machine during busy periods.

Some kind of a mix up occurred. Jack had sought a New Zealand pilot for the peak three months from June to August. In the event two Antipodean pilots turned up. They were neither of them going to suffer the indignity of using the Cub let alone the much lower acreage bonus encumbent with a smaller machine. The company possessed only two Pawnees and the Cub. Thus I was allocated the Cub.

A little needs to be explained at this stage to those both initiated and uninitiated in matters aeronautical. Mr Piper originally designed a superb little high winged monoplane called the Piper Cub (PA18) which came in a variety of marques with two seats in tandem and a small motor which would allow the machine to putter along at some 80-90 knots.

This was the machine with which I had become well acquainted during training in New Zealand. It was easy to fly and superbly aerodynamic. The Piper Super Cub was a very much more powerful aircraft of the same design designated the PA18A and was put to use in all manner of operations among which was the dispersion of chemicals both solid and liquid from the air. The machine, while a delight to fly and aerodynamically superb, was not very safe for agricultural work. When I was flying this particular version, an old sage from the Sudan who I met while working in Lincolnshire, warned me that should I find myself 'Going In' (about to crash!) it would be wise to raise the feet from the floor. Previous history suggested that the engine would come back and remove the pilot's legs at the knees. Fortunately, it was never my privilege to verify this most useful piece of information.

Presumably, as a result of early catastrophes Mr Piper put his thinking cap on and developed the Piper Pawnee (PA25). This was basically a PA18A but the wings were placed lower making it a low wing monoplane and the lift struts came down from the top of the fuselage into the top of the wings at a point approximately half way along the wingspan. This had a disastrous effect on the lifting capability and it has been suggested that the only useful lifting area of the wing was outboard of the lift struts. It had been my dubious privilege to fly this version back in 1966, fortunately not for agricultural purposes but purely for familiarization. With the 150hp engine originally meant for the PA18A the machine was hopelessly underpowered. The end result was the adoption of a 235hp engine which became standard for a number of years. It was easy to fly and relatively safe. It was in many ways an advanced piece of agricultural equipment rather than an aeroplane. The fact that it flew was purely coincidental to the operation of applying chemicals.

For several weeks I operated the Cub. There were major disadvantages not to mention the much lower acreage accrued in a day's work. The chemical tank was behind the pilot in what would have been the space occupied by the rear seat. The jettison (dump) mechanism was very different to the simple lever on the Pawnee and was long defunct anyway. The whole of the bottom of the tank was supposed to hinge open to release the load in an emergency. The release system consisted of a row of toggle clamps, connected with a gang bar. Working long hours I rigged up a cable from this gang bar up to a T handle on the cockpit dash panel. After lubrication of the neglected toggle clamps, it seemed to work well.

One day I found myself working off a private airstrip alongside the river Thames at Wallingford, spraying fruit trees. This was a quite unusual and not unpleasant job but I was to discover that my ingenuity in reviving the dump mechanism was no cause for self-congratulation. The strip ended where the river curved so a failure to take-off would mean getting wet. Over-confident towards the end of a long day, it seemed that to avoid two more loads to complete the job, if I took a slightly larger load, the work would be finished and I could head for home. The result was that upon reaching the end of the strip with the heavier load, the machine just refused to fly. Pushing the boundaries was frequently my downfall in those days and in desperation I pulled my carefully installed T-handle to dump the load. Insultingly, the cable broke and the T-handle came out of the dash panel in my hand.

The mind goes into overtime in these situations and I recalled a vague piece of advice collected sometime previously. Taking off with the Cub it is normal to use one notch of flap which gives a little extra lift. The second and only other notch is primarily extra drag for landing. However, if the flap lever is held halfway between the first and second notch a small increase in lift is evident. Pulling the lever up that extra fraction the machine became airborne and swooped low across the river as I gained a reasonable flying speed. Hard work in reviving the dump mechanism was a waste of time as I hadn't tried the obvious. Empty of chemical, the toggle clamps, with no load released easily. By definition, filling the tank applied far more downward pressure on the clamps and the force needed to release them was proportionately much higher. My proudly designed mechanism was simply inadequate for the job.

The pressure to pump liquid chemical from the boom mounted nozzles is provided on most agricultural aeroplanes by a bladed fan driven pump mounted between the main undercarriage legs. This pump also circulates the chemical and mixes it which is very necessary when using certain types, such as fungicide, which is a chemical suspension rather than a solution. A valve in the cockpit operated by the pilot switches the supply of chemical on when commencing a spray run and off at the end of it. A brake is also fitted such that the rotation of the pump can be stopped when the chemical runs out. A dry pump will over-speed, damage its bearings and seals and even disintegrate if the blades are not exactly balanced. The cub had a pump peculiar to itself and there seemed to be no spares available. The brake didn't work as the shoes were worn out and replacements couldn't be found. Worse, whereas the quantity of chemical remaining on the Pawnee could clearly be seen through the translucent chemical tank wall immediately in front of the cockpit, on the Cub there was a plastic tube running up the side of the cockpit which was supposed to show the level of chemical. Good for solutions such as insecticide but any suspension type liquids and the sight gauge became opaque and was useless.

I soon learned to judge the amount of chemical left using the spray pressure gauge and number and length of runs on each job. Inevitably, occasionally, I mis-judged and was greeted by the roar of an unloaded pump running away and threatening to self-destruct. The only answer was to land very quickly and this I did a number of times in any suitable grass field alongside the work area. Some worried citizens would drive post haste in the direction of the field to determine the reason for the sudden landing. Usually I had time to jump out, leaving the engine idling, loop a piece of light rope around the pump blades, kept at hand for the purpose to prevent rotation and head off back to the strip where the tanker was installed before there was too much interest from third parties.

These difficult days came to an abrupt and nearly tragic close. One of the New Zealanders was operating his Pawnee with an unserviceable starter motor. He presumably became a little too casual at hand swinging and caught his fingers in the prop when the engine fired. For him the season was finished as fingers were broken and needed time to heal. It could have been far worse. The bonus for me was that I had the Pawnee back but I would not have wished this accident on anyone. I was gratified to see that the starter motor was replaced immediately. Hand starting occasionally should be a reasonable procedure (reference my Australian experience!) but on a regular basis is not to be encouraged especially in the agricultural aviation business with plenty else to think about.

3. The Trivia of agricultural aviation

Events occur in this profession which would have mega consequences in any other form of aviation but are relatively insignificant when plying one's trade as an agricultural pilot. They occur regularly and vary in impact from trivial to just plain scary.

One day, proceeding up and down the fields dropping granular nitrogen fertilizer there was an impact with a small bird. This was not an unusual event and is similar in some respects to collateral damage caused to wildlife by road vehicles. However, on this occasion, the bird impacted the pitot tube which was completely torn off and disappeared into the slipstream. This small piece of equipment is a diminutive tube which, on the Pawnee, is attached to the underside of the port wing and faces into the oncoming airflow. It is away from the propeller generated slipstream and supplies the raw data which operates the cockpit airspeed indicator. The bird, sadly, presumably perished in the encounter but I found myself with no airspeed indicator.

The experienced aviator will say,

"How can you operate without an airspeed indicator?"

Quite probably glider pilots would have no problem. In their silent world they become tuned to the rush of the airflow and performance of their graceful steeds such that were the airspeed indicator to be blanked off they would simply fly by feel, sound and instinct. On one occasion, bush flying in North West Australia I found myself taking off with what appeared to be a sticky airspeed indicator. It was not sticky. Becoming airborne there was no airspeed indication whatsoever. The aircraft was a leased machine, hired while the company aircraft was on maintenance. The owner had lapsed into the cardinal sin of blanking off the pitot head with a precisely fitted plastic sheath. (I have to admit, it was red, the approved colour!). Vital parts of aircraft are always blanked off when the machine is not in use to prevent dust ingestion or insect blockages. I had missed it on the pre-flight inspection.

All covers and protective devices fitted to flying machines are by definition fitted with prominent red flags to prevent disastrous mishaps should they not be removed prior to flight. This pitot cover was not equipped with the vital flag. There are well documented accidents where larger aircraft and even airliners have crashed due to problems of this nature. Airspeed is a vital need-to-know facet of safe aviation. On that occasion, with a Cessna 206, I was so completely at home with the machine that I continued to destination and landed safely, guessing the airspeed for flap extension and approach, removing the offending cover after arrival. There were a few choice comments to the owner when I next saw him especially as he had the gall to say with a smile,

"Oh, you're the second person to be caught out by that!"

Coming back to the Pawnee, I was at that stage well experienced with the machine and finished the load without any airspeed indication. After landing to tell the loader what had occurred I returned to Enstone and politely requested a new pitot head.

"Take at least a week to get one!" was Jack's sharp response,

"Suggest you get back to work!"

And so I flew for a few days with no airspeed indicator and really found it was no problem.

Another incident which was potentially far more serious was entirely my own fault. Working near Newbury in Berkshire one of those annoying distractions occurred which caused a really unforgiveable omission.

The work was fast[1], that is to say I was landing to fill up with each load of granular fertilizer very frequently since the distance from the airstrip to the fields was comparatively small. After each landing it is important to keep track of the amount of material used, acreage remaining and where in the field the previous load has run out so that accurate continuation can occur with the next load. For this a notebook is kept to hand and the pilot usually develops his own shorthand to scribble down the essential details. Thus, the two to three minutes spent re-loading is quite intensively occupied.

On this particular morning a private pilot with an 'anorak' mentality insisted on standing next to the cockpit each time I landed and good manners dictated that I open the side screen and briefly pass the time of day. This was fine for one or two turn-arounds but when it became evident that this practice was going to continue for the duration I became increasingly irritated. No amount of hinting to the effect that he was impeding the operation put the message across. Finally in desperation I kept the side-screen closed and concentrated on the paperwork, ignoring the interloper. This was at best very rude but it did cause him eventually to disappear leaving me ill-humoured and not concentrating on the job.

---

1 Some top dressing can go really fast. While working for 'Bill' (see ch 11) I was given a wonderful job to the South of the town of Bedford. This was a massive block of several hundred acres and it was rectangular. The strip was a grass field alongside the block and was long enough for positioning the loader in the middle such that I could land, load and take off straight ahead. Taking slightly less than a full load of fertiliser worked out as exactly correct for one complete run down the field and I flew a whole afternoon of racetrack patterns. Take off, left turn spread the load in one run, left turn, land etc. This, on final calculation was 64 take-offs and landings in five and a half hours work.

The final ingredient to near catastrophe was the fact that, over the months I had gradually dispensed with pre-take-off checks. With the huge daily number of take-offs and landings, pre-departure and pre-landing checks, so vital to regular forms of aviation, could be largely ignored. It had become the habit to do a full pre-take-off check for the first flight of the day and following a break for any reason but otherwise ignore the practice completely.

Spreading the load immediately after the departure of 'anorak', I was proceeding down the crop, 100 mph and fifty feet above the ground when there was a sudden, unannounced total absence of noise. A micro second glance at the fuel sight gauge situated some way straight ahead down the Pawnee's long nose and the awful truth was confirmed. I had run out of fuel.

All good aviation practice was instantly forgotten. I threw the jettison lever forward, dumping the remainder of the load, heaved up the flap lever to apply full flap, full left stick, full right rudder, a ludicrous sideslip (never use sideslip with flap had been the advice since early days) and planted the machine in the tiny grass meadow at the end of the field being worked. Heavy braking followed by a sharp ground turn and I stopped sideways just before a line of tall elm trees. Had the engine stopped only milliseconds later it would probably have caused the premature demise of the aircraft and possibly me also.

The ensuing silence while I sat shaking and berating myself for being a complete and utter moron was deafening.

There was a farmhouse nearby. Collecting my scant remaining wits I walked slowly over to the dwelling and knocked on the back door. A cheery agricultural face appeared and I lamely confessed to my shortcomings.

"Wondered why the noise had stopped!" was the response,

"I guess you'll want to use the phone".

Eventually, the message was conveyed to my loader who on this occasion was an Australian summer worker and was the possessor of a commercial pilot licence. He was working as a loader while trying to obtain the all - important first flying job. Some thirty minutes later he arrived on the scene. He backed the truck up to the aircraft and we commenced re-fuelling. I have to admit that I simply wanted to fill the tank and get out of this embarrassing situation as quickly as possible. Aussie muttered through his bushy ragged beard,

"You're not going to fill it right up are you?"

Instantly I realised what he was saying. The meadow was tiny and the aircraft even completely empty would be struggling to make it over the hedge in the short distance available for take-off

"No, of course not!"

About five gallons had been pumped in and I stopped re-fuelling immediately. Hopefully my smiling gratitude conveyed heartfelt thanks for his timely and very professional suggestion. Shamefully 'loss of face' dictated that I didn't openly admit that he was right and I was being an ignoramus. For the second time that day the guardian angels looked favourably upon me.

After fuelling I started up, chose the longest run available where there were no trees at the end and set one notch of flap. Holding the machine on the brakes I wound up to full power. There was plenty of clearance as I made it over the boundary hedge but with full fuel that might well not have been the case.

Driving home that evening, mentally reviewing the day's work, I conducted a serious review as to the why's and wherefore's of pre-take off checks while operating the Piper Pawnee. There was a primary potential killer. This was engine failure for whatever reason. I made a procedural change to which I adhered rigidly for the remainder of my agricultural aviation days. On each take-off run for which I had not performed the full pre-take off check I would check the fuel quantity and engine oil pressure.

The following morning I felt confession time had arrived. These things have a habit of circumventing any attempt at a cover up. I said to Jack,

"Before it comes to you from another source I need to tell you that I ran out of fuel yesterday."

To my intense surprise he said with a half-smile,

"Such things have happened!"

The implication was that sometime in his history he had suffered the same ignominy. Indeed, it does seem endemic in agricultural aviation. In my Sudan days, some years before, one of the Kiwi pilots had run out of fuel, again with no damage to himself or the aircraft. Subsequently, a long term agricultural pilot with whom I had also worked in the Sudan mentioned in an exchange of letters that he had managed to perform exactly the same trick in New Zealand. The only difference was that the latter squarely blamed his loader-driver which seemed to me to be a little harsh.

4. Winter Months

The season gradually came to a close and by early September there was some serious thinking needed regarding the winter months. The pay had been good but there was little saved up for a winter of unemployment. A prospect came along for a winter contract spraying the Tsetse fly in Zambia. The money was acceptable and conditions looked good but by definition it had to be unaccompanied. I simply couldn't leave the wife and by then two offspring on their own for several months.

One morning Jack said, completely out of the blue,

"We want you to stay on for the winter."

He outlined what I would be doing and the prospect seemed both interesting and attractive. There would be very little flying but loading equipment needed a complete re-think, re-design and build. The aircraft spreaders needed improving and re-building and the company wanted to start a new base in Bedfordshire.

I jumped at the opportunity and it seemed that many problems were instantly solved and initially there seemed to be good prospects ahead for employment with the company long term. Regrettably terms of employment were not discussed. I just assumed that the pay would be reasonable.

Moving the family over to the Bedfordshire area, a pleasant rented house was quickly obtained. The daily drive to base at Enstone was long, nearly two hours each way. The use of another disused wartime airfield at Little Staughton in Bedfordshire was negotiated but it quickly became apparent that this was premature and the winter work was going to be at Enstone. This was easily solved. With fuel very cheap in those days, the company based the Cub at Little Staughton and I commuted the 20 minutes flying to Enstone in the morning and home in the evening in the Cub. It was amazing that with no blind flying instruments and no radio there were only about four days during the entire winter that I was forced to travel by road due to the weather. There were however two occasions when unscheduled landings in fields en-route were called for to wait for poor weather to improve.

The work was interesting and absorbing. A new loader was built based on an old army four-wheel-drive truck on which we mounted a Hyab hydraulic crane. For this we made our own sheet steel hopper with hydraulic gate mechanism and during the subsequent season it worked superbly. The time taken to load half a ton of fertiliser into the aircraft was reduced from about 4 minutes with the old equipment to thirty seconds once the operator became skilled with the new machine. The aircraft spreaders which hung under the aircraft and spread the fertilizer laterally were modified and improved and we managed to double the previous spread to great accuracy. All of this meant that in the subsequent season twice as much work was accomplished for the same amount of flying.

At the end of the first month Jack handed me a cheque representing a month's salary which was totally inadequate with the needs of a growing family. Humiliatingly I was forced to say that this was simply non-survivable. With a measure of bad grace the amount was increased by £30 with the codicil that the extra would be deducted from flying pay during the next season....which it was. Never having been in my nature to bargain over pay and conditions it was a deep disappointment that Jack chose to be so miserly when there were definite signs of prosperity within the company. There was little option but to struggle through to the new season when flying pay would become substantial again.

There was one amusing little flying incident during February. A slug baiting job came up. This was only about 20 acres in the vicinity of what was to become the New Town of Milton Keynes. One evening, with a good weather forecast for the following day I put several boxes of slug bait into the hopper of one of the Pawnees and flew the machine home to Little Staughton for the night instead of using the Cub. The following morning, cold clear and with a heavy frost I emptied the slug pellets from their damp proof packaging into the aircraft hopper and set off for the job.

This kind of work has its own dispersion problems in that the application rate is very low being literally a few pounds weight per acre. Gate settings need to be very precise in order to obtain some semblance of accuracy of application. This is very unlike the approximations required for one or two hundredweight per acre for granular fertilizer. However, granular fertilizer spread inaccurately, will cause yellow stripes in the crop which for obvious reasons is displeasing to the farmer. Slug bait spread inaccurately is not so serious. The slugs sniff it from some distance away and expedite their demise by seeking it out.

The job went well and while working, a Land-Rover appeared in the adjacent meadow. It was obviously the farmer watching me do the job.

It was a beautiful morning, there was no particular hurry to get back to Enstone and I felt a little PR was in order and decided at the conclusion of the work that the time was ripe to land and pass the time of day for a few minutes with the farmer. The adjacent meadow was large but as I landed aiming to stop alongside the Land-Rover it suddenly became obvious that the ground sloped downwards, not easily visible from the air and with the heavy frost there was zero braking. In increasing panic I shot past the vehicle and proceeded downhill into the boundary hedge, entering at about 5mph having fortunately remembered to pull the engine idle cut-off before doing so. There were fortunately no stumps or posts in the hedge and the farmer, emerging from his vehicle, helped me to extract the machine which was completely undamaged.

We spent a few minutes chatting. I politely declined the proffered cup of tea back at the farmhouse and headed back to Enstone. The departure and flight to base was uneventful.

5. Deeper Experience

The human existence is a curious business. At various times deep discussions occur. These can be over a quiet drink in some shady dive as beloved by aircrew or even in the middle of the chaos of a busy international airport. More often, they will occur completely unexpectedly during the long hours over the various oceans and landmasses of this beautiful planet.

"What really is life all about?"

The simple answer is,

"I don't know!"

What I do know is simply what has happened to me as initially described in chapter 9, section 1. Very occasionally other events and experiences have occurred which have left a deep feeling of humility and awe at the presence of the Almighty Creator of the universe, who Himself is right outside of the earthly phenomenon we call time. Indeed, He created time!

It was the spring of 1973. The new season had recently started. After initial teething problems had been ironed out, equipment built and perfected during the winter, was working well. After the shock of effectively being forced to take very low pay through the winter months, thoughts of a permanent position with this particular employer had vanished. There had to be a more stable and lucrative manner of earning a living.

Encompassed by these depressing thoughts I was working from a private airstrip to the South East of Swindon which was as smooth as a billiard table and would, under normal circumstances, have been a most pleasing experience. It was raining. Not torrential, just that steady continuous warm frontal rain so common in the British Isles. My loader was a man called Ted. He was a short strong middle aged little man, with a red weather-beaten face. A slim, hand rolled, untidy looking cigarette hung out of the corner of his mouth which he was obviously having great difficulty keeping alight. As always he was wearing a shapeless, dilapidated, brown felt hat and the rain dripped steadily from the brim. He seemed to be enjoying the morning as little as I was.

Each time I landed to re-load, he didn't look at me and I didn't look at him. There seemed to be unspoken vibrations in the ether which were causing intense displeasure to both of us, although not between us. Rather, he seemed to be ruminating darkly over some grudge of his own. I stopped to refuel. Ted passed me the re-fuel hose, climbed onto the back of the truck and commenced operating the hand pump while I directed the nozzle into the aircraft fuel tank. With the tank full, I handed the hose back and work re-commenced. The normal cheerful banter was starkly missing. We had exchanged not a word.

Flying the aircraft, despite good visibility which seems to be the norm under the cloud cover in warm frontal rain, life was wretched. The Pawnee has an air vent above and just in front of the pilot's head. This provides a vital air supply which is supposed to keep the occupant in fresh air, un-contaminated by the noxious fumes emanating from the chemical being applied. It can be opened or closed but it does not keep water out when it is raining regardless of its position. The water, a grey, highly acidic slurry caused by rain mixing with the fertilizer dust engrained in the vent filter, dripped steadily onto the front of my helmet and down over the visor onto my lap where I was keeping the windscreen rag to absorb as much as possible before it seeped through into the vitals.

Every so often at a re-loading stop I would open the side-screen and wring out the worst of this polluted mixture onto the wing.

Once again, I have no idea what happened. There are things going on in the Heavenlies which us mere humans are not party to.

I started to sing!

It was a simple little Christian song that I had known for many years and it is about God's love. Over the next hour the rain stopped, the sun came out, Ted's dark brooding countenance vanished and he became his normal light hearted self and all was well with the world. I sang that song quietly, to myself for three days. Weighty problems seemed to evaporate, long standing grudges were gone forever and I made the decision that at the end of the current season I would get a more sensible job.

6. A fine day in Essex

It was a good morning, in fact, it could even be said that it was a superb morning. The sun was shining, fleecy white cumulus clouds dotted the sky and an unusually warm Spring South Westerly breeze idled across the North Essex landscape. After the harsh cold weather of a week earlier with its marginal conditions for aerial topdressing this was sheer delight.

The airstrip, along with many others in East Anglia, was the remains of a wartime airfield from which heavily laden bombers departed night after night only some 25 years previously to drop their deadly cargoes on the dying Third Reich. Most of the hard surfaces had been dug up, the aggregate thus gained being used to fuel the rapidly growing motorway network which was the public and governmental passion of the 1960's and 70's. What remained was a narrow slither of concrete, very long and marginally wide enough for the Piper Pawnee allowing less than one metre of clearance either side of the undercarriage. This was adequate although it couldn't be described as generous. At approximately the mid-point of this strip of concrete was an enlarged area which was ideal for turning around and re-loading.

All went well for three hours or so. The work was primarily on large fields which enhanced the speed of the operation and being solid fertilizers was carried out at a reasonable height which made the problems of electricity and telephone wires of little consequence.

After a brief break for lunch during which the slightly taciturn loader and I sat munching our sandwiches simply enjoying the silence and the sunshine, the peace was destroyed by the roar of another agricultural aircraft from a rival operator arriving on the scene. This complicated the operation considerably. After a short discussion with the other pilot a mutual agreement was formulated. The Rival would use the North East end of the strip and I would use the South West end, the winds being such that each could land and take off, the Rival departing to the North East and landing South West and me taking off South West and landing North East both arriving at the centre re-loading pad without interfering with the other's operation.

During the morning, I had noticed a substantial wooden post toward the South West end and slightly to one side of the piece of concrete I was now restricted to. This was no problem with the light winds and being the only aircraft using the strip. However, it began to assume increasing significance as the afternoon wore on and the South Westerly breeze began to rise. Landing downwind, in order to stop by the loader, the touchdown point stretched further and further to the South West until towards the end of the afternoon on an otherwise normal landing run there was a loud bang under the right wing and I realized with some dismay that I had hit the post. Stopping the aircraft, a quick glance back confirmed that the post was no longer erect and a further check under the right wing revealed a small hole in the fabric towards the trailing edge but apparently no substantial damage.

The work continued but several take-offs' later things were definitely awry. At about 80 knots when the aircraft should have been lifting off it was showing no inclination whatsoever to do what it was designed to do. In addition there was an ominous shuddering and distinct inclination to turn to the right which had to be corrected with large amounts of left rudder. A furtive glance to the right revealed some kind of protrusion at the wing end of the lift strut which should not have been there. With the end of the airstrip approaching rather too rapidly and no indication whatsoever that this apparently perfectly viable flying machine was going to become airborne I decided that enough was enough and closed the throttle. The machine careered ingloriously into the ploughed field at the end of the strip. Fortunately, rather than by any pre-ordained skill or forethought, I hadn't dumped the load which would have been the correct thing to do when things were going wrong and as such the machine didn't nose over.

What had actually occurred was that the collision with the post had severely bashed the rear wing spar, denting the aluminium alloy extrusion of which it was made but not actually breaking it. In doing so the lift strut fairing had been loosened and after several take-offs the stress had caused the fairing to partially separate causing such interference to the airflow that the aircraft simply refused to fly.

This was an extraordinarily severe effect for the simple disruption of a lift strut fairing. The smooth merging of the over wing struts into the top of the wing was a fundamental necessity relating to the ability of the aircraft to fly. This miniscule fairing (a triangular piece of composite material some 150mm across) was critical and not to be tampered with.

The Boss and his sidekick chose this particular moment to arrive on the scene. There were some acid recriminations until the more practical aspects of the situation began to assert themselves. I climbed back into the cockpit and pushed the dump lever allowing the full load of fertilizer to drop into the field. After manually swinging the machine around to face the end of the strip which was no easy task in the ploughed field even with the load gone, the engine was started and with manpower on each wing and horsepower from the engine the machine was manoeuvered back onto the concrete. The hapless loader was summoned and instructed to bag up what he could of ½ ton of fertilizer now scattered among the furrows. This he proceeded to do with even less grace than his taciturn self normally allowed and he reminded me several times in the ensuing days what a chore it had been and to make sure that it didn't happen again.

The lift strut fairing was screwed back on, astonishingly for such a vital item it was only ever secured by one simple self-tapping screw and the day's operation was called off. Very chastened, I flew the machine back to base. Subsequently the repair to the aircraft was extremely simple. Mutterings from The Boss about the expense of a new wing or the work involved in replacing the rear spar proved totally incorrect and after an engineering inspection the spar was cold worked back to its correct alignment in the course of a single morning's work by the mechanics.

7. Flight Test

Inevitably the Department of Trade and Industry was on the case and insisting a UK licence be obtained rather than continuing with the validation of the Australian licence. With the intense work of the previous summer followed by absorbing projects of the winter it was hard to find the time to placate the authorities.

Eventually I did manage to sit the aviation law exam which was the only written requirement. After the practicality of Antipodean examinations the obscure demands of the powers that be, who seemed to be dwelling in the 1930's, were bizarre in the extreme. Clearly recollected is one of the examination questions which amongst a whole range of archaisms read:-

"What lights should an airship carry when riding at anchor at night?"

Presumably their Lordships in the Ministry had failed to update their examinations since pre-war days, that being the most recent period when viable airships plied the skies. Having studied hard I did know the answers and easily passed the examination.

Even more bizarre was a call from the Ministry out of the blue that informed me that I needed to pass a flight test to verify my aeronautical abilities. Enquiring as to the manner in which this was to be carried out I was informed that a flight test examination would be arranged and I was to present myself together with an aircraft at the appointed place and time for the purposes of this exercise. I pointed out that my validation was purely for agricultural work and that the authorised type was a single-seater which would not permit the presence of an examiner. The response came back that the examiner would observe and verify my flying abilities from the ground. With just under 5000 hours flying time, licenced to fly commercially in New Zealand, Australia and even Switzerland (licence obtained by post for a one off job) this did seem to be bureaucracy gone mad.

During the course of a normal morning's work I broke off and flew over to Sywell aerodrome in Northamptonshire. The examiner, a thin white faced gentleman wrapped up in a ministerial coat to protect him from the chill wind, met me outside the control tower and we shook hands. It is probable that he was a little shocked at my appearance. Dirty blue overalls and decrepit shoes, probably a little coated with the dust of nitrogen fertiliser encumbent with the operations, I did explain that I was in the middle of an intensive day's work.

"Well, never mind, we'll get this done as quickly as possible and you can go back to work!"

He was very helpful and presumably recognized that the entire exercise was a farce but ministerial instructions bode that he play the part.

"I would like to see you fly a couple of circuits with full stop landings and then come back to me and we will discuss the next detail."

"Would you like full procedural circuits or can I just do a couple of quick crop spraying circuits!"

His curiosity evidently outweighed protocol and he unwisely said slightly impatiently,

"A couple of crop spraying circuits will be fine."

Sywell was deserted, the aircraft was not possessed of a radio and anyway, during the week, there was no controller who might have required more dignified procedures.

Engine started, two minutes to settle the machine which was already warm and I was away. Two hundred feet above the ground, a procedural steep turn downwind at about 300 feet within the confines of the airfield boundary a steep turn on to final approach followed by a short full stop landing to avoid having to taxi back for the second circuit. Taking off straight ahead without backtracking, I repeated the procedure.

Taxiing over to the examiner after landing, I opened the side screen and he came alongside. He seemed a little perturbed at the exhibition so far but dignity kept him from speaking his mind.

"I would now like to see two stalls[1] followed by procedural recoveries."

"For that, especially with the drag of the spreader, I will need to go up to about 1500 feet." I replied,

"Will you be able to observe what I'm doing at that height?"

"Don't have much option, do I?"

A hint of a smile indicated that ministerial reserve was softening.

The Pawnee with the fertilizer spreader hanging underneath was an ugly sight in the stall and it was difficult not to lose considerable height in the recovery. I did the best possible through two of these manoeuvres and landed back again.

"I would now like to see a forced landing without power."

Up to 1500 feet again. Straight overhead I cut the engine back to idle and applied carburettor heat to avoid intake icing at low power. The simulated forced landing

1 Stalling. This is not to be confused with the engine stalling as on a motor car. A fixed wing aircraft (as opposed to rotary wing, e.g. helicopter) flies by means of its passage through the air. There is a certain minimum speed below which there is insufficient airflow and the aircraft will enter an aerodynamic stall. This usually accompanied by buffeting and subsequently a nose drop as effectively the aircraft falls earthwards. With some types, if the appropriate recovery action is not taken, this can result in the aircraft gyrating rapidly earthwards, semi out of control in what is referred to as a 'spin'.

manoeuvre was really most enjoyable. There was an insane desire to slow to near stalling, pull the idle cut off and stop the propeller for a real power off landing. This was not insane from the operational point of view. Agricultural pilots probably know their aircraft better than in any other branch of the profession and with a large wide open grass airfield below the procedure was 100% safe. However, the thought occurred that such an excessive compliance might dampen the examiners increasingly friendly attitude.

With the inbuilt drag of the un-aerodynamic Pawnee coupled with the oversized spreader that was a British home built design, the machine dropped like a stone. Keeping the speed well above the stall I plunged earthwards and planted it on the ground about thirty yards from the examiner. Heavy braking on the dry grass and I stopped up alongside him. Throwing the side-screen open and stopping the engine I asked,

"Was that okay?"

By this time there was a wide smile.

"I think I've seen enough, perhaps you ought to go back to work."

This was not the end of the story. Three weeks later, having heard nothing from the Ministry I cautiously telephoned the relevant department. Having finally achieved contact with an individual who was aware of my case I asked,

"About three weeks ago I performed a flight test and understood that this was the final requirement for me to obtain a UK commercial pilot licence. I have since heard nothing and am wondering if there is a problem?"

"Yes, as a matter of fact we are having some difficulty," was the guarded reply.

"You see, the issue of a Commercial Pilot Licence is for the carriage of passengers for hire or reward. The only aircraft you will be licenced to fly is a single seat machine which is not equipped to take even one passenger, so indeed we do have a problem. We are working on this and will eventually give you our decision!"

This was completely and utterly ridiculous. Racking my brains for a suitably ministerial solution I hit gold.

"The PA18A Piper Super Cub is also on my Australian licence and I have been operating this on the validation. This has the capability to carry a passenger when the spray tank is removed. Is that acceptable?"

I thought I heard a quiet sigh of relief at this information and the conversation was terminated in a friendly fashion. Within a few days the British commercial licence came through in the post.

8. Bewildering Beans

The manner of marking out the fields to enable the pilot to accurately drop chemicals has already been mentioned. There were occasions when a simpler method was used and this was known as "Human marking".

Two men, hopefully possessed of reasonable intelligence would be placed at each end of the field on which the chemical was to be applied. They would each be designated to carry a large fluorescent marker on the top of a stick and, holding this up in the air, walk the requisite number of paces across the field for each spray run. Instead of lining up on the static pre-placed markers the pilot would line up on the human markers and they would move after each run to show the correct positioning for the following and subsequent runs.

The ideal method was to work downwind and slightly to one side of these unfortunate individuals such that they were not sprayed nor in any danger of being hit by the aircraft. This type of operation was associated with the peak season when there was simply not time to mark out all the fields with fluorescent flags with the manpower available.

During my two seasons engaged whole time as a pilot in the profession there were two panic periods, each lasting about three weeks during which human markers were used. In June 1972 it was a fungus on Wheat crops known as "Rust" and in June 1973 there was a virulent attack of blackfly on bean crops, mainly in Suffolk and Essex.

There were many, many, problems, much more so with the beans than the wheat. There was absolutely no communication between the pilot and the human markers. The beans tended to grow tall, up to about 6 feet in height such that the hapless human markers could rarely see over the crop. The fields, especially in Suffolk, seemed to be generally of very irregular shape and quite hilly so much of the time the human markers didn't appreciate where they should be going in relation to the size and shape of the area to be treated. They were supposed to pace their way across the fields remaining on the upwind side of the spray runs such that they were not contaminated with the chemical being applied. Wind direction was obvious from the air but very hard to assess correctly on the ground so occasionally the work area simply could not be treated as the men were walking across the area in such a manner that they would receive the full force of the chemical.

One day, in the middle of all this, I was working in Suffolk for an agricultural agent who was contracted to treat several farms in his area. Under the terms of the job he was supplying the markers. It quickly became evident that they were completely unused to the procedure. Several fields were treated with marginal success and I began to realise that there was a particular problem with these two that I had not met before. Watching them jump into their van and drive to the next field all was explained. One was short and the other tall.

Part of the brief to the various agencies was that markers should check that their paces were similar prior to commencing work to avoid problems of mismatch. This they had manifestly failed to do. With some variations I managed to achieve most of the day's objectives and worked out that I needed to ignore the shorter paced man and 'freehand' straight runs on the taller personage who seemed to have more intelligence. To be fair, it was probable that Shorty was severely disadvantaged by his inability to see over the 6ft high crop. If I had stuck rigidly to their indications, on larger blocks of fields, I would very quickly finish flying in a totally different direction to that in which the job had commenced.

It was about mid-afternoon when things really fell apart. There was a particularly large block of fields which was an irregular shape, very hilly and intersected by a stream running down a small valley. The pair set off, one at each end, basically heading in the correct direction. They had even assessed the wind correctly and I was flying each run downwind of them. Shorty began to go astray. The irregular shape of the block coupled with the confusion caused by the hills and the stream were probably utterly confusing on the ground and he began to get disorientated. By the time he had turned at right angles to the intended direction I began to ignore him and concentrated on long-legs who was striding ahead with great confidence still maintaining a not unreasonable course.

By now, watching with not a little amusement, I observed Shorty heading at 180° to his original track, shaking his head and raising his fist in the air, expressing disapproval at my ignoring him. About half way through the job, long-legs also lost it. He came up against a small tongue of woodland that stretched into the block. Presumably he didn't have a map or was badly briefed since despite my circling and gesticulating he shrugged his shoulders and slowly began to make his way back to their van.

Finishing the job 'freehand' which was reasonable as there was a gentle wind which hopefully would carry the chemical to any areas I had missed I felt I should check on my markers. Long-legs was back at the van and looking around in a concerned fashion for his colleague who was nowhere to be seen. From my bird's eye view I examined the crop and saw a white patch in the middle of the beans which on closer examination proved to be the missing Shorty. He was lying on his back obviously fast asleep. A low run quickly awoke him and he guiltily rubbed his eyes. I pointed towards his van and he stumbled off in approximately the correct direction. There was other work still to be done in the area so I abandoned the job and commenced elsewhere. It was not right to 'freehand' more than where strictly necessary as farmers were paying good money for our services.

9. Ian

In the normal progress of a human life there are innumerable experiences, recollections and situations all of which are bound to affect the character of any individual. Some of these affect him or her deeply and others become totally dormant in the deep chasms of the long term memory. People affect people, sometimes for the better and other times for the worse and other times the end effect is ambivalent. Sometimes we remember throughout our lives incidents and the people involved therein and other times we lose the memory almost immediately following the occasion.

Loaders, generally obtained from the local labour exchange, were not paid very well and came and departed with monotonous regularity. We had one or two who stayed for a while and Ted, of a previous chapter, remained for the two seasons I was employed whole time in the industry. The work was hard and dirty especially manually handling hundredweight fertilizer bags to tip into the loader bin ready for the next load. When the liquid spraying season started the work was generally cleaner and less arduous as the chemical was mixed in a tank on the loading truck and then pumped into the aircraft using a standard Honda water pump.

Some characters were unforgettable. The Australian mentioned in an earlier chapter had a massive, black, bushy beard. I clearly remember the beard going blue in a day mixing blue fungicide powder with water in the mixing tank. Another red-headed character, who only lasted a few weeks, had a glass eye and a predilection to fierce anger. I will never forget his baleful glare as one eye glared at me and the other, presumably the artificial replacement, looked curiously over my shoulder when he had cause to complain about yet another of his constant gripes with the company. Another was a skinny profane hard worker who quit after about two weeks. He announced that he was better off on social security benefits than working for us. He had eight children.

Ian, yet another loader, was a character I will never forget. He was a bespectacled university student, working through the summer recess presumably to supplement the meagre or negligible income encumbent with his status. Small and slim without being dwarfish and possessed of a brilliant mind, his general radiance was a pleasing characteristic to have in a loader. The pilot works in this kind of operation in an isolated world where the only human contact comes on his brief ground stops to reload and a good rapport with a contented loader is a huge bonus. Ian had one flaw, if indeed it could be considered a flaw. He thought like a computer. That is to say, everything was reduced to binary codes of 0's and 1's, black and white. His analysis of all things sacred or profane simply had no room for non-positives or shades of grey.

One day I was going about my bounden duty in the Fens of East Anglia which is a major potato growing area in the UK. It was late August and the weather was fine. It was the third time these particular fields had been sprayed in this season which made the work easier as the layout and hazards, power cables etc., were clearly imprinted on the subconscious. The crop was potatoes; the chemical was fungicide, which is a potato blight prevention measure. The airstrip was a rectangular grass field along one side of which ran the river Nene and I had discovered that the best take off run was a diagonal from corner to corner with the run ending up over the river which conveniently had no raised bank but was about 300 metres wide, the water level being about 20 feet below the level of the airstrip.

In time honoured fashion the day started with a light load of about 60 gallons of chemical and this was gradually increased until the maximum that the aircraft would lift off this particular field had been reached which on this occasion was 80 gallons. Care had to be taken here also as a change in the wind strength however slight could make a dramatic difference to the take-off capability of the aircraft. The morning's work was straightforward and the company fieldsman appeared at lunchtime and operations ceased for refreshments. I sat myself in the fieldsman's van and, giving a parting instruction to Ian to 'Fill it up' for the next load after lunch, left him munching his sandwiches while the fieldsman drove us off to a local café.

On returning to the airstrip it seemed that the take-off conditions were similar but I also noted that a few anglers had appeared on the far bank of the Nene right across the take-off path. This theoretically was no problem as height could be gained crossing the river and while they might have to move a little for their own comfort the aircraft would be no danger to them on each departure.

I started the engine and ran it at high idle for about three minutes to warm up, checked the magnetos and then set off on the first load of the afternoon. Several seconds later a distinct lack of acceleration was clearly in evidence coupled with a curious sluggishness of performance. A quick check revealed a full fuel tank....Ian had filled it up as instructed, good oil pressure, full power engine revolutions, all appeared to be in order. A final split second glance at the level of chemical in the spray tank and the awful truth dawned. It was well in excess of the loads carried through the morning.

In mocking confirmation, flecks of chemical were appearing on the windshield which only ever occurred if the chemical tank was full or nearly full. A full tank held over 120 gallons so the load was well over the maximum that the machine was capable of lifting in the take-off distance available. On this particular day I was reluctant to dump the load. Chemical was expensive, the job needed to be done without too many delays and in a bout of outrageous foolishness I thought I might get away with it. I continued the take-off run to the edge of the river and made a final attempt to get airborne which proved to be a total and insulting waste of effort. The machine lurched over the bank and descended rapidly towards the river in a full aerodynamic stall. A momentary picture of the anglers on the far side running in all directions appeared as I found myself actually looking up at them. One fell backwards off his chair which in less straitened circumstances would have been hilariously funny.

At probably less than 5 feet above the water, in total panic, far too late in the day I pushed the jettison lever forwards. The aircraft, released of its load shot skywards like a cork out of a champagne bottle. Levelling off at about 300 feet to survey the damage there was a huge yellow stain rapidly expanding in the middle of the river and the anglers were packing up their gear having obviously decided against plying their trade in the face of such extreme aeronautical and chemical hazards.

More than a little shaken and mentally preparing a violent rebuke for Ian, I landed back on the field, parked by the tanker and stopped the engine. Opening the cockpit I yelled,

"What on earth did you fill it right up for?"

Looking slightly white and considerably disturbed Ian replied quietly,

"You told me to!"

"I meant, fill it up with the same load as we have carried all morning."

"Yes, but your actual words were "Fill it up" and that is what I did!"

With this I felt mildly chastened and had to admit that the hapless Ian had indeed followed my instructions to the letter.

Map of New Zealand, source Terralink International Ltd

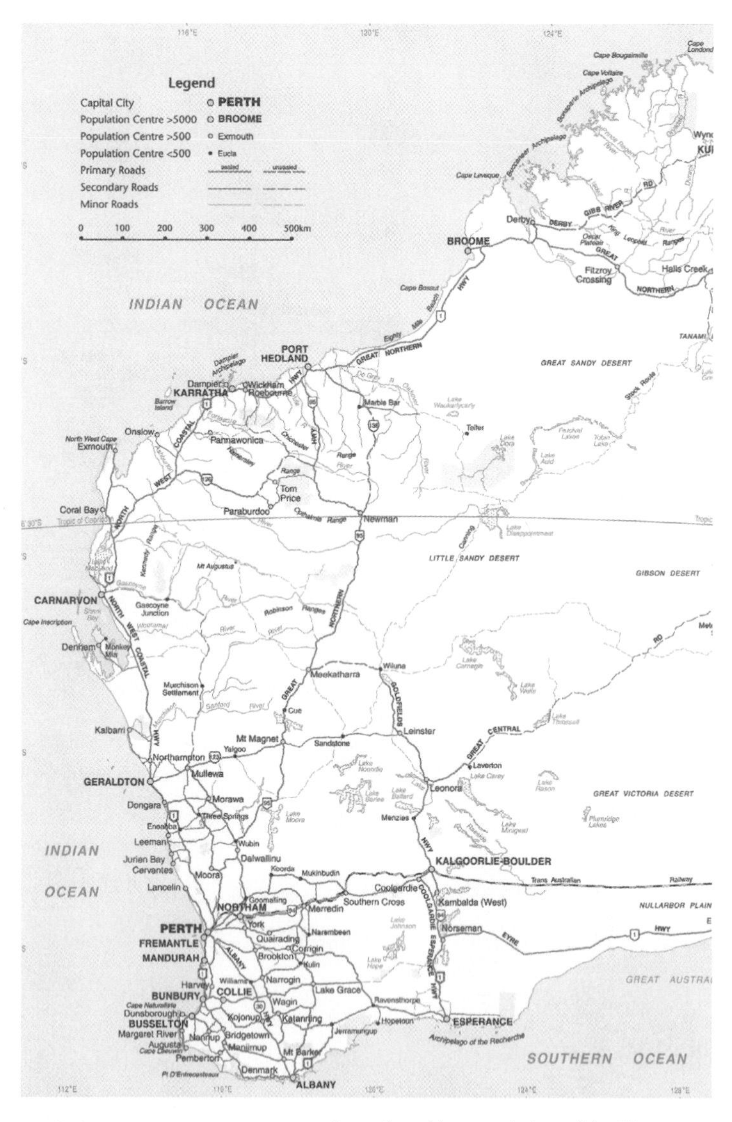

Legend
Capital City
PERTH
Population Centre >5000
BROOME
Population Centre >500
Exmouth
Population Centre <500
Eucla
Primary Roads
sealed
unsealed
Secondary Roads
Minor Roads
0 100 200 300 400 500km
INDIAN OCEAN
BROOME
Derby
Fitzroy Crossing
Halls Creek
PORT HEDLAND
KARRATHA
Dampier
Wickham
Roebourne
Onslow
Exmouth
Pannawonica
Tom Price
Paraburdoo
Marble Bar
Newman
Coral Bay
GREAT SANDY DESERT
LITTLE SANDY DESERT
GIBSON DESERT
CARNARVON
Gascoyne Junction
Denham
Meekatharra
Wiluna
Murchison Settlement
Cue
Kalbarri
Leinster
Mt Magnet
Sandstone
Northampton
Yalgoo
Mullewa
GERALDTON
Laverton
Leonora
GREAT VICTORIA DESERT
Dongara
Morawa
Three Springs
Menzies
Eneabba
Leeman
Wubin
Dalwallinu
Jurien Bay
Cervantes
KALGOORLIE-BOULDER
Moora
Lancelin
Coolgardie
Southern Cross
Kambalda (West)
NULLARBOR PLAIN
NORTHAM
Merredin
York
Norseman
PERTH
FREMANTLE
MANDURAH
Narrogin
BUNBURY
COLLIE
Lake Grace
Wagin
Ravensthorpe
BUSSELTON
Katanning
Hopetoun
ESPERANCE
Bridgetown
Manjimup
Mt Barker
Pemberton
Denmark
ALBANY
SOUTHERN OCEAN

Landgate

Cessna 205 Port Hedland

Beech 36 airborne in the Pilbara

Beech 58 on the ground at Perth

Piper PA25 Pawnee

Piper PA25 Pawnee at work, photo courtesy Pat Weeden

Beech 58 above the clouds. Western Australia

BOAC VC10 on approach to Hong Kong (Kai Tak airport)

Saudia Boeing 707, photo courtesy Wolfgang Mendorf

747-400

Empty 747

747-400 contrails

The Captain's view 747-400, Courtesy Captain Graham Ellison

Flight Engineers panel on 747-200, photo courtesy of Dieter Bongard

Prior departure from Seattle, destination Auckland, Left to right, Author, Captain Hugh Jenner, SF/O MartinWilcox, SF/O Adam Rhodes

Diane

Final Sydney Trip June 2009

Author at the rear standing between FSM Camilla Thwaites and SF/O James Butland. SF/O Chris Maddison kneeling front row. Two other London based crew unidentified. Remainder Hong Kong based and unidentified. This photo was sent to me by one of the male cabin crew... I think the man standing at the left. I have been unable to trace his name but thank you!

Frequently loaders were pilots in the making and such simple errors did not occur. Ian was of a distinctly different breed and no doubt has since become a world leader in Binary technology.

The chemical was fungicide which is an innocuous formula designed to coat the plant leaf and prevent the ingestion of blight spores into the crop. It could cause no irremediable harm to the river. The environmental impact had it been insecticide would have been very far reaching even though this was the early 1970's. Writing this over 40 years later such an incident today would have resulted in 'Questions in The House'. What did remain permanently in the memory was the delightful IAN!

10. Moving on again

The summer progressed and thoughts of more stable employment were never far away. I avidly scanned the back pages in Flight International and one day struck gold! There was a full page advertisement for Flight Engineers for the British Overseas Airways Corporation. Frequently when examining advertisements there was a shortfall between my qualifications and the requirements of the advertiser. For this situation I was more than qualified.

Before long, managing to obtain a day off mid-season, it was off to London Heathrow Airport and a day of testing and interviews at the now demolished Comet House. The psychometric tests during the morning were most enjoyable and seemed excessively simple. The afternoon interview was pleasant and unlike threatening situations that seem to abound when one's future is at stake, things were relaxed and all seemed to be on my side. There was one penetrating and mildly disturbing question which caused much food for thought.

"With all your flying experience are you going to find yourself constantly wanting to be in the pilot's seat instead of at the Flight Engineer's panel?"

The answer was honest and from the heart.

"No, I've only ever been a light aircraft pilot and what I'm really after is a reasonable, consistent salary and some stability for my wife and family."

A week or so later there was a letter in the mail from BOAC. All requirements had been met but they regretted that they were going to delay the next intake of Flight Engineers for about 12 months due to a change in the commercial programme. Writing this some forty years after the event and with many years of airline employment intervening I have to ask myself as did King Solomon some 3000 years ago,

"Is there anything new under the sun?"

Any airline flight crew will know exactly what I mean!

Taking advice from home I replied somewhat flippantly thanking them for their letter and asking if they had any vacancies for pilots. This was impudence. I had no airline experience and no UK instrument rating. The latter is an additional qualification which I had obtained in Australia but would have to be added to my UK Commercial Pilot licence at some considerable expense before being employable by any airline.

To my complete and utter astonishment I was summoned back to Comet House. One, Mr Kelly, who seemed enthusiastic for my case, spent a half hour or so discussing things. He couldn't promise a job but if I would like to obtain a UK instrument rating he would arrange another interview, this time for a pilot position.

By now it was the end of August and the crop spraying season was waning. I gave in my notice to Jack who didn't seem to think I was serious.

Borrowing money from the bank it was off to the flying school at Oxford Kidlington airport.

The course was bizarre. Despite having operated for several years with a full instrument rating in Australia it seemed like starting from scratch. Three weeks later I was the proud possessor of a UK instrument rating and not really a clue about what was going on. There had been a series of procedural hoops to be negotiated both in the Link trainer and the aircraft. They had even predicted a partial failure in the final flight test. This occurred exactly as expected and after a re-test on the failed item a UK instrument rating was issued. The intensely practical nature of the training in Australia seemed to be irrelevant and here I was, virtually clueless, yet qualified to fly at least small aircraft with commercial passengers in instrument flying conditions. There was not even a requirement for me to land the Piper

Seneca twin engine aircraft I had trained on.

By this time, answering advertisements, and with one completely unsolicited approach, there were no less than four potential openings. The un-solicited was a start-up crop spraying company who wanted me to be chief pilot and operations manager. Having decided to remove myself from agricultural aviation the answer was 'No' immediately but that did not stop them telephoning and they even sent someone round to my home to see me. It was intriguing. They had three Percival EP9's which had been crated up since new some 15 years before and had never been used or flown. I believe it was Charlie, the German chief engineer of the Sudan days who knew all about EP9's that I eventually managed to contact. The simple advice was,

"Don't have anything to do with it!"

Another was as a DC3 co-pilot on oil supply work in Scotland. I drove to Edinburgh for interview but while the job was offered, the characters interviewing were far from appealing as employers.

The third was flying a Beech Baron Charter aircraft from Peterborough. This was very tempting. The pay was reasonable, I knew the aircraft from Australian days and the whole set up was appealing.

The fourth, as previously mentioned, was BOAC.

Mr Kelly arranged a pilot interview. BOAC and its European counterpart, British European Airways, had been taking pilots from the ab-initio schemes at Hamble, Oxford and Perth (Scotland) for a number of years. There was a suggestion that the 'powers that be' were becoming increasingly concerned at the lack of experience levels amongst co-pilots, especially with a large number of captain retirements taking place. There were to be 140 direct entry pilots from the armed services and other airlines. Where I fitted into this I have never understood!

The interview was with a VC10 captain and a Boeing

747 captain. Mr Kelly also attended but sat to one side. The VC10 captain seized upon my log books and after a brief examination of the contents he began to ask questions. These were not about my potential suitability to work for the airline but about my Australian flying and work in agricultural aviation. I began to relax. There ensued a pleasing discussion and a rapport that gradually became more enjoyable. I later discovered his name was 'Phil' and I was to encounter him in training and work with him on the line on various occasions in the future. He was well liked and respected throughout the airline. Having finally learned all he needed to know about my dubious past, he looked over to his colleague,

"You will want to ask some questions."

The dour faced 747 Captain had sat thus far in brooding silence. He glared at me through black rimmed spectacles and asked,

"What do you know about 'INS'?"

Brought back to earth with a bump and instantly recalling the serious nature of the interview I haltingly queried,

"Inertial Navigation System?"

It seemed that I had hit gold. There was a satisfying smile and Mr Kelly nodded approvingly. Once again I have to thank 'Flight International'. Reading the columns in that worthy publication I had learned of the existence of this magical new box called INS[1].

About a week later there came a letter with a contract from BOAC and a course date for commencement of VC10 training at Cranebank on the Eastern side of Heathrow Airport. There was little need to think too hard about which of the potential employments to accept.

1 Inertial Navigation system. See glossary for expanded explanation.

11. Postscript to Ag flying

"The dog returns to his own vomit
And the sow to her wallowing in the mire."
(The Apostle Peter quoting from Proverbs!)

Despite resolutions to the contrary there was more work in Agricultural Aviation during the coming years.

About two years after commencing work with BOAC there seemed to be excessive leisure time. With a cash hungry growing family a little extra income would be a great asset. There was some casual building work for a friend but I also dabbled with agricultural aviation for several years. The time spent was comparatively small, about 10 days per year and most of this during the midsummer peak season. Because of the ministerial very strict flight time limitations all extra flying was co-ordinated with my primary employer but there was never a conflict. During these years the sum total of annual flying hours including both airline and agricultural work, rarely amounted to more than 600 and these were amongst the lowest annual totals of my entire flying career.

This time the operator was a well-established, very straightforward character who operated from his own private airstrip at Rush Green near Luton. Bill ran a good organisation. His aircraft were cared for and maintained in pristine condition. He ran two Piper Pawnees, a Cessna Ag-wagon and a Grumman Ag-cat all of which on various occasions I was to operate.

He was a great innovator, mostly very useful devices that enhanced the operation. All the aircraft had VHF radios with a microphone button on the control stick which was particularly helpful when operating near or out of the sundry active military airfields in East Anglia. Some of the Pawnees were fitted with non-standard extended, turned down wing tips which enhanced distribution of liquid spray. The cockpit hopper opening devices were strong and weren't subject to frequent breakage. The manually operated spray control valves could be electrically operated by a button on the stick.

There was another extraordinary device for self-marking which was better than human markers but not as good as fixed markers. This was operated by yet another button on the stick which, when pressed, released a square piece of cardboard with white tissue paper attached from a magazine mounted on the wing. The cardboard/tissue was supposed to drop onto the crop to give an indication for positioning of the next spray run. It was only viable when used from the low distribution heights associated with liquid spray and was subject to various problems and idiosyncrasies! Sometimes the magazine held up and didn't discharge a marker. Other times, especially on beans, the marker fell down into the crop and disappeared from view rendering it useless.

Proceeding down the field after lining up, in addition to the usual manoeuvring, crossing the field boundary you pressed one button on the stick to start the spray discharge. Following this you then pressed another button to discharge a marker and then, on larger fields it was desirable to drop another marker towards the end of the run followed by switching off the spray and climbing away for turning around for the next run.

The chaos came when working near a military airfield. Controllers had a habit of calling while in the middle of a run down the field. It was easy to become confused with the various buttons on the stick. I found myself discharging a marker when I should have been pressing the radio transmit button or switching off the spray valve when I should have been dropping a marker. There were other chaotic combinations which would have delighted Walt Disney.

Later on Bill introduced some brand new Pawnees which had manufacturer - installed fuel tanks in the outboard sections of the wings as opposed to the original design where there was one fuel tank in the nose between the engine and the chemical tank.

This new design had an unexpected drawback which gave me a big fright. On the standard Pawnee you could steep turn as tightly as possible until buffeting occurred indicating the onset of a stall. With one notch of flap you could then tighten up the turn but when buffeting occurred with that flap setting, the turn could not be tightened any further without the risk of a catastrophic stall.

Early on, using this new machine, I was operating normally, pulling up into steep turns at about 200 feet above the ground at the end of each run. As the day progressed and confidence built after weeks of airline flying, I began to tighten the turns until suddenly, with no warning buffet, the down side wing dropped in a stall leaving me in a vertical turn uncomfortably close to the ground. Fortunately, years of experience enabled a quick recovery simply by easing off the backward pressure on the stick and then correcting the bank.

A colleague was not so fortunate and crashed. The machine was a write off but with the superb safety aspects of the Pawnee he was unhurt. It was however seriously expensive for Bill and there was all the usual aggravation associated with an accident of this kind. There was an amusing aside to this disaster, although no accident is amusing. It was said that a lady had been leaning on the gate of the field watching my colleague applying fertilizer. Seeing the aircraft about to crash she leapt clear and fortunately also escaped any injury. Her shoes were found under the centre of the wreckage.

The Cessna 188 Ag-wagon was a very different machine. Considerably faster and carrying a greater load than the Pawnee it was much more sophisticated and flew like a thoroughbred compared to a carthorse. With a constant speed propeller it was more complex but this addition seemed to involve little added hassle. Very quickly, I learned when reducing power after take-off to bring both throttle lever and propeller pitch control back together. They are situated on the same quadrant on the left side of the cockpit. Setting the required power for working came completely naturally. The one drawback I did encounter was its behaviour in crosswinds.

One afternoon, working at Bourne in Cambridgeshire, the fertilizer in the standard hundredweight bags had been unloaded on the ground next to the threshold of a runway that was across the wind direction. We didn't have the ground equipment to move the fertilizer to a more suitable position. Other than a long taxi to the runway facing into wind for each new load there was no option other than to take off and land across the wind. The material was prilled nitrogen fertilizer and being fairly heavy the stronger winds were no inhibition for a good accurate spread on the fields to be treated. Landing seemed to be no problem but taking off became more and more difficult as the wind steadily increased during the afternoon. The wind was from the right and eventually full left rudder was not keeping the aircraft straight in the early part of the take-off run. It became necessary to use a little left brake as well. Using brake on the take-off roll does not by definition improve the ability of the machine to accelerate and so reluctantly I had to taxi the several minutes to the other runway for each load. Aerial work of this nature relies on speed to be commercially viable and the job slowed down hopelessly. It is my contention that a basic design flaw in this machine was too small a rudder.

The Grumman Ag-Cat, a much heavier machine capable of carrying double the load of the Pawnee, was an aircraft that I flew too little to appreciate. It is well spoken of in the industry but in my small amount of flying on this type I found it comparatively heavy on the controls and physically wearying for a whole day's work. Two other problems were the reduced vision, so vital for work at very low level caused by the fact that it was a bi-plane and by definition the upper main-planes (wings) obstructed all round vision. Also it lacked the comfort of a cockpit heater. A morning of slug baiting in February left me shivering as I had arrived for work with no thermal clothing completely forgetting the machine's lack of this basic facility.

As a final note on the subject of agricultural flying the only really life-threatening incident in all my work of this nature occurred while I was doing casual work for Bill. The work was liquid spray and the aircraft a Pawnee.

Wires potentially hazardous to agricultural flying come in three varieties in the UK. These are, National Grid cables mounted on steel pylons, local electric distribution cables strung along wooden poles and thin telephone wires, also on wooden poles. The easiest to avoid were the National Grid cables on steel pylons. They were easily visible, not just the pylons but also the wires themselves and their height meant that using caution they had little effect on the work even when operating right underneath them.

Telephone wires, at the other end of the scale, were likewise not a serious hazard. They were almost invisible but their presence was obvious from the line of poles on which they were supported. In the event that the aircraft flew into them they would rarely cause much damage. I did not have the misfortune to validate this information but naturally, avoiding them was most important to maintain good relations with British Telecom and the general public.

The real danger was the local electricity supply cables on wooden poles. Again, they were barely visible against the background of fields and hedgerows and the pilot estimated their presence by means of the poles. It was usually safer when using liquid spray to fly under rather than over these cables provided there was sufficient space. Flying over, it was difficult to assess their height and a misjudgement could cause contact with the undercarriage and drag you into the crop. Flying under, there was a knife edged bar up the front of the windshield which would either deflect or cut the wire in the event of contact and a deflector cable from the top of the cockpit to the top of the fin. There was a completely ludicrous tendency to duck the head when flying under wires! If the line of poles was along a hedgerow there was generally too little space to fly underneath.

Operating in the South of Cambridgeshire I very nearly came to grief. The field being sprayed was long and narrow and a line of poles ran lengthwise down the middle. Along one side was a substantial wooded area. Taking note of the various obstructions I began work. There were four or five runs along the length of the field away from the wood on one side of the wires and these were completed satisfactorily. It was then time to treat the other side of the line of poles, adjacent to the wood.

On the first run, passing over the hedge there was a tremendous jolt and out of the corner of my eye I observed the left wing tip being torn off. The machine kept flying and was nearly full of chemical which was a bonus as there was good inertia. I climbed up a little and examined the situation. The machine seemed to be airworthy despite being seriously out of trim. Left to its own devices it was trying to turn left which required some opposite rudder and aileron. I then had a look at the field and realised that from one of the posts a set of wires went at right angles into the wood and the next and subsequent poles on that line were buried in the trees. This was a nasty trap set by the Eastern Electricity board precisely for the purposes of catching out the unwary like me.

Assessment of the damage to the aircraft was impossible while flying but since all seemed manageable I finished the load before flying back to base rather than the operating strip. The damage was serious. The leading edge of the left wing was severely dented and torn, the left wingtip was missing and the propeller was damaged enough to be beyond repair. There was also damage to the undercarriage legs.

Right through to 1979 I continued to carry out the odd day's work for Bill and overall it was a useful income supplement and a pleasant experience.

Some years later, after leaving the employment of a Middle Eastern Airline, I ventured briefly back into the industry with a day's work on a Pawnee spraying potatoes in Romney Marsh. It was astonishing how quickly it all came back. After a couple of hours I was back at home in the machine and the industry as if I'd never left. That was my final experience in agricultural aviation. A week or so later, the one man operator I worked for lost his machine with the great Hurricane of October 1987 which hit the South East of England. This storm damaged or destroyed a number of aircraft at Headcorn airfield in Kent where the machine was based.

SECTION III

AIRLINES

1. Introduction to BOAC

Some thirty trainees started with the airline in the autumn of 1973. The planned one hundred and forty was reduced due to the looming fuel crisis and only those who had actually commenced their employment were retained. I was amongst the thirty. These were primarily from the RAF, a very few from the Royal Navy and even less coming from civil aviation backgrounds. Over the next very pleasant six years it became evident that for more than one reason we were surplus to the company's requirements.

The VC10 course was long and intensive. The "Need to know" computer based aircraft type rating courses of this day and age were still well into the future. Having worked on the type at Vickers as an apprentice, much was familiar, especially the electrical system.

Towards Christmas, simulator training started.

To begin with there were many new concepts to be absorbed. I have never been a fast learner but the time allocated was adequate and it gradually all came together. Inertia and trim were discussed at length. Unlike a light aircraft it is vital to plan ahead. Manoeuvring 150 tonnes of metal around the sky is very different to the agility afforded by a machine weighing less than 5 tonnes.

In the greater world, the fuel crisis became more and more serious. Sheik Yamani, the Saudi oil minister, appeared nightly on our television screens delighting in the sudden power wielded by OPEC. I began to wonder how much longer this potentially superb employment would last. I need not have worried. Things were very different in those days. It was a government airline and other than committing the gravest of offences, it was a job for life with a handsome pension accruing for retirement. It was difficult to have much faith in this, especially with my background where personal advances in the world of aviation had always involved a struggle.

Sometime in January 1974 we trainees piled into a VC10 with a bunch of training captains, spares and engineers and it was off to Bahrain in the Persian Gulf for about ten days. Fuel was expensive and hard to obtain in the UK with the on-going crisis. The company's simple solution to this problem was to carry out base training in the Gulf, from whence the fuel originated.

No expense was spared and each of us was given more than adequate training to the standard required to release us to the line. This was all immensely enjoyable and flying the aircraft was much easier than trying to do the same in the antiquated analogue computer based simulators at Heathrow. With my light aircraft background I tended to an inferiority complex but there was no problem. Handling this, to me, huge machine was very straightforward. Landing it was also easily mastered. The simulator and classroom training had been excellent.

Back in London line training began in earnest over the coming weeks. This took place on regular operating trips on the company's scheduled route network and the world rapidly became a smaller place. Initially this was as an extra crew member and then full absorption into the industry took place.

It was hard work. Having operated on my own as single crew for so long the concepts of working multi crew were completely foreign. It is probable that the ex-military trainees who had come from single seat fighters suffered similar difficulties. I had to learn to do my designated duties, well and efficiently but still keep an eye on the whole operation in a monitoring role.

One of the greatest problems was in the understanding of foreign accents on the radios. All the experience to that time had been talking to operators whose mother tongue was English. I learned to restrict transmissions to standard phraseology and to anticipate replies with heavy barely decipherable accents by listening to what I expected them to say rather than trying to work it out from scratch. Flying over the Balkans seemed to be particularly difficult in this respect. Probably the trainee in this day and age has Hollywood to thank for much improved aircraft communications as spoken English, the *lingua franca* of aeronautical operations, has improved by leaps and bounds.

HF radio was yet another steep learning curve. I had been used to excellent equipment both in aircraft and the responding ground stations in Australia. The Indian subcontinent and Africa were a culture all of their own in matters of HF communications. It should never be necessary to yell on aircraft radios! I learned to use a high pitched tone with strong emphasis on key words, requests and acknowledgements. The responding ground equipment seemed to be trusty and reliable if a little antiquated and with persistence one eventually achieved a satisfactory understanding of the clearances or instructions being transmitted. With diurnal and seasonal variations and the interference of tropical thunderstorms there were many, many problems communicating using HF.

At this stage of development in the industry the Radio Operator had only recently disappeared from Flight Decks. Immediately post World War 2 the standard flight deck crew on long haul-aircraft was five. These were, Captain, Co-pilot, Flight Engineer, Navigator and Radio Operator. On the VC10 in 1974 we carried a standard crew of 4. These were, Captain, two co-pilots (First Officers), and a Flight Engineer. One of the co-pilots doubled up as a navigator and was the holder of the requisite Navigator's licence. Within the first two years this was reduced to three man flight deck crews as INS was introduced. This wonderful new navigation device was pilot operated so the services of a navigator became unnecessary.

By April 1974 I was released to the line as a fully qualified First Officer.

2. Some notes on the VC 10 and heavy aircraft operation

The reader who is less interested in the technical side of aviation might like to skip this chapter.

The VC10 and its sister, the Super VC10 were designed and built with the so called 'Empire routes' in mind. With four engines mounted on the rear fuselage and 'clean' wings it was possessed of startling performance, the original objective being to enable operation from 'hot and high' airfields in the Middle East and Africa. Nairobi direct London, one of the major routes, was achievable with a full payload, which for early jet airliners was a unique capability. Nairobi is 5500 feet above sea level and averages fairly high temperatures. These two factors combined result in considerably less dense air. This requires a significant increase in aircraft performance to become airborne compared to operating at sea level.

There was a serious downside to the design which I only really began to grasp as time went by. This was primarily the very high basic weight of the machine due to the rear fuselage mounted engines. Other aircraft manufacturers of the time, namely Boeing, Convair and Douglas hung the engines under the wings. While this 'dirtied up' the wings making them less aerodynamically efficient there were two major plusses. These were to do with basic aircraft weight and versatility of engine types. A long range aeroplane by default needs to carry large amounts of fuel. The only sensible place to carry this fuel is in the wings and if the engines, the other major weight after fuel, are hung from these lifting surfaces the structural weight of the entire aircraft is significantly reduced. Lower weight means lower fuel consumption which in turn means smaller fuel tanks and again less weight etc. (In many modern long-haul aircraft a relatively small amount of fuel is also carried in the tail-plane, in the case of the Super VC10 this was in the fin.) If the designer places the engines anywhere other than on the wings there is some heavy structure needed to carry the not inconsiderable weight of these units and also to transmit the thrust that they generate to propel the machine forward.

Consequently, the beautifully designed and engineered VC10 with its wing skins milled out of solid alloy and heavy fuselage structure enabling rear mounted engines, was a commercial disaster. The fuel consumption was very high compared to its American rivals. Due to the placing of the engines the emerging fan type developments with their much lower fuel consumption could not be adapted to the tandem rear fuselage mounting. The aircraft became affectionately, sometimes derisively known as 'The Iron Duck!'

The Boeing 707 and to a lesser extent the Douglas DC8 gradually became the world's workhorses. The designs could be easily adapted to modern, more efficient engine designs with no major changes to the airframe configuration.

Completely new to me with a background in light aviation was the critical speed control associated with retracting flaps after take-off and extending them prior to landing with a heavy aircraft.

In essence, the 'messy' protuberances associated with flying machines, i.e. flaps and wheels are surplus to requirements when the machine is in its true element, flying clean and fast through the skies at altitude. However, aircraft have to be operated on the ground both at the beginning and end of each flight simply because there would be no reason to have aircraft if they didn't carry, collect and deliver a viable payload, quite apart from the need to re-fuel. Wheels are needed for ground operation and flaps allow a reduction in flying speed such that a machine can travel slowly enough to take-off and land. Air is a viscous fluid and the higher the speed of an object passing through it, the greater the effects of aerodynamic drag. High speeds and economic operation would be impossible if the various devices to enable a landing were not stowed away as speed increases.

So, on departure the wheels are raised. Heavy, complicated devices with their brakes, anti-skid equipment, oleo legs, doors and other paraphernalia, they fold themselves up into their appointed spaces and their doors close over them. This is activated from the cockpit, or flight deck, by means of a simple lever or switch. The effort required by the pilot to set this enormously complex function in operation is little more than that required to operate a domestic light switch...unless the mechanism develops a fault in which case it is another story!

Operation of the wing flaps, both on the leading edge and trailing edge of the wings is a far more subtle and potentially lethal aerodynamic operation. Leading edge and trailing edge flaps are usually system coupled and operated by one lever. They have several positions, usually about 5 detents on the flap lever quadrant on the flight deck control pedestal depending on the aircraft type. They enable two complimentary functions. These are, increase the area of the wing and adjustment of the camber or shape of the wing.

Both functions operate to enable flight at an acceptably low speed for take-off and landing. Typically, less flap is used for take–off than for landing. Descending the machine requires much lower power settings and greater drag is beneficial. To give some typical numbers, at high weights, take-off speed could be of the order of 170kts (195mph), landing speed, when most of the fuel has been used, of the order of 135kts (155mph). Cruise speeds with all landing devices retracted are of the order of 480kts (552mph). Normal cruising speeds could not be achieved with any of these devices extended both for structural reasons and the aerodynamic drag encumbent with their operation.

After raising the wheels almost immediately after take-off, there is initially a climb to about fifteen hundred feet when power is reduced from that required to get the aircraft off the ground to a less strenuous setting for the climb. At this stage a steady acceleration begins. There are other factors that come into this procedure, noise abatement and procedural turns to name two, so departures are rarely identical. Proceeding with the acceleration the flap retraction commences. There is a minimum and a maximum speed for each flap setting and keeping the speed strictly within these parameters is paramount. The minimums are associated with aerodynamic stalling speed which varies with the amount of flap in use and the maximums are associated with the structural limitations on the flaps and their very complex mechanism. Too slow and the machine could enter an aerodynamic stall. Too fast and the flaps will be damaged or worse, detach from the aircraft. At take-off weights close to the maximum for the aircraft type the permitted speed envelope for each flap setting can be very small and crew operate the flaps and monitor this phase of the flight very intensively.

Landing also requires considerable preparation as the speed reduction is commenced typically back to 250kts at 10,000 feet on descent and then, depending on the peculiarities of each destination, extending flap accompanied by slowing up as more and more flap is extended. This commences in the last 15-20 miles of the flight. The wheels are lowered before the final flap positions are selected. Usually all is completed prior to 1000 feet on final approach when the speed should be stabilised on or close to the computed final approach speed with everything configured for landing.

3. Line Flying

The weeks progressed into months and the months into years. My flying log book began to fill with multitudinous global destinations. Alphabetically; Abu Dhabi, Amman and Amsterdam; Baghdad, Beirut, Bermuda, Brisbane and Brunei; Cairo, Calcutta, Chicago and Colombo; Damascus, Dar-es-Salaam, Delhi, Detroit, and Dhaka; and so on through almost all the letters of the alphabet, finishing with Z for Zurich.

To begin with the routes were Eastern and Southern, that is Africa, the Middle East, India, the Far East and Australia. After a few months there was an introduction to the USA. Trans-Atlantic procedures were complex. Operations into and out of the Eastern seaboard of the USA were very different from those elsewhere in the world. In the course of time I came to respect American procedures, which while very foreign to British and European systems possessed a pleasing ambience all of their own.

Being very junior I tended to collect unpopular trips. There is recollection of a particular expedition where we operated to Bahrain and after a night off went passenger (deadheaded) to Singapore. From there, after another night off, we operated to Tokyo transiting Hong Kong en-route. After a brief stopover we then deadheaded back to London on a Boeing 747 via Anchorage, Alaska over the North Pole. This saga was in essence, round the world in five and a half days and it took a week to recover from the ensuing jet lag.

World weather held a fascination all of its own. I was to become used to early morning fog in the Persian Gulf, freezing fog in the European winter, unexpected clear air turbulence at altitude, the sudden clamp down with snow and ice causing very difficult operating conditions on the Eastern seaboard of the USA, to name a few. Thunderstorms in the tropics around the ITCZ[1] appeared, on occasion, to rise well above our cruising levels to at least 60,000 feet. Meteorological knowledge of the day said that there was no cloud above the layer known as the Tropopause[2] at around 40,000 feet. Similarly, outside air temperatures at altitude varied from as low as -60°C in equatorial regions to -75°C in Northerly latitudes. Perverse meteorological wisdom of the day stated that the lowest temperatures at altitude were to be found in the Tropical regions.

With regard to Captains and the crew in general I can only remember really delightful folk who seemed to have infinite patience and were really pleasant to work with. There were a very few crusty old captains, (when I say old, the retirement age was a mandatory 55 at the time so they were actually not that old!) but they were few and far between and not encountered very often. There were in fact a very few thorny younger captains who seemed to be out to make a name for themselves but they were even rarer. Crew stayed together for each trip but other than that, there were usually new faces every time you went to work. As time went by more and more familiar faces would re-appear but with about 18 aircraft on the fleet and eight crews per aircraft this took some time. It was a regular event to turn up for a trip and not know any of the crew.

Looking back over the years I have come to realise that the whole BOAC experience was an incomparable apprenticeship into the Airline trade. The many and varied experiences enabled me to grasp the good and shun the bad such that in future years, when I became a Captain, there was a wide grounding upon which to base decisions. Some captains were colourful to the point of obduracy. Others appeared to make decisions which were unnecessarily severe but subsequently wisdom was revealed.

1 ITCZ See glossary

2 Tropopause See glossary

Very early on, sitting in the aircraft doing pre-departure checks, the commander decided the windscreens were dirty. He had left it rather late in the day and there was a minor altercation with the ground engineer since having them cleaned was going to cause additional delay to a service already running late. Stupidly I added my bit by saying I didn't think they were too bad. (It was comparatively recently that I had been scraping cow slurry off the Pawnee's windshield to be able to see anything at all!) The captain, at least 20 years my senior, was large, florid and portly. He turned to face me and I sensed I had incurred his displeasure. In sonorous tones, something akin to The House of Lords or 1930's Royalty, double chin quivering, he growled,

"This is BOAC. We don't fly with dirty windscreens!"

The engineer took the hint and hurried away to comply.

The captain was of course absolutely correct. There is no problem unless there is a dawn or dusk arrival straight into the sun. In these conditions it can be very difficult to see a runway to enable a safe landing without the exaggerated effects of dirty windscreens.

On another occasion, leaving Heathrow, we were assigned an aircraft that was seriously in need of a paint job. The captain, again an older gentleman refused to board.

"I'm not taking an aircraft down route in that condition!" he bawled at the ground engineer.

The engineer shot off to the ramp telephone and returned shortly after.

"I've called my supervisor and he's going to try and find another aircraft."

This turned out to be delaying tactics. A senior hangar manger arrived and in obsequious tones implored the captain to take the machine. Apparently it was scheduled for a re-paint immediately following the trip and there was none other available to operate the flight. Grudgingly the captain accepted the aircraft muttering about how things weren't what they used to be.

A really ridiculous incident occurred at the recently opened Charles De Gaulle airport on the Northern outskirts of Paris. We were operating a sub-contract for Air Ceylon and were on our way home after a week-long trip which had taken in Paris, Rome, Dubai and Colombo and return via the same route. I think we had been scheduled to stop at Paris Orly but for reasons I fail to remember we landed at Charles De Gaulle. The flight engineer and I were looking forward to a 45 minute transit and then the short trip home to London. The cabin crew being Sri Lankan and grossly overworked weren't particularly bothered about where they ended up for the night anyway. Being a base so far not used by VC10's the ground staff were having trouble borrowing the required back-up ground equipment. The ground engineer casually mentioned that he would be using a Boeing 707 tow-bar to push us back as there wasn't a VC10 unit available. The very young captain asked,

"What's the difference between a 707 and a VC10 tow-bar?"

"The shear pins have a different breaking strain", the engineer replied.

"Then it's illegal and unacceptable!" the captain said flatly.

The engineer looked completely non-plussed. There was no point in arguing. The captain had said no and a VC10 tow-bar would have to be located. We had picked up the service from another crew in Dubai and operated via Rome and were running out of flying hours to remain legal. The engineer did some telephoning and arranged for a tow-bar to be brought by road from Orly. It was going to take at least three hours.

We ran out of duty time and both crew and passengers were accommodated in a hotel for the night at presumably, horrendous cost. It was difficult to see the logic behind the captain's reasoning. If the tow-bar had broken during the push back (and they do very occasionally break) there would have been no damage and anyway it would have been the engineer's responsibility and not that of the crew. I filed this incident away under the column headed 'how not to do things'!

On another occasion I arrived at Heathrow for a multiple Atlantic crossing trip. To my deep disappointment the Captain was newly promoted and as such was required procedurally to do all the flying himself. This was to be about ten days of shuttling London, New York, Prestwick, Manchester, Prestwick, Montreal, Toronto, back again to Manchester etc, finishing up in New York for the last night before return to London. I would not be doing any of the handling.

As the trip progressed I observed that the Captain's operating skills were as near perfect as I could ever imagine. His departures, approaches and landings and the entire operation was performed impeccably. It seemed to me that if I was ever going to be captain material I would have to get my act together in some considerable measure before I would attain a standard anywhere near this performance.

On the last day we had an evening departure from New York's Kennedy airport. It had been snowing during the day but in the manner of Eastern seaboard airports runways were cleared as the snow fell but taxiways were generally covered and could only be identified clearly by the yellow frangible posts that marked their boundaries. We taxied out following the rapid fire instructions of the ground controller. Approaching a 90° turn I was horrified to see the Captain begin to turn the aircraft before the designated taxiway which would have taken us into an unpaved area or worse, possibly a ditch. I called a warning and at the same time grabbed the tiller to straighten the machine up. Fortunately the VC10 had a tiller on the co-pilot's side as well as that of the captain. Not all aircraft of that era were so equipped. The captain realised his mistake and took control again after a brief word of thanks.

A few minutes later at the holding point when we had a few minutes wait before departure he thanked me profusely for preventing a potentially very embarrassing incident. The overall message I have never forgotten. Firstly, in aviation never be too proud to admit you have made a mistake and secondly, if you thank your co-pilot when he stops you making a fool of yourself he will feel free to communicate anytime he feels things are going wrong even if he is not sure.

Another Captain with whom I worked fairly early on needs to be mentioned. His name was/is Bob Rowe, no pseudonym on this occasion. I still see him from time to time in retirement.

In 1975 there was an extended Far East/Australia/Africa trip and Bob Rowe was the captain. My log book records that we worked our way through Singapore, Melbourne, Brisbane and back to Melbourne again, Perth, Colombo, Seychelles, Dar-es-Salaam, Nairobi and back to London. All of this took some fifteen days. Since there were two co-pilots I only handled two of the legs for the entire trip. One of these was into Dar-es-Salaam which at the time had no approach aids at all, not even VASIS (Visual Approach Slope Indicators). With my chequered background it did not occur to me that there was anything special about this approach. It was fully visual and most of my previous flying had been fully visual. To have to judge the correct approach angle with no aids did not cross my mind as being particularly noteworthy. Thus I was slightly bemused when Bob was pleasantly and highly complementary when we were chatting on the way back to London. It was of sufficient significance not to be forgotten. Many years later in a completely different environment, Bob was more than kind for reasons which will be described much further on in this volume.

Airline flying, contrary to the popular impression in some sections of the community is never boring. The only really boring aviation I have encountered has been agricultural aviation. This is probably not the impression given by the ag flying section of this epitome but it needs to be appreciated that other than the incidents described, flying up and down the fields endlessly, day after day dropping one form of noxious material or another does become extremely monotonous.

As a boy I really enjoyed the variations in the toil on the farm through the seasons. To spend most of one's working hours day after day for some six months of the year merely applying chemicals would be abhorrent to those whose lives are spent on the land. The fact that this is performed with an airborne device makes little difference.

Worldwide flying with the constantly changing, incredible sunsets and sunrises, indescribably beautiful vistas of the clouds, amazing views of the stars and the moon at night, and generally, the constantly changing Glories of Creation could never in a million years be described as boring. To rise majestically from the clag of a November Heathrow to the blinding sunshine a few hundred feet above and some 8 or 10 hours later descend into a pristine tropical paradise was a thrill which has lost none of its staggering beauty even after more than forty years of flying.

The destinations with the multiple ethnic variety of peoples, curious and sometimes even difficult approaches and airports, the characters I worked with not to mention the sheer pleasure of flying a beautiful machine so at home in its environment is indescribable and I consider myself very privileged to have spent most of a lifetime in this occupation.

There have been downsides. There was the very occasional colleague who was difficult to get on with. Also, there was the equally very occasional impatient simulator instructor on routine bi-annual checks who probably had his own 'issues'. Situations such as these were extremely rare in BOAC. They were much more common in my next employment.

4. INS

I will never forget the first time I used Inertial Navigation. It was on a London – Bermuda flight and as installation was progressive on each aircraft, there was only one set fitted.

Half way to Bermuda our navigator scratched his head and said,

"I'm wasting my time. This machine is doing a far better job than I will ever be capable of."

The early INS sets were very crude compared to the state of the art systems used today. A total of nine waypoints could be inserted. These were entered one by one in terms of latitude and longitude to the nearest decimal point of one minute in both axes.

There were jokes, emanating from the Boeing 747 fleet, about the 'Jumbo Graveyard'. The 747 was the first commercial aircraft ever to be fitted with INS as standard. After 9 waypoints, if you didn't re-programme the equipment, the machine was said to proceed to N00'00.0 and W000'00.0 which is a point in mid ocean to the South of West Africa where both latitude and longitude are zero. The machine would theoretically circle that waypoint until the inevitable fuel starvation. I am fairly certain that by the time INS arrived on the VC10 fleet, if you failed to re-programme, the machine would just turn around and go back to the position programmed in waypoint number one.

Gradually all the VC10's were equipped with dual INS and the third pilot/navigator was surplus to requirements. The airline reduced the flight deck to three man crews. This was excellent from my point of view in one sense. Most Captains simply flew leg and leg about[1] so my handling time increased dramatically. The down side was that by definition the airline was one third over-crewed.

1 Leg and leg about. See glossary.

5. An unusual incident

There was only one scary incident during those years. This is the way airline flying should be. If there were continuous scary incidents the general public would quite rightly shun travelling by air.

The company ran a once-a-week service from Johannesburg to Tokyo and back. The stops en-route were Seychelles, Colombo and Hong Kong in both directions.

Once on this route we were over Madagascar heading for Johannesburg. In this part of the world are to be found the worst thunderstorms the elements seem capable of contriving.

The captain, who was flying the leg, was busy avoiding the storms using the weather radar. It was night and continuous nagging turbulence added to the general feeling of dissatisfaction. I was trying to talk on HF to the en-route controller based at a ground station called Tananarive. The background noise and static caused by the storms was chronic. In the middle of all this the clear voice of an Australian oceanic radio controller in Perth, talking to another flight came through over the ether. He was many thousands of miles away but in the manner of HF, which uses the ionosphere to bounce radio transmissions back to the surface, we were exactly placed for clear communication. I recognised the voice and although not recommended practice I couldn't resist briefly passing the time of day. He could hear me as clearly as I could hear him and for a few brief moments it was like old times and we exchanged pleasantries.

The flight continued and some sort of communication was established with the ground stations. Over Laurenco Marques, Mozambique (now known as Maputo), as the sun rose behind us, we began to talk to a South African controller on VHF and were also able to pick up the

Automatic Terminal Information Service (ATIS) giving us the arrival weather for Johannesburg, now less than an hour away. All the weather was fine, as had been the forecast for Johannesburg when we departed the Seychelles.

At the top of descent with about 100 miles to run to Johannesburg, there was an unsolicited and slightly worried controller's voice on the VHF advising that low cloud and fog were rolling in fast at our destination. We immediately enquired as to the state of our number one alternate, Bloemfontein. The controller advised that this was the same as Johannesburg, low cloud and fog rolling in. Asking about Waterkloof, the number two and rather unsatisfactory military alternate, we were told flatly that this was closed on Sunday Mornings. This was Sunday Morning.

Options were running out. The VC10 was fitted with auto-land but this was effectively de-activated as it had never been satisfactory. The flight engineer was hard at work making some calculations. With about 10 minutes to run to destination as we were slowing up and extending flap he announced that if we went to Durban where we had been advised the weather was clear, we would arrive at the same time as the fuel ran out.

The captain flew down the instrument landing system with impeccable accuracy and approaching the minimum altitude, just as we were about to make a missed approach, we saw the runway and landed. We taxied off towards the terminal. As we parked we saw that the cloud had descended to the extent that the tops of the standard lamp poles around the terminal had disappeared into the overcast. This was a lucky escape.

There are things one can do in desperation. An airport that is unsuitable for a heavy jet could be used but this would probably result in severe damage or write off of the aircraft even if lives were saved. On this occasion we did not have to resort to such extremes and, indeed, in the industry as a whole such situations are extremely rare.

6. The star of Bethlehem

Beautiful, almost ethereal experiences occasionally occurred completely unexpectedly. One of these stands out in the memory.

It was December, shortly before Christmas. We were heading from Heathrow to Amman, Jordan. The flight departed in the early afternoon but since we were headed east, darkness fell very quickly. As we encountered the politically and aeronautically tricky region in the North Eastern Mediterranean where the airway transited a corner of Cyprus it was as black as pitch outside. The radio work to which I was entrusted was pandemonium. Even today this area is difficult. It is necessary to communicate with three different controllers at the same time. These are a station on the Turkish coast called Inkirlik, Nicosia on the island of Cyprus and Damascus in Syria.

The Captain was lending a hand where possible. As we streaked across the coast of Syria at Banias riding on a 100kt tailwind we collectively breathed a sigh of relief as Damascus became the only controlling station. The route then proceeded about 100 miles further East to a turning point in Syria required by the politics of the region and then we turned back heading South East to Amman. We were heading in the direction of Israel but would be descending and landing in Amman, Jordan well before risking being shot down by infringing the very sensitive Israeli air-space.

There was about 5 minutes of silence which I used to arrange the charts for the descent and approach into Amman which from previous experience I knew was going to be fairly intensive with the radio work. Straight ahead in the pristine night sky was a brilliant star which unlike the normal beautiful clusters, stood out dominating all else.

All three of us were momentarily mesmerised. It was probably the planet Venus. I have no idea what the thoughts of my two colleagues were but I couldn't help thinking of a similar situation two thousand years before. Wise men from the East who were probably Jewish exiles from Babylon, made the hazardous journey to see the new born King of the Jews, guided by the star.

7. Are we over-paid ?

Another trip of interest concerns Baghdad. It was a destination that was unpopular amongst crew for a number of reasons, not the least of which was the allowances being paid in non-negotiable currency. Thus my juniority dictated that I spend many days at this destination as the schedule was twice weekly. By default the crew would have to wait for the next scheduled flight onwards or back to Heathrow.

On this particular trip we were billeted at a very luxurious hotel on the shores of Lake Habbaniya. Staying in the same hotel was the temporary BOAC station manager for Baghdad who was a very pleasant young man and being on his own he socialised with the crew. He did have an issue. Although unspoken directly he made it plain that he felt flight crew, especially pilots, were overpaid prima donnas. When the time came for us to return to Heathrow the manager came on the flight with us as the permanent manager had returned from annual leave. The aircraft was full and the manager travelled as a passenger on the flight deck in the jump seat.

It was a smooth flight back to the top of descent into London but en-route, a few comments had been dropped by our flight deck passenger to the effect that we really did have an easy well paid path to retirement and how he wished he had pursued a similarly decadent career.

The ATIS (Automatic terminal information service) indicated that things were far from pleasant on the ground. Heathrow, unusually, were using the now defunct runway 23 (230° magnetic) with very strong gusting southerly surface winds which were too strong to allow use of the normal East West runways. We descended in clear beautiful winter sunshine and were surprised to find the clearly delineated top of all the cloud in the area at around 10,000 feet. Normally with bad weather forecast, unless it is fog, serious cloud begins much higher on the descent.

Leaving 10,000 feet and entering the cloud it was incredibly turbulent accompanied by very heavy rain and hail. The latter is associated with thunderstorms and as everybody in the industry knows, cloud with tops less than 10,000 feet does not contain embedded thunderstorms

The Captain was flying. The aircraft registered immediate disapproval of the turbulence with a loud aural warning as the auto-pilot disconnected. The Captain tried to re-engage but the equipment stubbornly resisted. This was always a flaw with the gentlemanly VC10. The auto-pilot noisily and ungraciously defied any attempt to use it when it was most needed. Manual flying in moderate turbulence was really hard work and I noticed renewed interest from our flight deck passenger as the Captain manfully coped with most unpleasant conditions.

Gradually, we were radar vectored on to final approach. I cannot remember the wind strengths but I do remember everything was in slow time as we were flying South West into incredibly strong winds thus our speed over the ground was unusually low. Intercepting the Glide Path on the instrument landing system at about 4000 feet the turbulence became really bad and then to our astonishment there was a brilliant flash as lightning struck the machine on the nose. I doubt anybody has ever heard of thunderstorms with tops lower than 10,000 feet and I had never heard of this before or since this incident.

I advised air traffic control of the lightning strike for the benefit of other aircraft on the approach and while doing so glanced back to see how our passenger was faring. He was gripping both sides of the seat, his knuckles white. His face was green and evincing distinct signs of terror.

The turbulence continued throughout the approach and

the captain managed a landing which, given the conditions, was surprisingly orderly helped by the unusually slow groundspeed.

We parked and while carrying out the shut-down procedures our passenger thanked us profusely for getting him on the ground safely. I never met him again but have often wondered whether his philosophy has changed since that approach to allow him to feel that pilots sometimes earn their money.

8. Khartoum

Gradually over the years the Christian faith which hit me at the age of 21, began to solidify. From initial conversion to full and firm conviction was a lengthy process and writing these lines more than 45 years later is still going on. It was not my way to be overt in my beliefs in work situations but when opportunities came, discussions inevitably arose. There were those of my colleagues, few and far between, who were overt in their Christian Faith and preached at anybody and everybody. They have my total admiration. These things are serious. As I said to a colleague of mine, recently retired, who was suffering from terminal cancer and has since passed away,

"Eternity goes on for an awfully long time."

There was a long stopover in Khartoum lasting for some four days.

Sitting by the pool at the Sudan Club, a previously very British establishment dating from colonial times, I engaged in serious conversation with the flight engineer who had brought his teenage son along for the trip. I cannot remember how the conversation came around to matters of faith. Both the Engineer and his son seemed fascinated by my Christian beliefs. Two things emanated from this conversation all those years ago which have stuck in the memory. The lad, amongst many other questions, asked,

"Who created God?"

As a fairly new Believer myself, this floored me for a minute but I came up with an answer which I have never had reason to revise or question. I said,

"I guess God always was and always will be."

Thinking this over in the intervening years, it makes more and more sense. While God is totally in contact with man everywhere through the unseen presence of The Holy

Spirit, He is right outside of this universe which He created. Everything to do with our microscopic little individual existence is governed by Time. We cannot conceive of a dimension where Time doesn't control. God made and designed this universe, one of whose fundamentals is the dimension of Time. God having made Time is not subject to its strictures.

Much more could be said but this is an autobiography, aviation based and not a theological treatise. I would be as out of my depth trying to write Theology as a Bishop would be in the flight deck of an aeroplane.

I said two things emanated from the conversation with the flight engineer and his son. In those days before radical Islam held sway in the Sudan, some of the hotels had the statutory Gideon Bible in the rooms. When we eventually departed to the next destination, settling down to the usual routine in the cruise, the engineer tapped me on the shoulder. I turned around and was astonished to see him brandishing a Bible which he had retrieved from his briefcase. He said,

"Do you think God will mind that I stole this from the hotel?!"

To which I had no answer.

9. 'E dun er in!"

This chapter is a digression from aviation. A biography is by definition an infinitesimally inadequate description of the sojourn of just one miserable human on this planet and this discourse is no exception. A little sobering colour to the otherwise interesting incidents of aviation probably adds some human interest to the general picture.

There were totally unpredictable absences from home, both short and long while in the services of BOAC which was associated with being very low on the seniority list. Overall I was home far more than the average nine to five employee but for my wife, bringing up three young children with unpredictable absences of the husband, was no mean task. Lovely friends at the local church were a great help but even that was insufficient.

When things in this area became untenable the options were stark. Either I had to hire a nanny which on my relatively meagre salary as a co-pilot was impossible, or I needed to leave the company and find employment which afforded a more regular lifestyle. The ultimate solution which proved a boon for several years was the employment of au-pair girls.

These young ladies come to the UK for short or long stays to assist with children and infants in family homes on very small salaries or allowances. The payback is their immersion into the family such that they can improve their fluency in the English language.

So, for several years au-pair girls came to the home. Some stayed a month or so, some stayed much longer. They were from many countries, mainly European but one came from Ecuador and another from Korea. They were also from many different cultures and behaviourally there were some shocks and no doubt this worked both ways. With regard to their care of the children they were generally very good and some were exceptionally good. Only one was absolutely awful in all respects but that is not the subject of this discourse.

One girl, who came for a longer period on two successive summers, was a quiet, well behaved French girl of Algerian descent. She was superb with the children and while not uncommunicative she mostly maintained a discreet presence, only really opening up when communicating with her young charges. Part of the contract was a whole day off per week and every Wednesday Ayesha would disappear in the morning and be home regular as clockwork at 6pm.

There came a Wednesday when she didn't come home at 6pm. By 8pm I was really worried and called the Police. Shortly after, a little Ford Anglia Panda car with a blue light on top parked outside our Cambridgeshire home and there was a knock on the door. Two uniformed officers entered the house and I sat down at the kitchen table with them and told them what had happened. There was not much to tell. Our disciplined, well behaved French/Algerian au pair had failed to return home after her day off.

Plod an older officer with greying hair, quiet and friendly sat and listened while Sherlock, his young, eager colleague began plying me with questions.

The questions gradually became interrogation and the interrogation became increasingly hostile. He was born in the wrong place and the wrong era. The Gestapo or the KGB would have been proud of him.

His young face, badly shaven, hot breath accompanied by sporadic issuances of spittle came closer and closer to mine across the table as I tried to draw back. Over some thirty minutes the questions came thick and fast and I found myself contradicting earlier answers and stumbling with my replies. It was very embarrassing and I was regularly colouring up each time he caused me to contradict myself.

Eventually, Plod gently interrupted and suggested that they needed to look at the girl's room.

While Plod went to check the room, Sherlock, having no doubt decided that I had committed the ultimate crime and hidden the body, sat silently, leering at me across the table.

After some 10 minutes Plod came downstairs. He announced to his colleague that, other than a diary written in French, there was little to indicate where the girl might be and suggested that there was nothing more to be done for the time being. They would file a missing person's report back at the Station. I gave them the girl's reference paper which contained all her details and a photo. There was a menacing parting glare from Sherlock accompanied by a threatening statement,

"We'll no doubt be back!"

As they left I perceived a barely perceptible wink from Plod over the shoulder of his departing colleague but then, it might have been wishful thinking. It came as a drop of water comes to a dying man in the desert. Had I really done the girl in? I knew I hadn't but then, after the interrogation, I wasn't really sure of anything!

There was to be no sleep. 10pm came and went and so did midnight. Shortly after, I thought I heard a vehicle parking quietly outside. Looking out of the window, there was the Panda car and in the poor illumination provided by a street lamp I could make out that there were three people. Plod emerged, the driver who I imagine was Sherlock, stayed in the car and wonder of wonders, Plod was helping Ayesha out of the back seat. I shot downstairs and let them in. Ayesha fled up to her room with a profuse apology in my direction and Plod explained what had happened.

"She went to Birmingham on the bus to see her friend which she does every Wednesday. She missed the 4pm bus back and the only other one departed at 10pm. She didn't know how to use a public phone and anyway she didn't have your phone number. We were sitting in the town square when she got off the bus and recognised her from the photo you gave us."

My gratitude was profound. There was the overriding relief that the girl was safe but also, any more interrogation or suspicion was by default terminated. It would have been good manners to have offered the officers a cup of tea but the thought of facing Sherlock again was unthinkable.

There was a sleepless night. I got to thinking about how easily a man could be convicted for a crime he did not commit. What if the girl had just disappeared, never to be seen again? How many injustices have there been in the past where citizens have even been put to death for crimes which they were not guilty of? The ultimate in this regard was the conviction and crucifixion some 2000 years ago of an innocent man. On that occasion the endemic evil in mankind surpassed anything else in history. They put to death the Only Begotten Son of God.

10. Off her trolley!

Late one Friday night we were flying from Jeddah to Abu Dhabi, the final leg of a service originating in London. With the relatively short sector, we were light on fuel and since it was the last leg of the service the payload was similarly light. As a result we were not only flying high, 41,000 feet, but also making excellent time being right in the core of the sub-tropical jet stream providing a very fast speed over the ground.

Crossing the Kingdom of Saudi Arabia involved a fairly straight leg East to overhead the capital, Riyadh, a turn to the North East proceeding almost to Bahrain before turning South East down the Gulf to the destination. The lengthy dog-leg was due to a military flying zone in Eastern Saudi Arabia. I had flown this sector before but the Captain had not.

It occurred to me that being the Islamic week-end, the military area would be inactive and clearance might be negotiable direct from Riyadh to Abu Dhabi saving well over one hundred track miles. This had been granted on previous similar trips. The Captain agreed for me to request such a clearance from Air Traffic Control. It was immediately granted,

"Speedbird __, proceed direct destination, Abu Dhabi!"

The remaining distance was very short and, as mentioned, we were riding a very strong tailwind. A few minutes later it became obvious that the Captain had forgotten the much reduced distance to destination and we were rapidly getting very high for the descent and arrival. I said, tentatively,

"Just wondering if I should ask for descent Captain?"

"Yes, go ahead," was the slightly disconnected response. The captain was still unaware of what was happening.

I requested descent clearance and this was granted to an initial level coupled with the instruction to change to the Bahrain area control frequency.

With an oath, the captain suddenly came alive. By now we had only 80 miles to run and were still at 41,000 feet, going very fast. We should have commenced descent about 60 miles before.

He acted quickly. Pulling all four thrust levers back to idle, he rapidly spun the auto pilot trim wheels forward to initiate the descent and pulled the speed brake lever fully aft. The machine precipitated into a dramatic dive earthwards with an unhealthy amount of negative 'g'. The nose down deck angle became most undignified for a civil airliner.

There was an ominous rumble followed by a horrendous crash from behind. A first class food trolley burst through the flight deck door with a very harassed looking stewardess, also out of control, in hot pursuit. Coming to an abrupt halt, it smashed into the central control pedestal spewing all manner of delicacies onto the auto pilot and radio control panels. Grabbing the backs of the pilot's seats with each hand the stewardess just managed to prevent herself landing in a heap on top of it all. Various bits of cutlery and broken crockery scattered all over the flight deck, some even disappearing under the rudder pedals on the floor in front of us.

The stewardess was loud in her apologies obeying the protocol of the time (I suspect in this day and age things would have been a little different!) Summoning additional help from the cabin, two of them did their best to clear up the wreckage while we were more than hands full with rapid descent and arrival procedures.

Landing and parking a few minutes later we completed the shut-down checks and switched on the cockpit flood light.

The first ground staff member to arrive on the flight deck was the station manager. He was an older man with a military bearing complete with moustache. His supercilious nasal tones could be likened to 1920's aristocracy, Heathrow air traffic controllers or the late Field Marshall Sir Bernard Montgomery.

He surveyed the scene of chaos, broken crockery and scattered cutlery. Some expensive looking relish was dripping from the flap handle. With a tone of disgust bordering on contempt he said,

"Having a party, are we chaps?"

Later on, in the crew bus, the captain being a complete gentleman apologised to the cabin crew and when we eventually reached the hotel it was drinks on him. Many captains of the era would not have been so gracious.

11. Another move

There was a serious over-staffing situation caused by the introduction of INS. With normal expansion the crew would have been absorbed but there was no expansion. There was retraction as routes were cut with passenger numbers dropping in straitened global economic times. Those amongst my more sagacious colleagues, equally junior to me, saw the 'writing on the wall' and began to leave. Most went to Cathay Pacific who were expanding rapidly and hiring pilots accordingly.

By the time the penny dropped in my private little world that there was scant future in the current situation, the industry was retracting world-wide.

Rather late in the day I started writing letters again. To my surprise there were several openings but a rebuttal from Cathay Pacific. They were only hiring ex-RAF pilots. Job offers came from Laker Airways, Invicta Airways and Saudi Arabian Airlines.

Rightly or wrongly I accepted a job with Saudia, commencing work with them in September 1979. It was very sad leaving BOAC which in the interim had metamorphosed into BA. They had been good years with a good company and I remain forever grateful for the introduction to airline operations amongst such grand colleagues. Invicta disappeared off the radar screen shortly after. Laker went out of business about three years later. The one possible regret was Cathay Pacific who called me in for interview after I had started with Saudia. This time I heeded my mother's advice of many years previously.

"It's no good changing horses in mid-stream."

The BA VC10 fleet wound down and ceased operations completely about eighteen months after I left the company. The very few of my remaining direct entry colleagues were put on semi-permanent leave and were re-absorbed back into the airline in 1984 when they started re-hiring.

In the 1990's, as a Captain flying for Virgin Atlantic, a few of the men who had gone to Cathay appeared as my co-pilots having fallen out of Cathay at 55 years of age which was their mandatory retirement age. Very occasionally I was to meet two of those who had joined BOAC with me in 1973 and had remained with BA. One in particular was a very senior co-pilot on the 747-400 fleet. He appeared to be generally fed up with life and longing for retirement. This alone confirmed that I made the right move in leaving when I did. Whether or not it was a good thing going to Saudia I leave for Eternity to decide. Certainly the next few years could be considered character building.

SECTION IV

ARABIA

1. Saudi Arabian Airlines

The airline was a whole new world in all aspects. Initially there was a week in Jeddah for induction. Never have I seen such paperwork. Anything and everything required reams of paper with at least three passport photos attached to each item. The fifty such portraits brought with me should have been preparation enough. Not so. After three days there was a necessity to purchase a further one hundred. Almost all were consumed by the end of the week.

There was a residence permit for the Kingdom of Saudi Arabia and an exit/re-entry visa not to mention umpteen other passes for various functions. All the initiation having been accomplished, $US6000 in open traveller's cheques appeared together with round trip airline tickets to and from Kansas City, Missouri, USA. I was instructed to go and learn to fly a Boeing 707.

The Boeing 707 course was run by the now long defunct Trans World Airlines. Other than a few hours of actual flying on the aircraft all classroom and simulator instruction was conducted in a downtown city office block in Kansas City. It seemed a little bizarre to enter a simulator in a fourth storey office block in the middle of a bustling city. Simulators are normally to be found in the environs of airports and occasionally on industrial estates but never in City Office blocks.

The training was excellent and friendly and the few

hours flying training on the actual aircraft at Kansas City airport and at a neighbouring satellite field were all quite enjoyable despite the inevitable hard work associated with these pressurised courses.

The 'chickens came home to roost' with a vengeance on return to Jeddah. There was a leisurely week or so of a 'differences course' as the Saudi 707's varied significantly from those we had studied for the type rating course and then one morning I reported to the airport with four other trainees for base training.

There was a Saudi training captain and an American flight engineer. The trainees consisted of two 707 Captains from a Lebanese airline and three First Officers. Two of the F/O's were Americans and then there was me. None of us three First Officers were experienced on the type except for the minimal TWA training but the two Lebanese Captains were well qualified long term captains on 707's. After a briefing session we climbed aboard with one of the Lebanese in the captain's seat, the Saudi Training Captain in the right hand seat, flight engineer at his station behind and the rest of us in the passenger cabin.

We departed for Taif, only 20 minutes flying away to the East in the mountains. After take-off, us non-operating trainees stood in the back of the flight deck to observe. All seemed to be proceeding well until half way to Taif the training captain, who had previously introduced himself as 'Sammy', instructed the trainee to do a steep turn at 45° of bank angle through 360°. He was to roll out of the turn on the current South Easterly heading. This should have been no problem as it had been included in the simulator training and unlike in the UK, satisfactory demonstration of this manoeuvre is a requirement for operations under the FAA (Federal Aviation Administration of the USA) under whose rules the airline operated.

Watching from the flight deck door we could see that

the turn was poorly executed but not disastrously so. The Lebanese Captain managed to lose 200 feet in the turn. This was not good and I was fairly confident when it came to my turn I could hold the height accurately. What happened next was, in my experience completely unbelievable.

With a wave of the hand, thumb pointed to the rear Sammy said to the trainee,

"Leave the flight deck. Your performance is not up to Saudia standard." The message was clear and uncompromising. The man had been sacked on the spot.

The second Lebanese Captain climbed nervously into the Left hand seat at Sammy's invitation. We proceeded to the Taif area.

Taif airport is 5000 feet up in the mountains with much higher peaks all around. The man was instructed to carry out a procedural two engine approach to Taif in simulated instrument conditions. Sammy put two cabin pillows up against the windscreen in front of the trainee, blocking all forward vision such that the only reference to flight path was from the aircraft instruments. He then pulled two engines on one side back to idle and initially the trainee coped well. This is a difficult manoeuvre at the best of times and precision is difficult especially with the 707 engine configuration giving severe yaw in the direction of the idling engines. This is countered by rudder and rudder trim but due to necessary engine power changes on the good engines the yaw is uncomfortably variable. Having said that, with the adequate simulator training, there should have been no problem.

With the thermal turbulence generated by the high outside air temperature and mountainous terrain accurate flying was well-nigh impossible. Watching from the rear of the flight deck I thought the overall performance was reasonable. We approached the runway, Sammy pulled the pillows away at the approved minimum descent altitude and we landed.

Another wave of the hand, thumb pointed to the rear and Sammy dismissed the second trainee as below Saudia standard.

By this time, we three First Officer recruits were wondering just what we had got ourselves into. I had left a potential good job for life and never for one minute anticipated anything like this. One of the American First Officers was invited into the Right hand seat while Sammy moved himself over to the Captain's position.

This time things went well. No extreme procedures were called for and the trainee was sent back after about 45 minutes of departures, approaches and landings. Much of the airborne manoeuvring was with the pillows up, forcing real instrument flying. Sammy announced that the trainee had passed his base check.

Next was my turn. I settled in well and all the needles seemed to be in the right place at the right time through several approaches and landings some of which were on three engines. I began what was obviously going to be the final requirement, an approach using the VOR[1]. This approach has no vertical guidance on older aircraft and the descent is calculated and operated using a mixture of mental arithmetic and good old fashioned judgement. I lined up correctly on the runway using the VOR with the pillows blocking all outside vision. It is critical on this kind of manoeuvre to be sure the aircraft is tracking correctly before commencing the final approach descent. I delayed, probably no more than 10 seconds while making sure all was in order when Sammy started screaming,

"Can't you read the English on your chart? We should be descending, not flying level!"

It seemed that the fact that I was about to do precisely that was of no interest. Also, there was plenty of room for

1 See glossary

the descent prior to the runway and no hurry to get down at all. Instant gloom descended and I could see myself looking for another job. Sammy allowed me to continue flying and removed the pillows at the statutory minimum altitude. The runway was gratifyingly straight ahead and I was at the correct height to make an orderly landing. After touchdown, I applied reverse power, allowed the machine to roll a little and followed this with gentle braking to stop on the runway as instructed.

Sammy gave the now familiar wave of the hand, thumb pointing back indicating that my session was finished. I was expecting the phrase, 'not up to Saudia standard'. Instead, he said,

"Good work Trevor!" and shook my hand.

And so it continued for seven long years. My immediate managers, in terms of personalities varied from a few who were good men of integrity to a minority who were capricious, unpredictable and deeply suspicious of the foreigners they were forced to employ. I was to discover that politics, whether international or internal, within the airline, was to play a big part in our lives. It was quite possible that the instantaneous sacking of the two Lebanese Captains was for reasons other than their supposed lack of flying ability

Amongst the flight deck employees, about half were Saudi Nationals and the rest were made up of many of the world's nationalities particularly US citizens. Most were reasonably easy to get along with but by no means all. Some had very colourful backgrounds. Others were bordering on the obnoxious. A few were possessed of such extraordinary behaviour that one could only speculate that they were probably 'wanted' in their respective home countries. There were two whose characteristics suggested that there might be mental misalignment. One, a US citizen, of whom more later, and the other a Saudi who I was later to fly with on the 747 fleet and who was reputed to carry a certificate verifying that he was sane. While pleasant to fly with he was certainly 'curious'! The pure aviation side was fascinating but much that went with it, in terms of living in Jeddah and the capricious nature of the Saudis, was not so pleasant. The pressures of the local regime and the behaviour of a few particularly unsavoury expatriates, who had nothing to do with the airline, made for a generally very unhappy period of my life.

A postscript is worth writing with regard to Captain Sammy. Not much more than three years later, when I was well established as a co-pilot on the Boeing 747 aircraft, Captain Sammy arrived, newly checked out on the fleet. He was a completely different character. Gone was the blustering superiority. He was just a regular Captain grappling to come to terms with this new and very large machine. He was right out of the comfort zone he had established for himself as a result of many years on the 707 and was actually very pleasant to work with!

2. Flying the Boeing 707

Although designed as a long haul aircraft, Saudia used the Boeing 707 for a mixture of long and short haul. The aircraft design was simplistic in the extreme compared to the VC10. Of the three primary controls, that is ailerons, elevators and rudder, the first two were manually controlled assisted by cleverly designed trim tabs. The rudder was endowed with power assist known as 'rudder boost'. The machine, generally, took some getting used to, especially the ailerons. With the four engines strung out along the wings, the ailerons, providing roll control were very heavy and initially I found that on final approach it was easy to over correct resulting in an unstable rolling motion. With a little practise this was easily cured and thereafter, no longer required any particular effort.

Some of the destinations were familiar from BOAC days, others were new to me. The very small fleet, six aircraft and occasionally seven, when the engineers weren't robbing the oldest machine for spares, worked a large network. West to North Africa with all points to Casablanca, North to Amman, Damascus and Istanbul, East to Kuwait and some of the gulf states, South to Sanaa, Aden, Mogadishu and Nairobi as well as many destinations inside Saudi Arabia.

3. Perspicacity

It was very early days for me in Saudia. There was little assurance of the competency of some of the captains I was flying with. Much of this came from folklore in the ex-pat community. Some was simply xenophobia and some, as was later demonstrated, not without reason. However, there were occasions when I was to witness a measure of competence which was unequalled.

One morning we set off from Jeddah for a Northerly destination. The captain, a Saudi who I had not met before, was handling. On the flight deck, in addition to the three operating crew was an American ground engineer complete with toolbox, destination Amman. He was required to fix one of the other Boeing 707's grounded in Amman for technical reasons. Shortly after take-off the captain called,

"Gear up," in time honoured fashion.

I complied with this command by moving the appropriate lever to the 'up' position but was interested to note that while the main trucks retracted, the nose gear remained firmly in the 'down' configuration. This was confirmed firstly by the green nose gear 'down' indication light remaining on and secondly by the fact that there had been no sound from the nose gear retraction; normally clearly, if not offensively audible as the unit was positioned right below the flight deck. The captain maintained speed, delaying flap retraction and commanded me to re-cycle the gear. I selected down and waited for the main gears to show green and after a suitable pause moved the lever to the 'up' position again. Precisely the same sequence re-occurred. The main gears retracted and the nose gear didn't move.

The Captain commanded

"Gear down", again and the indications were good that all three units were down and locked..

Before departure we had noted a write-up in the aircraft technical log regarding the landing gear. The previous crew had been forced to lower the gear manually on arrival at Jeddah early the same morning, due to a hydraulic fault. When this action is taken there is a manual pin that has to be inserted in the nose gear mechanism under the flight deck floor. This procedure calls for the flight engineer to descend into a dreadfully cramped bay and release a manual pin which engages into a rotating drum which is part of the nose gear mechanism. Insertion of this pin mechanically locks the nose gear in the down position.

Addressing the flight engineer who was a Saudi, the captain said,

"Did you check the nose gear pin prior to departure?"

This procedure was part of the pre-flight duties of the Flight Engineer but many of the less dedicated ignored the requirement as it was an awkward and dirty business descending into the compartment known as the 'lower 41'[1].

"Yes, of course Captain!" was the immediate response.

The nervous tone suggested that he had done no such thing and was trying to 'keep face' desperately hoping the pin was not in and the problem was un-related.

The American ground engineer entered the discussion un-solicited,

"Captain, would you like me to go down and have a look?"

The captain thought for a minute and said,

"Okay, go ahead."

The American raised the hatch in the rear of the flight deck floor, descended into the depths for about two minutes and emerged saying,

"Pin was in, Captain, I have released it so we can raise the gear and be on our way."

1 See glossary.

I reached over to the gear lever. This was out of order as there had been no command from the captain. A hand shot out and stopped me. It was the captain.

"Wait, I need to think about this!"

Meanwhile we were climbing slowly in the take-off configuration and I had advised the Jeddah departure frequency that we were having a minor technical problem and would advise intentions shortly.

A full three minutes or so later the captain announced.

"We are returning to Jeddah."

He instructed the American to go back down into the lower 41 and re-insert the pin.

I have to confess that I was non-plussed. All seemed to me to be in order and why were we not raising the gear and going on our way?

We landed back at base, parked and shut down the engines. Two or three ground engineers arrived and inspected the nose gear from outside. Shortly after a voice came on the ground/flight intercom,

"Nose gear's in a mess, captain, this machine will have to go to the hangar.

We off-loaded the passengers. There was no other aircraft available to fly the service so we were released from duty.

Being of an engineering background I needed to know the full story for my own satisfaction. A few days later, encountering a hangar engineer who happened to be an Englishman all was revealed. Cycling the nose gear twice with the pin inserted had seriously damaged the retraction mechanism. If we had retracted a third time after releasing the pin we would have destroyed the mechanism completely. There would have been a crash landing with the nose gear partially extended.

It was humbling to realise that the captain was far ahead of me in his knowledge of the aircraft despite my roots being in aircraft engineering. Most of the Saudi's were severely lacking in technical understanding simply because they were born of a non-technical society. I was never to meet this captain again during my time with the airline.

4. 'No Problem!'

For a while I seemed to meet and fly regularly with a Saudi Captain by the name of Ali. He was easy to work with and pleasingly lacking the 'hang-ups' some of the Saudis seemed to bear against ex-pat crew. If he had a defect it was a tendency to recklessness in his operation of the 707. The origins of this serious aeronautical flaw I was never to determine. It might have been Islamic 'Will of Allah' mentality which dictated that no matter what you did or how you behaved, when your time came, your time came. As I got to know him I concluded that this was unlikely. The problem could well have been lack of the healthy respect needed for all things aeronautical which, in the Western World, is taught in every facet of the profession.

Saudia descended their Boeing 707's at 350 knots indicated airspeed (IAS)[1]. This is fast! Standard airline practice is to descend a jet airliner at 280 to 320kts depending on the aircraft type and the flying conditions. There is always a requirement to reduce to an approved turbulence speed in rough air.

Captain Ali descended at 350kts regardless of conditions. I clearly recollect descending towards Riyadh at his usual 350kts and seeing a broken layer of cumulus cloud at around 18,000 feet with thick haze below indicating thermal turbulence. We barged on through it and the stresses and strains on the aircraft could only be guessed at. It was certainly very uncomfortable and I couldn't help thinking of the BOAC Boeing 707 which had broken up not many years before in severe turbulence in the vicinity of Mt Fuji in Japan.

One day we were in Medina heading north. Many northbound flights transited Medina some 40 minutes flying from Jeddah. The airport was possessed of a tricky runway. To the north, west and east there were mountains.

1 See glossary.

Immediately to the south there was a ridge of black lava from some geologically recent volcano which was 70-100 feet high. Transit outbound through Medina always seemed to be in the morning. The temperature would be rising rapidly and the winds were very fickle. We would always be at maximum take-off weight to reduce the need to purchase expensive fuel outside the Kingdom for the return trip.

I worked out the take-off data card and mentioned to Captain Ali that it might be a good idea to allow for a small unfavourable wind change and a slight increase in temperature.

"This is not necessary. Use the current temperature and winds. This is no problem!" said Ali confidently.

Having seen a debacle in this regard at the same airport previously I was not so sure. On that occasion we had de-fuelled. De-fuelling is never a good idea. The valves rarely seem to work as they are little used and a bowser has to be found as it is not permitted to return the fuel to ground storage after being contaminated in aircraft fuel tanks.

Sure enough, when the time came to depart the temperature had risen by two degrees and the wind, from a light northerly breeze of 5 knots or so was southerly less than 5 kts.

Departure to the South was completely impossible anyway as we were about 25 tonnes overweight according to the data tables. For departure to the North we were also too heavy by approximately 5 tonnes. I had even surreptitiously allowed for a rise in temperature and less favourable winds but this was not enough. I pointed all this out to the captain.

"This is no problem. The take-off data tables are far too restricting!"

I was unhappy but this was Saudia and not BOAC.

Take-off was normal and I began to think that the take-off data tables might indeed be too conservative. It quickly became evident that they were accurate. The problem was not the actual take-off; it was what is known in performance language as "the second segment climb".

The mountain range was looming large in the windscreen and we didn't seem to be climbing fast enough. There was no room for turning. The runway direction led naturally into a valley straight ahead. We entered this fairly wide defile but it became evident that the valley floor was rising faster than our pitiful rate of climb. Retracting flaps was impossible as we were unable to gain sufficient minimum speed to enable us to commence this procedure. We were at full power and rapidly approaching the limit for this setting which was 5 minutes.

It was a nerve racking experience as we clawed our way up the valley floor, unable to accelerate, unable to increase the rate of climb and unable to reduce power. After what seemed like an age, during which Ali had reduced from his usual chirpy self to white faced anxiety we scraped over the highest point of the valley floor with little more than 300 feet between us and the rocky ridge below. The ground fell away and we were able to accelerate and retract the flaps. Until passing the top of the valley we had not risen more than 500 feet above the terrain and that dizzy achievement had occurred immediately after take-off.

The end eventually came for Captain Ali. He was flying with an American co-pilot, a New Yorker named Bill, who was a good friend of mine.

Bill described how they had landed at Riyadh at the end of a long day's work. The captain taxied in at some forty knots in his usual flamboyant style (taxiing speed is normally 15-20kts especially in high temperatures). Before the ground controller had time to direct him to park in the designated parking bay the captain parked in the first bay he came to. Ground control advised that he was supposed to be parked two bays down past a stationary Boeing 737.

"No problem", said the captain.

Ali taxied forward onto the service road between the parking bays and the terminal building. This road was for ramp vehicles and probably wasn't even stressed for heavy aircraft. Apart from anything else it just wasn't wide enough for the big machine. He turned left up the road in front of the parked 737.

Bill's by now vociferous protests at this extraordinary manoeuvre fell on deaf ears. There was not enough room. The left wing tip of the 707 scraped the windscreen of the parked 737. Ali then turned left past the 737, out onto the taxiway and after a 180° turn parked correctly. After shutting down the engines the captain and the flight engineer, also a Saudi, disembarked the aircraft with Bill chasing after them.

"Aren't you going to write this up in the aircraft technical log?" Asked Bill.

"What is this that needs to be written up?" demanded Ali.

Bill pointed to the damaged wing tip, torn metal with navigation light hanging down like an eye out of its socket and then to the damaged nose of the 737.

"This and that!" said Bill.

"This and that is no problem!" said Ali.

Bill subsequently received a letter from the company blaming him for not directing the captain correctly. The long diatribe finished with the statement,

"Nothing in this letter should be construed to suggest that the co-pilot should ever override the captain!"

At the subsequent court of enquiry Ali was relieved of flying duties. Apparently he was relegated to a company cost centre which existed for folk who remained on the payroll but would never be required to work. I suppose this was necessary but I was rather sad on his behalf as he was a good pilot and easy to work with. There was just a lack of discipline which surely could have been sorted.

5. Bird strike

One day flying north, I was working with a diminutive, jolly American Captain. There was a Saudi Flight Engineer and also an extra crew member in the flight deck. The latter was a chatty little Iranian ground engineer by the name of Freddie. He was what is called a 'flying spanner'. Freddie was on board because, the Boeing 707, similar to the VC10, was heavily dependent on ground equipment for transits as it did not have its own Auxiliary Power unit (APU). The company did not have a resident ground engineer at our destination.

We were on final approach into a hot, steamy, hazy Summer Istanbul. Hovering straight ahead was a large bird of prey. It was so large that we could see that its ample rear end was presented insultingly in our direction. It must have been deaf. The 707 was not a quiet aeroplane. Too late it heard or sensed impending doom and despite its not unsubstantial bulk, made a surprisingly rapid manoeuvre to the right. Which only meant that instead of us having a windscreen obliterated by blood, guts and feathers, the bird terminated its earthly sojourn with a substantial thump which shook the entire aeroplane as it entered the number three engine.

The operating flight engineer was oblivious to the drama but Freddie, like the captain and myself had observed the process from start to finish. We were still at about 1500 feet and according to the engine instruments, the number three engine seemed to have swallowed the bird without effort but there was some unusual vibration and Freddie voiced the fact that the number 3 EGT (Exhaust Gas Temperature) seemed to be slowly rising.

There was no call to carry out any emergency procedures such as shutting down the engine and we landed normally. Freddie went out to inspect the damage.

"Some fan blades bended," he announced on his return a few minutes later in his peculiar brand of Iranian English.

Facetiously I said,

"How did the bird get on?"

Freddie disappeared.

A few minutes later he re-appeared with an enormous smelly carcass of feathers, blood and gore and dropped the gross morass on the flight deck floor. He was grinning,

"I think it no alive!" He declared.

All of us went out to inspect the damage. It didn't look good. At the front of number three engine, four fan blades were severely bent at the tips. Others had suffered some damage. My personal, unvoiced diagnosis was that we had a stopover of three or four days while a new engine was located and fitted. The Captain probably had similar thoughts as he announced that we would book into an airport hotel.

It had been a long day already with a very early start and after checking into a room I fell asleep. It was still daylight when I awoke to the sound of the telephone. It was the captain.

"Freddie says he has fixed the engine. Can you be ready for pick up in about ten minutes?" I agreed.

There was nothing to pack as I had not brought an overnight bag. I looked at my watch and realised I had slept for about four hours.

Freddie had fixed the engine. He was evasive when questioned but I suspect he had either purloined some spare blades from Turkish Airlines and fitted them or more likely, removed the bent blades and managed to straighten them before re-fitting. Either way, he had fixed the machine and had signed it off for flight which he was fully qualified to do.

The flight home via Medina was without incident except that we really had to stretch the flight time limitation rules to extremes to get home and still remain legal. There was a subsequent letter that we each received from the company thanking us for our diligence.

Bird strikes were not infrequent over the years but normally passed unnoticed, just a sad mark on the fuselage or leading edges of the wings where the unfortunate had collided with the aircraft. The Istanbul incident stands out as the only severe incident of this nature I was ever to encounter.

6. Three more captains

There were many extraordinary and colourful characters in the airline, some already mentioned. To do justice to them all would require a separate volume. It behoves me to pick out another three on the 707 fleet for special mention. All three were captains.

Captain Andy was a Norwegian. He was one of several who, as ex-pat co-pilots, we referred to under the generic term as 'African Bush Pilots'. The characteristic of this group was superb flying ability coupled with a total lack of any aviation discipline. In their previous lives they had worked on Boeing 707's and Douglas DC8's for all sorts of nefarious African operators carrying passengers and freight all over that vast continent. From the tales they told it was obvious that at least some of the operations they were involved in were of questionable legitimacy.

I first met Captain Andy on a Casablanca flight. We transited Tripoli, Tunis and Algiers en-route uneventfully. Arriving overhead Casablanca after a long day's work there was a thick dust haze and we were carrying out a procedural approach prior to intercepting the Instrument Landing System. There was no terminal radar control and little traffic in the area.

Andy suddenly called out,

"I've got it!" and commenced a steep turn to the left calling for gear down and full flap.

I realised he was saying he had visually sighted the runway but there was no reason whatsoever for not continuing with an orderly procedure to intercept the ILS and carry out a dignified landing.

Having been employed by BOAC for the previous six years with their high standards of aviation discipline and lugubrious safety conscious procedures, behaviour like this, with a heavy jet transport, was beyond belief. With the ease of handling a crop-sprayer Andy continued the steep descending turn and put the machine down accurately on the runway. I had barely enough time to obtain landing clearance. It is difficult to imagine the fear engendered in our long suffering passengers by this unseemly dive for the ground.

It was not my place to say anything. Other than describing the incident to my co-pilot peers on return to Jeddah, it was not discussed further. However, enough feedback somehow found its way back to management and the more wild behaviour of the 'African Bush Pilots' gradually declined.

Andy was a likeable character as were most of the other pilots with Scandinavian origins and I was to operate regularly with him on the 707 fleet.

A further incident with Andy bears recounting if only to demonstrate what an utterly different culture Saudi Arabia was.

One night we were headed back from a North African airport to Jeddah when a Saudi steward came onto the flight deck and announced that a passenger was bleeding seriously from the mouth and nose. He asked the captain what should be done. Leaving the control of the aircraft to me, Andy went back to investigate. This should not have been necessary. Cabin crew generally are better trained and far more au fait with medical problems and to consult the flight deck usually means the situation is serious enough to warrant a possible diversion to get the sufferer to the nearest available professional medical help. Andy returned about ten minutes later. He described what had occurred.

He had been taken down to the very back of the aircraft to find the male passenger, indeed bleeding heavily from the mouth and nose, and sitting on a toilet. There had been no first aid attempted. Andy asked,

"Shouldn't he be lying down?"

The steward grabbed the passenger by the heels and pulled him off the toilet seat onto the floor. The subject's head suffered a heavy encounter with the toilet bowl rim on the way down.

"How's that Captain?" asked the steward, rubbing his hands together, pleased with a job well done.

The subject lay head back on the floor now bleeding profusely, barely conscious and groaning with pain.

By this time we were closer to Jeddah than any other destination with medical facilities and thus continued. I have no idea whether this passenger survived the incident.

Then there was Captain D____ of East African/Asian ethnic background. He gradually acquired a reputation for poor flying and general inconsistency.

One stormy night, on final approach to Tunis which was an intermediate stop en-route Madrid to Jeddah, Captain D____ was handling the aircraft. It was bad weather for the arrival with heavy rain and the control tower advising a strong quartering cross wind for the landing. All seemed to me to be in order and the crosswind was within the prescribed limits for the 707. With about three miles to go Captain D____ turned his head in my direction and with blatant terror manifested on his face said,

"Is it safe to land?"

I could see no reason for his apprehension or the question. We were fully configured for landing, speed was good, we were on the correct approach path and the runway was in sight albeit a little blurred through the heavy rain even with the wipers set to 'high'. There was absolutely nothing untoward about the situation. I said,

"Well, captain, I don't envisage any problems, what is it that is concerning you?"

There was no reply and we continued to a shaky landing. To this day, I have no idea of the reason for this aberration.

Professional pilots have great respect for the many possible snares and pitfalls that can be encountered during the practice of their trade but they are not afraid of the machines they fly. There might be transient under-confidence, especially in the period after transferring to a new aircraft type or operating in an unfamiliar environment but neither of these situations applied on that night.

On another flight with Captain D____ there was a further incident of bizarre behaviour if not downright incompetence.

The flight engineer on this occasion was a likeable, older American who was my next door neighbour in the company housing compound in Jeddah. His name was Joe. We knew each other well and he was particularly pleasant to work with. In the manner of many of the American Flight Engineers he was also a pilot but was neither licenced nor qualified to operate in that capacity with Saudia.

The route was Casablanca direct to Jeddah through the night, some seven and a half hours flight time. Captain D____ had designated me as the handling pilot.

We became airborne and after raising the landing gear I flew the aircraft manually through the flap retraction and up to about 10,000 feet. It was time to engage the auto pilot and I moved the appropriate switch. Nothing happened. It simply refused to engage. Unlike the VC10, the 707 had only one auto pilot but again, unlike the VC10 it was usually very reliable. This one was the exception. It was no problem other than the fact that it was going to be a very long night.

Jet transports are not difficult to control manually at cruising altitudes provided the control inputs are tiny and excursions from the flight path, especially in pitch, are not allowed to amplify. It is necessary to apply absolutely minimal backward or forward pressure on the control column to achieve stable flight and this is best achieved by gluing the eyes to any trend on the Vertical Speed Indicator.

It is also vital to keep the elevator trim[1] set very precisely, the adjustments required being very small. Roll control, in my experience, seems to be far less exacting. Some two hours into the flight I was getting very tired and also needed to go to the bathroom. I said to Captain D____,

"I need to go back for a couple of minutes, do you mind taking over?"

"Okay, but don't be long will you?" was the under-confident reply.

Leaving the flight deck I felt the machine begin to lurch in pitch with increasing excursions and the cabin seat belt sign illuminated. Trying to use the toilet with alternating positive and negative 'g' was an exercise requiring considerable skill. Returning to the flight deck with literally indecent haste, I found the flight engineer, Joe, sitting in my seat hands on the controls and gradually bringing the machine back to stable flight. Captain D____ was hands away from the controls, looking straight ahead through the windscreen into the blackness, red faced with embarrassment.

Eventually, when Joe had us in straight and level flight, he turned around and said,

"Would you like to get back in now?"

"Fine," I replied.

Joe left my seat and I slipped in quickly and took control.

A further two hours or so passed by which time I was not only completely exhausted but also hungry. Drinking cups of coffee while flying one handed was no problem but it was not practicable to have a meal. Joe said,

"Want to go back for a meal and a snooze?"

I looked over to Captain D____. He nodded assent. I slipped out of the seat and Joe sat in and took over.

---

1 Elevator trim. See expanded description in glossary.

First Class was only half full and I sank into a vacant seat. Thoughts of a meal were lost in instant sleep.

There was a tap on the shoulder. It was a stewardess waking me up with a cup of coffee. I rubbed my eyes and gradually became aware of the fact that I had been asleep and of what had transpired on the flight so far. I looked at my watch. I had been away from the flight deck for two hours!

Quick loo stop, splash of water over the face and back to the flight deck. A very weary Joe was still flying and very thankful to see me back. The remainder of the flight proceeded without incident.

Captain D____ was an exception. The general standard of competence of pilots of all nationalities was very high. How this Captain slipped through the system and achieved his position was an unanswerable conundrum.

Joe, a heavy smoker, sadly passed away as a result of throat cancer some three years after this incident.

Finally, there was Captain Mike.

A word of warning to the reader. The rest of this chapter has little to do with aviation!

Back in the mid 1970's there was a vitriolic letter published in the 'Your Letters' columns in 'Flight International'. The exact content I don't recall. It had something to do with the difficulties civil aviation pilots were experiencing trying to obtain first employments. While I couldn't agree with the tone of the letter, the overall implications I had personally been well aware of. The name of the writer stuck in the memory and lo and behold, one day I arrived for work and my captain was the self-same author of the letter.

Along with a number of others he had become unemployed when a substantial UK cargo operator went out of business. Many of the redundant crew from this airline were to come to Saudia.

Mike was tall, slim, dark haired and a great character. He usually wore a cynical, almost supercilious smile and was passionate to the point of fanaticism on a number of subjects, some quite trivial. One of the more serious and justified of these passions was to do with the smoking habit. He did not allow smoking on the flight deck. In fact, his anti-smoking campaign was conducted with an evangelical zeal that was marvellous to behold even to the point of regular letters to the British Prime Minister. Being unable to practice the smoking habit while flying with Captain Mike infuriated some of the Saudi National crew members many of whom were inveterate smokers.

The reader might be aware that the writer is classified with regard to creed as a 'Born again Christian'. Mike is the only person I have ever met who could be described as a 'Born again Atheist'. He had thought the whole issue through and decided there was nothing there. The likes of me were, therefore, interesting folk to talk to. As such he would discuss things for hours on the many occasions I was to work with him with no rancour, condemnation or embarrassment. He neither ridiculed nor decried anything I said, just listened and discussed the matter in a gentlemanly fashion in proportion to the true gentleman he really was.

Mike asked many penetrating questions. It could be considered bad publicity for my Faith to repeat the following but I firmly believe that Almighty God has no problems with honesty.

We were in Madrid, Spain. Coming from Saudi Arabia, technically a 'dry nation', that is to say, alcoholic beverages and the consumption thereof were banned in the Kingdom, most expatriates would head for the nearest available bar and have a drink. Thus, after arrival, along with the Flight Engineer, I was invited to Mike's hotel room. The cork from a bottle of Champagne was popped over the balcony to the street below and discussion commenced. Conversation ranged far and wide through the early evening and later when we adjourned to a restaurant for dinner.

On this occasion we really went to town on religion. I had reasonable answers, usually Biblically based, to most of Mike's questions but then out of the blue came the devastating cruncher,

"You say if I don't believe in Jesus Christ as the son of God, I will end up in Hell?"

Wondering what this was leading up to I cautiously replied,

"That is what the Bible says and implies in more than one instance. God is the Creator of everything and man is in rebellion against his Creator. Forgiveness is freely and wonderfully available to anyone who cares to ask for it."

"So," said Mike, "What kind of a God is it who creates me knowing I'm going to end up in Hell?"

A theologian would probably have a better answer than I had on that occasion. My own dear father would occasionally discuss similar questions in depth. He was not scared of them either. He had a simple answer. When all is said and done, this life is past and we are in the presence of The Almighty, the Righteousness of God will not be in question. I appreciate this is far from a perfect answer. From my own point of view I have seen enough and experienced enough in my short life to accept this answer as the best that will be revealed this side of the grave.

Mike and I maintained friendship and correspondence for some 27 years until he passed away in 2008. He now knows all the answers. In Saudia I flew as his co-pilot. In my next airline, he flew as my co-pilot. Being an inveterate radical with regard to employees' rights, he crossed swords with the management of our next employer sometime in the early '90's and left under a bit of a cloud. This was a great shame from my point of view, but knowing the character of the man, it was not entirely surprising.

I was once asked how I could have a friend like Michael since we were so diametrically opposed in belief. The reason is simple. He was a total gentleman, completely honest and a delight to work with. His one serious flaw was a predilection to occasional almost menopausal outbursts over matters which were not always of great importance.

A final thought on my good friend Michael. After his death a heart rending but fascinating letter from his widow indicated to me that even he was not entirely satisfied with his belief system. It is my fervent hope that in the Hereafter he will be present with his good humour and semi supercilious smile. He certainly 'held out the cup of cold water'[1] to me during times of great personal difficulty which were to follow shortly after I left the 707 fleet.

1 "Cup of cold water" Matthew 10.42 Christian New Testament. I am not theologically equipped to define whether this is appropriate to this situation but I would fondly hope that it is!

7. Fleet change

My sojourn on the 707 fleet lasted little more than two years. At interview prior to joining the company there was an assurance that promotion to 737 Captain would be about 18 months after starting work with Saudia. This proved completely incorrect and was a deep disappointment. The next move was to the new Boeing 747 fleet as a co-pilot. Not many years later, in retrospect, I was most thankful for the time on the 747. This enabled me to get my last and best airline job by far. It would not have been possible without 747 experience.

The course was very rapid, only just over a month, and again, it was provided by TWA, this time in New York. On return to Jeddah things were very different to the initiation encountered when joining the company on the 707. The base training on the aircraft was with a very pleasant captain and two of us first officer trainees were allowed a whole two hours each of general handling, approaches and landings. In this day and age of high fuel costs, things are very different. Provided the trainee has experience on other jet airliners he will operate his first flight on a new type on a regular passenger schedule with a training captain and having only previously flown the simulator.

And so it was off on the line again. A very different route structure emerged with a similar mix of long and short haul but other than some of the same destinations within Saudi Arabia, we ranged from New York in the west to Seoul (South Korea) in the East and many points in between.

Again, there were fascinating routes, destinations and characters along the way.

A little general information about the Boeing 747 is called for. This design which emerged in the early 1970's was to become the backbone of the world's long-haul airlines for many years. In a variety of marques and fitted with various engines it continues to this day albeit, more recently, many long-haul routes have been taken over by twin engine aircraft and the larger Airbus A380.

At two and a half times the gross weight of any other aircraft in service at the time, Boeing, in the initial design phase, were concerned that there wouldn't be enough passengers to fill such a huge machine. Hence the upper deck concept came into being which allowed a freight door in the nose with the flight deck above and slightly aft. In fact, the freight door in the nose was only ever to appear on the pure freighter version. Such was the explosion of passenger travel in the 1960's and 70's that the designers' fears were not realised.

It was a good solid functional design and the engineering was superb. It had the sophistication of the VC10 combined with the practical commercial aspects of the Boeing 707.

At inception the Saudia fleet consisted of about ten, -100 series aircraft fitted with Rolls Royce engines and a further two Boeing 747 SP's. The SP stood for 'Special Performance' and they were originally designed for ultra-long haul routes. They had a shorter fuselage and increased fuel tankage and were grossly over-powered with the 4 Rolls Royce engines. The design had already been superseded by the -200 series which had become available from Boeing. It is possible that the entire fleet been designated for another carrier who had failed to take up their options.

Saudia used their SP aircraft for the route west from Jeddah to New York and the route east from Jeddah to Seoul, South Korea via Riyadh. An indication of the excess power available on these machines was occasionally demonstrated spectacularly.

One evening we arrived in Riyadh after the 15 hour flight from Seoul and the payload and fuel load for the last leg to Jeddah were both minimal. The cruising altitude was planned at 43,000 feet. I timed the beginning of the take-off roll to reaching cruising altitude and it was 12 minutes. The altimeter was winding up like a demented clock bereft of its pendulum. The rate of climb would be insignificant on certain military machines but was extraordinary for a civil transport.

8. Three Captains on the Boeing 747 fleet

Brian, an Englishman, was a delightful character, stocky with a body that seemed slightly too elongated for his legs; ebullient, full of sage aviation folklore, critical of much of the goings on in Saudi Arabian Airlines and openly and loudly xenophobic. The latter trait could be highly embarrassing although the comments probably went completely over the heads of the intended recipients.

Somewhere in my youth I learned the dubious delights of winding people up on sensitive subjects. This, in retrospect, was a defect that probably caused serious offence on occasion and it was only in middle age that comments from my younger brother awoke me to its needless provocation.

Brian had two passions which he had regularly expressed on previous occasions when I had flown with him. Firstly, he adored the Boeing 707 and felt that it was the only worthwhile aircraft that had ever been built. Secondly, he despised the airline seniority system where, as a training captain, he frequently checked out trainee Saudi Captains only to have them advance above him on the seniority list. The latter was based on date of joining for each rank and governed bidding rights for the all-important crew rosters.

We were heading East as occurred on approximately ninety percent of the Saudia 747 flights. It was about 2am (another characteristic of the airline was the preponderance of 747 night departures all of which seemed to commence in Jeddah and transit Riyadh before heading for all points East). There was a Saudi Flight Engineer, Brian was the Captain, and I was the First Officer. In the jump seat was a United Air Carriers First Officer in uniform who was positioning to Riyadh to commence a flight with his airline. The aircraft was full, every seat taken with regular passengers so the positioning crewmember had been assigned the jump seat.

Settling into the cruise for the one hour and thirty minutes flight to Riyadh I decided it was time to wind Brian up.

"Wonderful to be shot of those dreadful old 707's", I declared innocently.

Brian hit the roof.

"The 707 is a superb aircraft and there will never be anything built to compare with it ever again…!"

He ranted on for a full fifteen minutes on the subject before gradually cooling down.

It was time for phase two.

"At least the seniority system in this airline is fair to all of us unlike the dreadful system we had in BA."

Brian almost leapt out of his seat.

"The seniority system in this airline is _____. Every time I check out a new Saudi captain he jumps ahead of me on the seniority list and I lose out on my London trips. What kind of a system is that?"

This time he wouldn't let go and the passions rose as he tried to convince me of the injustice of the system.

By this time we were well on the descent into Riyadh. The deadheading first officer was showing signs of unease as the haranguing bore no signs of abating while we should have been concentrating on the final critical stage of the approach. Landing gear down, full flap selected, the last 4 miles of the flight and Brian finally fell silent as he concentrated on the landing.

Departing Riyadh we set course down the Persian Gulf with a full load. The night sky was moonless and the pitch darkness was intense except for the stars. I contemplated the long night duty ahead.

The winter visibility at altitude over the Gulf seemed, sometimes, to be unnaturally good. Dead ahead was a bright light on the horizon seemingly beaming straight at us. We looked at it. I didn't know whether it was aircraft landing lights, frequently left on in the cruise in these busy airways, or whether it was a planet. It was far too bright to be a star.

With the wisdom of umpteen thousands of flying hours and many more years of aviation than me, Brian looked over and said sagely,

"Venus!"

I wasn't sure and didn't say anything.

A full 15 minutes later with a closing speed of some 1200 mph the landing lights of an opposite direction aircraft passed 2000 feet overhead, rotating beacon flashing. Desperate to enquire whether Venus had been equipped with a rotating beacon I glanced at Brian. He sat statuesque, looking straight ahead and I thought it best to remain silent.

Some while later another bright light appeared dead ahead. This time I couldn't resist it,

"Mars!" I said, ..."And Venus is just landing at Riyadh!"

Brian snorted.

Of course there is always a payback. In future years with my next airline, when I was a Captain and was flying with a particularly abrasive First Officer I was 'wound up' similarly. I only realised this was the case because being a USA West Coast flight we had two co-pilot's. The other man, a quiet very pleasant character had the grace to politely tell me when his companion was off the flight deck.

Brian was really good company and a lovely man to work with. I was to value the friendship greatly during really difficult personal times in the years ahead.

Then there was Matt.

Matt was greying, slightly portly, always with a smile on his face and an American. He was very easy to work with as were many of his nationality. I'm not sure if his background was military. Most US crewmembers had seen service in the military in Vietnam. Most didn't talk about it.

Matt was a good pilot but there was definitely a screw loose somewhere. As with others of his race he waged a constant battle with the US Internal Revenue service (IRS) who unlike their UK counterparts subjected their citizens to taxation regardless of domicile. Matt alleviated this irritation by declaring himself a 'Minister of Religion' which enabled a whole plethora of allowances against tax unobtainable by normal citizens. Matt was not religious. He would discuss religion at length and was most knowledgeable but his behaviour suggested that any spiritual tendencies were associated with their convenience to himself.

In Bangkok, good clothing, fancy dress, uniforms, or any other article of clothing could be ordered and made up incredibly quickly and cheaply. Matt ordered a uniform. This was not a regular uniform but the type that is worn in movies by quasi-military South American gangsters. It was jungle green with a slight surface sheen, there was a polished cap loaded with gold scrambled egg, there were ridiculous gold epaulettes like huge brushes on each shoulder and rows and rows of outsized medals emblazoned across the chest.

Matt came down to the reception in the quite up-market Inter-Continental hotel in Bangkok dressed in this extraordinary garb. He advised the receptionist that he was expecting a call and that he would be at the poolside.

Many eyes turned to view this extraordinary figure as he sat down heavily on a poolside seat. After a few minutes, sure enough, over the public address system came an announcement,

"Would Captain Matt ___, Saudi Arabian Airlines, please come to reception where there is a personage awaiting him.

This time every eye in the populated pool area turned to watch as this amazing spectacle raised itself to its feet, adjusted the uniform and slowly walk the long way around the pool back to reception puffing heavily on his gigantic cigar.

Matt's motivation in this farce was impossible to determine. Was he trying to make a mockery of his employer? I don't think so. One doesn't kill the goose that lays the golden egg! I think he just suffered from a minor form of subtle harmless insanity which is no doubt definable by some lengthy medical nomenclature.

This account fails to do justice to the many fascinating characters I encountered in the airline but there is room for one more.

During my seven years in Saudi Arabia there were regular aviation incidents of a quite serious nature although none were to affect me personally. These varied from hijacks of which there were no less than four, to serious accidents, one of which hit the international headlines. The hijacks were all nasty and the details remain sketchy in the memory except that one, on the 737 fleet, resulted in the killing of the perpetrator and severe injury and maiming of a Saudi training captain.

The worst accident was the loss of a Lockheed Tristar after an on-board fire. The machine landed safely at Riyadh but subsequently burned up with the loss of all on board. Much has been written and there have been two movies produced on the subject. I happened to be on a night stop in Riyadh when this accident occurred

One of the incidents that didn't become international news was the near loss of a 747SP. The relief captain, a reserved Rhodesian by the name of Ray, related the story to me over a quiet drink in some oriental bar on a trip shortly after.

Writing in 2011, 29 years after the incident, I was able to contact Ray who has retired in Montana, USA. The story comes verbatim from him at the end of this chapter with the exceptions that I have abbreviated it a little and deleted the surnames of the folk involved.

I was to work many times with Ray. He was slim,

exceptionally quiet but easy going and very professional with it. He was reputed to have been in the SAS[1].

Another incident bears recording if only because it was extremely unusual.

Working with Ray we were arriving into Bombay (now Mumbai) on a dirty night in the middle of the monsoon season.

Weather radar is an essential device and the Saudi 747 fleet was possessed of the newly developed coloured screens. We had been negotiating our way around the red blobs indicating monsoonal storm cells all the way down the descent and for the initial part of the approach. Weather radar shows precipitation in the form of rain, hail, and to a lesser extent sleet and snow. It does not give wind shear[2] warnings. The latter using Doppler technology is detected on modern aircraft systems but at the time such sophistication had not even been thought of.

We emerged out of the bottom of the overcast on the instrument landing system to Bombay's runway 27 at about 1500 feet above the ground. There was very heavy rain but the poor street lighting of the city was visible on the ground and the runway lighting, a watery blur through the wipers, was visible ahead.

At about 300 feet above the ground the airspeed began to drop off alarmingly. I was handling and added power on all four engines to compensate. The speed continued to drop and I added more power. This was repeated until the thrust levers were so far forward on the quadrant that we must have been close to go-around power. Concentrating on the runway ahead there was no time to look at the engine gauges but the whole situation was bizarre and highly dangerous. There was an audible sharp intake of breath from Ray's direction. By some amazing good fortune we touched down gently and I quickly pulled the thrust levers back to

1 Ray has since confirmed that he was in the SAS.
2 Wind shear. Expanded description in glossary

idle and lowering the nose engaged reverse power. Bombay's runway is very long so despite being at maximum landing weight there was no problem stopping.

Later, in the late 1980's and early 1990's, the mechanics of thunderstorms, at the time not fully understood were analysed by scientists and meteorologists following a series of accidents which occurred in the vicinity of these dragons of nature. Wind-shear warning devices were developed for aircraft and terms such as 'downburst' were coined. We had encountered a downburst [1] and survived unscathed.

SP incident as related by Captain Ray Smith

(Author's note. In the following it should be noted for the non-aviation reader that this description is quite technical. For the aviation reader it needs to be pointed out that when this incident occurred we none of us had been operating the Boeing 747 for more than a year as it was a new fleet.)

"The incident happened in the evening of December 27th 1982. Allen was the captain, Aubrey, his flight engineer; I do not remember the Saudi first officer's name. They made up the first crew. I, along with Richard, my flight engineer made up the second crew. If you remember we only had one first officer to make up a heavy crew. Two captains, two flight engineers and one first officer made a heavy crew in those days.

We took off from Jeddah bound for JFK New York at night, fourteen hours with a full load of fuel and a full passenger load. I sat upstairs in the upper passenger deck forward facing on the right side; Richard was upstairs with me. We had one flight attendant upstairs, rear facing sitting on her jump seat on the left side.

Just after liftoff out of Jeddah and at about 700 feet I heard a very loud noise which I thought was the nose gear coming up through the floor of the aircraft. If you remember

1 Downburst. See glossary

a few months earlier we had an incident over the Persian Gulf where part of the main wheel of an L-1011 Tri-Star came up through the bottom of the aircraft, it made a huge hole and sucked out two small children. I thought we had a gear problem; the noise was followed by a loud grating sound. The cabin attendant who was rear facing saw, as she later described, a shower of sparks and fire coming from the wing, she thought we had hit another aircraft.

It took all of five seconds for me to unbuckle and enter the flight deck where the first thing I saw and heard was the red oil pressure light of the number two engine illuminated along with the low pressure hydraulic light on the centre panel and a shout from Aubrey, "S___, I pulled the wrong fire handle". (He had been looking at his engineer panel when he pulled the fire handle and saw the white transit light illuminate on the number one engine fuel panel instead of the number two and made the expletive). I then saw the red oil light and the amber hydraulic light for the number one engine light up.

'That is when I thought we were toast'. 'Two engines out on the same side'.

Aubrey tried to push the fire handle back in, but if you remember, the yellow flag ejects and turns to prevent pushing the fire handle back. (A safety feature in order to prevent inadvertently pushing the handle back in after a genuine shut down. All the fluids are shut off from the engine when you pull the handle). One must twist the flag and push in the fire handle. I think with everything going on at the time and shutting down the number one engine by mistake Aubrey must have been a little spooked and forgot.

I then slid into the jump seat, pulling the number two fire handle at the same time and told Aubrey to get back onto his panel. I shouted to Alan, "You fly the aircraft and I will relight number one". While he concentrated on doing just that I twisted the yellow flag, rammed the number one fire handle back in, recycled the fuel and ignition switch and later, according to the flight data recorder, had the engine relit in seventy-seven seconds, that is from shut down to relight. As I pushed the number one throttle back into Alan's hand he was already coming back on number three and four throttles. What saved us was the fact it was the SP. We had enough power for those few seconds before relight of the number one engine.

My flight engineer, Richard barreled through the flight deck door right after me, took a right turn and threw every switch on the fuel dump panel, eighteen in all and we dumped seventeen tons of fuel in the seventeen minutes we took to get back on the runway.

Most of the cabin attendants were New York based British girls. The supervisor came onto the flight deck during all the hoopla and asked if they should do a crash and ditching drill to which I replied, "Yes". I had looked outside and on the SP, if you remember; you can see the number two engine from the flight deck. Not possible from the regular 747's. I saw that the engine was hung down at the back and slewed up at an angle on the pylon. It should have separated but did not. I thought anything could happen; either we make the runway or the Red Sea.

Alan had his hands full flying with leading edge flap up on the failed side, (Duct failure), coupled with turbulence from the air flow going over the number two engine angled up. Aubrey could not read the check list due to the vibration so we all figured we would wing it, if you will excuse the pun. I told Alan just to fly and we would handle the rest. I told the first officer to declare an emergency and have emergency crew standing by on the ground. We took off on 34L. There are three parallel runways in Jeddah. When all was done we landed back on 16R which is thirteen thousand feet long. (The same slab of concrete from which we took off).

Alan flew well, he did a great job, we flew out over the desert far enough to make a turn to land back on 16R. We landed overweight, flap 25 and a threshold speed of 200Kts.

At the time I had forgotten where the number two engine sits in relation to the wing gear. I thought if it detaches on landing we might run over it with the landing gear. Now I know, the number two engine is well outside of the wing gear but with all the excitement I could not remember. I had mentioned to Alan,

"Try not to use reverse thrust on number one engine just in case the number two engine shakes loose and we roll over it with the wing gear".

Of course with the amount of speed we had over the fence and during the landing roll he shouted,

"I need to use reverse on number one".

As it came into reverse and the resultant vibration I was expecting the worst.

During our approach to 16R we did happen to notice all the fire tenders were neatly lined up next to 16C which of course is a few miles away. There were no fire trucks anywhere near us when we did land even though the first officer had told them we would be landing on 16R.

"Well, I guess we could not expect much to go right that night".

I recommended we clear the runway and stop but Allan decided to taxi all the way back to the terminal. The result of course was more heat buildup in the wheels resulting in all the tires deflating as the fuse plugs melted out. (400°f).

On the post flight walk around all the tires, one after the other began to deflate, under the left wing there was a huge hole where most of the turbine section of the number two engine disappeared. Some debris hit the main fuselage and some hit the number one engine. One passenger had passed out during the course of the cabin attendant emergency briefing so had to be carried off on a stretcher. One of the ground mechanics while looking up through the large hole in the wing stated, 'The hole was just a few inches from one of the main fuel tanks'. He also stated, and I must agree, 'Boeing builds a good aircraft'. 'That it would take a lot to bring one down'. His statement did bring some comfort especially at the time.

After gawking at all the damage for a while and the passengers had departed we were taken back to operations. By this time a few people from management had arrived.

Allan and his crew went home until the investigation was complete. I was not so lucky!! They soon found a 747-100, rounded up another crew, if I remember it was Tony N and some other poor souls. After an hour or two they dispatched us to Shannon, Ireland to refuel as the 747-100 could not make it direct, then on to New York.

This time I was first crew as I figured since my adrenaline level and heart rate would take a while to settle down I would be wide awake. In retrospect I think they should have given us a day off. Maybe a few days?? Maybe not as I remember they sell beer in NY. After seven hours to Shannon it was my turn to hit the bunk for the rest of the flight to NY. I did sleep as I had been up since morning in Jeddah, twenty four hours previously.

The problem on the flight deck happened just after liftoff. They had an AVM (Vibration) light on the number two engine illuminate right after rotation, it comes on if the meter reads over 2.5: Rolls had put out a series of procedures in the form of a Circular which called for shutting down the engine if the AVM light came on, if the oil differential indicator goes over 12.5, if the oil pressure light comes on, and a few more items which I cannot remember. It was a design problem which I understand was never rectified since there were other similar failures on the RB211. The rear engine bearing apparently was not getting the necessary oil flow to get the lubrication required. When the light came on Allan retarded the throttle and the vibration indication returned to normal.

At about 700 feet and since everything had returned to normal Allan thought he would try opening up the throttle again. He mentioned later that he figured since we had a whole bunch of people bound for New York and a full fuel load and everything was back to normal he would continue.

Unbeknown to him the rear engine bearing had melted due to lack of lubrication and welded to the main core. When he opened up the throttle, power came up and the turbine section just torqued out of the engine resulting in a total disintegration and destruction of the engine itself. Just a few months earlier they had fitted a fan catcher which may have saved the compressor section and maybe us??

Allan was relegated to first officer for seventy hours for not following 'Circular Instructions' as mentioned. The instructions came out in a Circular and were not yet in the operating manual. Aubrey was fired and the first officer escaped. He just did as he was asked. Poor fellow thought, much like all of us, that we were heading for the dirt. (Maybe a sand dune)

After returning to Jeddah from NY they called me in to get my take on what happened. They asked me at that time if I would have Aubrey as a flight engineer on future flights. I replied that I would. Obviously that did not hold too much sway as they fired him anyway. He managed to join a DC-8 outfit back in the States and was back a few months later doing Hajj flights.

Allan passed away a few years after leaving Saudia. He had returned to Australia. I met the first officer a few years later when he came up to me one day and mentioned he was the first officer on the flight but I did not recognize him although I pretended I did."

9. Of dreams and infidelity

It would be a fair assumption that the entire human race are subject to at least the occasional nocturnal or even daytime dream. After a hard day's work or a particularly traumatic time the inner workings of the human mind reproduce the stresses in ordered, sometimes disordered, sometimes completely confused recollection. Other times dreams come unsolicited and completely remote from anything that has occurred in our lives. There has been much written, professional and unprofessional about these visitations of the night and there is historical record, especially Biblical, of those who have been enabled to interpret dreams and visions.

In Australian days there was a particularly vivid dream. In it, my Mother, to whom I was always very close, was killed in a car crash. I awoke suddenly feeling horror and dismay. There was recourse to my new found faith and I pleaded with God not to let my mother be taken. Some years later I was driving with one of my brothers in Sussex in the UK. I have forgotten the reason for the journey but at a particular spot on the road that seemed vaguely familiar my brother said, completely un-solicited,

"This is where Mother had that awful car accident. The car was badly damaged but she was unhurt."

It was the same place where in my dream I had seen her killed. Nobody had even mentioned her accident to me before and that was not unreasonable since she wasn't hurt and I was, at the time, on the other side of the world.

Coming back to Saudi Arabia, things were bad at home. The reason for this constantly plagued my mind but then I never have been particularly smart at solving obtuse conundrums.

There was a contact from Jim, a Christian Pastor in the

UK and also a good friend. He had worked for many years in the 'London City Mission' and had seen more than his fair share of the devious conniving of humanity. Man can try his utmost to hide his nefarious activities but there is a God in Heaven before whom all is laid bare, whether we like it or not.

Jim gently let me in on his knowledge.

An elderly lady in his Church had suffered a vivid and awful dream that I was in trouble. She had shared it with the Church and the immediate assumption was that this had something to do with my flying. However, other information came to the Pastor and he was able to put it all together and other than giving a specific name, which he simply didn't know, it became obvious that my wife was having an extra marital affair. From Jim's extraordinarily detailed information it was not hard for me to figure out who the other party was.

Challenging my wife there was immediate acknowledgement that indeed there was a relationship in progress with a 'third party'.

My world was unravelling.

The following night it was off to Bangkok. Had it been BOAC, immediate compassionate leave would have been granted. This was not BOAC. The only compassionate leave allowed was for locals and they used this facility regularly, especially when they simply didn't want to go to work.

The crew was a little unusual. There was a senior Saudi management captain and a portly German flight engineer who also held a position in management. The Captain was a familiar figure from previous flights but the Flight Engineer was not known to me.

We headed east to Riyadh landing sometime around midnight. With full fuel tanks and a heavy payload we then set off for Bangkok. This was a regular route, a daily schedule and I had flown it many times before. We always carried as much fuel as possible out of Saudi Arabia since this was much cheaper than purchasing it overseas even though the percentage of additional fuel used in carrying the extra weight was significant.

As we progressed down the Persian Gulf, Captain Fuad and Karl, the rotund flight engineer, exchanged greater and greater insults which at one stage became seriously xenophobic. Had I been in a normal state of mind it would have been very funny.

We crossed the Arabian Sea followed by India. It is said that crossing India you can smell the curry at 33,000 feet. I was more interested in trying to get through to the controllers on the over busy HF frequencies. These days it is all VHF and very professional over India.

As the sun rose, dead ahead, dazzling our tired eyes, we crossed the Indian coastline well to the South of Calcutta and headed out over the Bay of Bengal. Very sensibly Captain Fuad insisted that in turn we each have 20 minutes shut-eye. Not the norm in those days and positively frowned upon but later to become a very sensible and accepted practice. It is amazing how quickly the human spirit revives with a short break.

We landed into Bangkok in the steamy morning heat of that capital city and after the fairly rapid bus ride to the downtown hotel I slept soundly, the first time for some forty eight hours.

In the early evening there was an unexpected phone call. It was Captain Fuad. In his thick, heavily accented English he said,

"I would like you to come out to dinner with Karl and myself?"

In the manner of the Saudi's it was less of a question, more a command.

This was so out of character I mentally fell over backwards. Saudia was not a social airline. This kind of invitation simply did not happen unless it was a case of going for a meal with an expatriate crewmember of previous acquaintance. Completely mis-interpreting my hesitation he added,

"I'm paying!"

"Yes, of course I'll come", I replied and "Of course I'll pay my share."

We assembled shortly after in the hotel lobby, a taxi was summoned and we proceeded to a reasonably upmarket restaurant a few blocks away.

During the meal, still feeling thoroughly miserable I communicated little but Fuad and Karl continued their pseudo antagonism in heavily accented English which was presumably their only common language. Their voices increased as more and more wine was consumed until we had the undivided attention of most of the restaurant.

Unfortunately, in the manner of many conversing in a language other than their respective mother tongues, they both assumed that the use of various adjectives which they had collected from profane American and English colleagues was normal polite conversation.

Eventually I felt the need to intervene.

"Do you think we ought to tone it down a bit....I think we might be embarrassing the ladies with the strong language."

"Strong language?" yelled Captain Fuad,

"I'm not using _____ strong language! You have never heard me using _______strong language. If I was using _____ strong language you'd know all about it!" he roared.

I was gratified to note that the two of them did tone things down a little.

About an hour later with more empty carafes' on the table it was decided to return to the hotel. During this time there had been major indiscretions uttered, both political and with regard to our employer, which would cause both of them serious embarrassment should their disparaging remarks ever reach home base. This was especially true for Fuad as in the Saudi society of the time (and probably still now) these things could result in big trouble.

As we rose to go, Fuad thumped me in the chest with his not inconsiderable sized fist,

"Trevor, don't you ever forget, I'm still a Saudi!"

The message was simple; don't repeat anything that has been said to anyone else.

The following morning we met in the lobby. The Captain and Karl were trying to hide humungous hangovers and were not succeeding very well. It had previously been decided that the Captain would fly the two sectors outbound and I would fly the two back to Jeddah.

We departed for Riyadh. As usual the payload (Zero Fuel Weight[1] in aviation terms) was at maximum. The flight to Riyadh took some eight hours against the prevailing headwinds. The surface temperature at Riyadh was in the high forties (°C) and the thermal turbulence at low levels was considerable.

By now I had been operating in the region for several years and knew most of the pitfalls. We approached the Northerly runway and predictably, as we crossed the threshold the machine started to sink rapidly. This is caused by less dense air over the iron hot tarmac whereas the sand of the desert before the threshold was not so hot. I was ready for it. The natural reaction is to increase the flare angle by adding more back pressure on the control column. This can not only cause a tail strike but also, because the gear trucks are behind the centre of pressure about which the longitudinal axis of the aircraft rotates, the trucks can be driven into the ground and a heavy landing results. I maintained the flare angle and added power on all four engines, squeezing the thrust levers forward easing the inevitable thump into the ground. It was not a tidy landing.

1 Zero fuel weight. See glossary.

I applied full reverse power and slowing to about 80kts, applied gentle braking. The brakes on the classic 747 were prone to overheating very quickly with high outside air temperatures and unlike in temperate zones it was unwise to use them at high speed. Cancelling reverse I took the next high speed turn-off and said to Fuad,

"Sorry about the landing there wasn't much else I could do with the shear in the flare."

"That was a very good landing and most first officers would have sat and watched it happen. You increased the power which prevented a heavy landing."

It is a silly thing but to have their somewhat coarse companionship the night before and then a word of professional encouragement in the middle of dire personal circumstances was a boost to the morale that I have never forgotten.

In very difficult times like these, real friends came out of the woodwork. I have already mentioned Mike and Brian but there were many others whose kindness I will never forget including Captain Fuad who seemed to perceive well beyond the information that he was party to. There were Christian friends also, to whom I owe much.

The marital situation was patched up for a while but about a year later things were obviously bad again. I was assured there was no-one else involved but the lady wanted a divorce.

Cutting a long and very sad story short, there was yet another man. Gradually I came to terms with the fact that the marriage was over. If I didn't care for the children nobody would and so for the next few years I was to find myself trying to hold down a job and bring up three children on my own.

This chapter began with dreams and ends with another dream.

Was it dream or was it a vision? I will not know this side of the grave. I was carried to another world, dimension, call it what you will. This was in the middle of the, to date, most difficult time of my life, the marriage break up. I saw things which are too precious to be described indeed, there would be insufficient human language available were I to try and describe them. The most accurate description is to repeat the words of a man going through a severe personal crisis following the great fire of Chicago of 1871…

"I had such an experience of *His* love that I had to ask *Him* to stay *His* hand."

10. Conflict with Customs

"All Hell let loose" is an expression in the English language relating to extreme, almost freak disorder in human situations. As mere mortals we have little idea what is really going on in the Heavenlies or spiritual realms. In fact, I have long held the view that as Westerners, where the culture has been heavily dumbed down since the almost universal acceptance of the theories of Charles Darwin, we have largely closed our mind to Spiritual things, whether sacred or profane. Orientals are not so inhibited albeit there is a tendency to go to wild extremes in either direction.

In my years in Saudi Arabia I was to experience a day when All Hell seemed to have been let loose. I can make no comment other than that said above but will tell it like it happened and the reader can rationalise or agree according to where the individual mind is coming from.

The seeds of the situation were sown sometime around late 1982. As the first officer on a 747 crew I was transiting Dhahran en-route to Riyadh, final destination Jeddah, having left the Indian sub-continent early the same morning.

It was a facet of my time in the Kingdom that customs would turn out the suitcases of passengers and crew on each and every entry to Saudi Arabia.

Since conversion at the age of twenty-one I have always carried a Christian Bible on my travels. This has never been an ostentatious religious tome but small and un-attention-getting. Generally Saudi customs would open it up, thumb through the pages and return it to the suitcase. Those who realised what it was frequently gave me a knowing look and occasionally there was a nod of approval. I guess they felt that evidence of a real Christian was better than nothing and the Koran refers to Christians as "The People of the Book". Amongst the Moslems who knew I was a Believing

Christian I was referred to, not unkindly, as "Mu-min" or "Believer" and sometimes as "Messiahi" presumably meaning a Believer in Christ as the Messiah, or Son of God.

On this occasion the young customs officer took a long look at my Bible as he thumbed through the pages and eventually threw it back into my suitcase and said angrily,

"This is Bible. This is illegal in Saudi Arabia. I will let you take it but leave it at your house and don't bring it through customs again!"

I said nothing. Sorting out the disorder caused by his rummaging, I closed and locked the suitcase and returned to the aircraft.

Some eighteen months later and shortly before I was to transfer to the Boeing 737 fleet there was a similar trip. I had transited Dhahran many times in the interim without encountering further problems. This particular morning, queuing for the statutory rummage I espied my enemy on the other side of the customs hall. Fortunately I was not in a queue anywhere near his. Regrettably he must have seen me.

His queue was effectively dismissed and he was looking straight at me and beckoning for me to come over. With a sinking feeling about the inevitable I went over to his position. He opened my suitcase and very quickly found what he was looking for. He held it high with one hand.

"This is Bible. It is illegal in Saudi Arabia and I have told you this before. I am confiscating this item," he shouted.

Many heads turned curiously in our direction.

As a Christian I am supposed to be gentle, forgiving and turn the other cheek. I failed in all respects. I was furious.

"If you take that away I can no longer work in Saudi Arabia", I shouted in return.

He threw my Bible into a box behind him and indicated that I should go. Meanwhile a small crowd of officials had gathered amongst whom I recognised several station staff employed by the airline. They were generally indicating some sympathy with my misfortune and there was a loud argument in Arabic developing. I was so angry I slammed my suitcase shut, locked it and strode back across the tarmac to the aircraft.

Making my way to the upper deck I passed the Captain reclined in a lounge seat having a siesta. He had obviously managed a fast transit of customs and was unaware of all the fuss. He was a Saudi National. I did not see any point in waking him up to bemoan my misfortune. I sat in my seat and began to prepare for the next leg to Riyadh. I was not concentrating but this was a 'bread and butter' route and I could almost load the INS waypoints without even referring to the charts.

Halfway through this procedure, anger gradually subsiding, I happened to glance outside. The sight that met my eyes was bizarre in extremis. There was an entourage of some fifteen uniformed figures proceeding in the direction of the aircraft. In the lead, waving my Bible above his head as if it was some kind of a rallying banner was one of our ground staff. Shortly after there was a clatter of feet up the stairs behind me and a spectacular babble of raised voices. It was obviously about the fuss I had caused. With a measure of un-Christian obduracy I decided that if they wanted me they could come and get me.

Inevitably, shortly after, a head appeared round the flight deck door.

"Captain wants you to come back to the lounge to discuss the … er, incident in customs."

The small lounge area, semi-circular configuration with a table in the middle, was crowded. Some were sitting, some standing. In the centre of the table was the offending article.

My enemy was arguing heatedly with the captain but then it might not have been an argument. Sometimes in

Saudi Arabia a normal conversation could sound like a declaration of war. With my very limited knowledge of the language it seemed that the Captain was arguing my case and suggesting that I was only an ignorant foreigner and had no plans to corrupt Islam while the customs officer was insisting that he was doing his duty.

Finally, the Captain, an older man, turned to me and said wearily,

"Customs are going to permit you to take your book on the flight back to Jeddah. The local customs office in Jeddah will meet the flight and take it from you there for further examination."

The next sector to Riyadh was uneventful but things began to go wrong on departure for Jeddah. Opening up the engines for take-off a loud intermittent horn sounded.

All airliners are fitted with a device known as the Take-off Configuration Warning. This is an intermittent horn that sounds if any major discrepancy is detected in the configuration of the aircraft for take-off. Usually there are five items that must be correctly set. These include, leading edge and trailing edge flaps, stabiliser trim, speed brakes fully stowed and parking brake released.

Several times over the years I have encountered this warning. Usually it has been a faulty micro switch or stabiliser trim anomaly where the aircraft centre of gravity has been detected incorrectly by the on-board sensors. This time and for the only time in my entire aviation career, it was for real. It was highly embarrassing. With three flight deck crew members, all having independently checked the stabiliser trim setting, not to mention the appearance of this item twice in the check-lists, it had not been set.

The captain stopped the take-off, we set the stabiliser to its correct position all of which took about twenty seconds, and considerably shaken we were on our way.

Descending into the Jeddah area about an hour and

fifteen minutes later I changed to the Jeddah terminal control frequency when instructed and we were greeted by mayhem.

Jeddah is a very busy airport. It was eventually discernible that the terminal area radar had failed. In my seven years based there I had never known the airport to operate without terminal radar. Indeed, large international airports are supposed to have enough back-up systems for this never to happen.

The obviously panic-stricken Saudi controller was manfully trying to cope with a situation which, probably in his worst nightmares, he could never have imagined. The captain slowed the aircraft while I tried to get a word in on the saturated airwaves. Eventually, with everybody stepping on everyone else's transmissions, I was heard.

The controller rattled off a holding position and altitude. His instruction was reasonably clear but there was a possible ambiguity and I strove for clarification. Eventually I just gave up as there were other aircraft in a far worse situation than us, some getting short of fuel as they had been holding for so long.

I had a fairly clear picture in my mind from the controller's instruction that we were to hold on the 311° radial at twenty miles from Jeddah, 7000 feet. The captain had an equally clear picture in his mind that we were to hold on the (reciprocal) 131° radial at twenty miles, 7000 feet. One was 20 miles North West of Jeddah and the other 20 miles South East. There was no point in arguing about it. The captain is the captain and he has the last word in these situations. Anyway, I wasn't sure enough of my ground to dig my heels in. We held to the South East.

There was no traffic collision avoidance equipment fitted or available in those days so we were keeping the best possible lookout for other aircraft in the conditions of a thick Saudi dust haze.

After about twenty minutes of continuing mayhem on

the frequency during which we didn't see a single other aircraft despite their being some thirty or more in the vicinity a solid calm American voice took over the frequency. He was probably a senior manager who had been called in to rectify the highly dangerous situation. He demanded silence and gradually worked through the list of aircraft in the area and worked to get the low fuel cases to a rapid landing. Being a fairly late arrival on the scene it was some time before he called our flight. When he did so his first question was for us to state our position and altitude. I did so and there was a pregnant pause...

"Say, I have you guys holding on the 311° radial at twenty miles, what took you down there?"...

There was alarm in his voice and before I could reply,

"Turn immediate heading 270, descend 6000 feet, expedite."

I acknowledged and the Captain grunted, complying with the instruction as quickly as possible.

The truth will never be known but it was fairly obvious that we were holding in the wrong place and probably in conflict with another aircraft holding at the same place and same altitude. By some miracle we didn't collide. There were further instructions and eventually we proceeded to the Jeddah VOR and carried out a procedural ILS approach to land some twenty minutes later.

As we parked my mind went back to the incident in Dhahran. We were now an internal flight but a yellow customs car was approaching the aircraft. I had hoped they would quietly forget the fuss over my Bible but it was not to be.

A local, quite friendly customs officer arrived on the flight deck and apologetically took the offending article.

"Come to the customs office in three days when we will have had time to examine it and you will be able to have it back."

Three days later I went to the customs office and stated my case at the reception desk. I was ushered into an immense office on an upper floor and the door was closed behind me. The sole occupant of the plush, magnificently furnished suite was a skinny bearded older man behind a huge polished mahogany desk. He was dressed impeccably in starched white Arab dress. He had ink black, hostile eyes. The only item on the desk was my Bible.

He glared at me for a minute or two until the situation began to feel embarrassing. Finally he said in broken English,

"This is Bible. You take it to your house and keep it there until you leave Saudi Arabia at the end of your contract. If you try to take it in and out of the country before then, we will take it from you and you will not have it returned."

The interview was clearly over. I picked up my Bible, left the office and went home. It was definitely time to think about a future other than in Saudi Arabia. Two years later this came to pass in not quite as orderly a manner as I would have hoped.

Shortly after this I was rostered to fly with the same captain again. He failed to turn up for the duty citing 'family reasons'! A standby captain was called out to replace him. One assumes that he had decided that I was bad medicine and to fly with me again was not a good idea.

There are two postscripts to this chapter.

The underlying problem was easily solved. Not long after this incident, while in Nairobi, Kenya, I found a Bible in a Christian bookshop with a cover that made it look like any ordinary novel. I carried this with me on trips for the remainder of my time in Saudi and it never aroused any undue attention.

A number of years after I left Saudi Arabia, there was a tragic mid-air collision between a Saudia Boeing 747 and another airliner. This occurred over India in the vicinity of Delhi. But for the Grace of God I could have been part of a similar statistic in the manner described in this chapter.

11. Boeing 737

After five years in the airline the change to a command on the Boeing 737 fleet finally arrived. Like most things associated with Saudia it was not a happy experience. It is not a good thing to change to an unfamiliar aircraft type when being promoted to command. The ideal is simply to upgrade to Captain on an aircraft type familiar to the trainee. The rigours of the airline's sometimes overt dislike of foreigners exacerbated the trial.

The 737 fleet consisted of the older -200 variety which had an all up weight of about 50 tonnes. The flight deck crew consisted of two pilots. The controls for the air conditioning, electrics and hydraulics, etc. were on a large overhead panel easily reachable by either pilot. In one aspect things were familiar, it was a typical Boeing so, to me after flying the 707 and 747, the scenario was not entirely unfriendly.

The course was conducted in Saudi Arabia and after the ground school and aircraft type rating there were primarily young Saudi National training captains to contend with.

Some were good, a few were indifferent and a few were very difficult and determined to cause any ex-pat to fail the course. They succeeded. Of sixteen ex-pat starters only a very few (I think three) completed the course successfully. I was one of the few. There was little to suggest that my performance was better than the failures. It was simply there were enough problems with the home situation without all the hassles of having to find another job. I just stuck at it through all the harassment whereas others said,

"Why should I, an experienced professional pilot, put up with all this stupidity?"

There were a few situations where I scored points which eased the journey.

On one training flight, when we were on the ground in Sharurah, the only airport in the 'Empty Quarter' of Saudi Arabia there was a problem. When we were ready to depart, the air-stairs failed to retract. There was no ground engineer. These days, passengers usually embark/disembark via a jetty or very occasionally using a set of external steps. The Boeing 737's in Saudia were equipped with air-stairs which extended and retracted into and out of the fuselage as a part of the integral equipment of the aircraft.

The training Captain and I examined the obdurate device and then, to my astonishment, the Captain grabbed a stainless steel culinary knife from the galley and started trying to prise open the relevant electrical control panel mounted on the fuselage wall. In engineering terms this was not only stupid but dangerous as there was high voltage associated. I persuaded him to stop and asked if I could have a few minutes to examine the mechanism prior to the next step which would be to call maintenance in Jeddah for advice.

Knowledge gleaned in ground school suggested that there were a number of micro switches in the system all of which had to be satisfied before the mechanism would operate. I fiddled with the side rails for a couple of minutes and asked the captain if he would operate the retraction switch. It worked! From then on, with this particular training captain, I could do nothing wrong!

Another training captain, possessed of a particularly evil disposition, was making life difficult. With regard to my operation of the aircraft things had been going well and this seemed to exacerbate his endemic irritable tendencies. One day, on the leg from Nejran to Abha, he briefly fell asleep. For him to be asleep was much better for me than when he was awake and I made no steps to change the status quo except that, procedurally I was duty bound to wake him up for the landing. Intercepting the final approach course he suddenly woke up, glanced at the chart followed by the altimeter and screamed,

"What is this 13,000 feet? We should be 15,000 feet. This is no good, this is failure. It is not possible for you to be captain with these errors!"

I pointed to a footnote on the chart which permitted 13,000 feet if the approach direction was from the South East. There was a subdued silence. Nothing else was said but he was much easier to work with from that time on.

Once checked out things were reasonably good. The routes were 90% within the country and there were some intriguing destinations, particularly those buried in the mountains down the Western escarpment of Saudi Arabia.

12. Captain

After a total of eleven years as a co-pilot in two different airlines it was a dramatic psychological and not un-enjoyable change to be a captain. The co-pilots were all Saudi nationals, generally very good at their job and friendly. There were exceptions, usually due to innate arrogance associated with being in their home country employed by their national airline which could generate a tendency to demean ex-pat captains. I quickly learned to ignore this attitude as invariably, there would be some stupid operational blunder resulting in 'loss of face' followed by a measure of humility.

By the nature of the rostering system on the fleet, it was normal to fly for a whole month with the same co-pilot. Generally this was fine but on the very rare occasion that the co-pilot was un-friendly or un-co-operative it could be awful.

One of the very few obnoxious young men was overt in his dislike of me and his hostility increased as the month went along. It came to the stage that I even considered going in to the fleet office and making an official complaint. It is not pleasant to work in such an atmosphere and it is not unknown for this kind of behaviour to be a contributory factor in aircraft accidents. I need not have worried.

One dark night we were flying the very short leg from Abha in the mountains to Gizan on the Red Sea coast. I think the leg is 55 nautical miles which with orderly departure and arrival procedures takes 15 to 20 minutes. Starting at Abha, some 7000 feet above sea level with my fractious colleague handling the aircraft, we climbed over the Western Saudi escarpment and then descended rapidly to Gizan which is at sea level. Not being party to his thinking processes I observed that everything was well flown and completely in order until the touch-down. For indeterminate reasons he then literally drove the aircraft into the ground with the worst landing I was ever to see on a Boeing 737. I suspect it was a simple matter of over-confidence and inexperience. The temperature at Gizan was some 20°C higher than at Abha and he may have forgotten the simple need for circumspection in the flare when there is a high surface temperature. He was a very subdued young man as we parked and his loss of face was exacerbated when a steward arrived on the flight deck and said to me,

"What happened Captain?"

Cabin crew in Saudia rarely if ever commented on flight deck performance so the effects in the cabin must have been dramatic.

I could see that the young man was severely chastened. The ground engineer happened to be a very friendly ex-pat and I felt the need to avoid writing a report if at all possible. I explained what had happened and asked if he would do a good check of the undercarriage and anything else that might have been affected. He returned after about 15 minutes and advised that all was in order so we went on our way. The 737 is a sturdy little aircraft and puts up with much mal-treatment during the rigours of its short haul existence. The co-pilot's attitude underwent instant transformation and he was easy to work with for the remainder of the month

Mankind is by nature greedy and the traditional ploy on the 737 fleet was to fly the cruise section of each flight at Mach 0.72 whereas the official company designated speed was Mach 0.78. This by definition increased the flight time and thereby frequently resulted in lucrative overtime payments. I flew the official speed of Mach 0.78 in the cruise. This generated hostility from a few of the more mercenary minded co-pilots but also resulted in a most amusing incident.

One day, flying in the vicinity of Hail and Gassim in the middle of the country there was a call on the local air traffic frequency for me to contact the caller on the company frequency on our number two VHF radio. This I did and was greeted with a grilling from a management captain as to why a certain leg on our route had taken longer than scheduled. I replied with the explanation that we had taken the exact planned time and were cruising at the official company speed. The caller failed to check his figures as I was requested to be at flight operations at 10am the following morning to explain the alleged discrepancies.

Having a completely clear conscience on the matter I arrived at operations at the appointed hour the following morning knowing there was no case to answer. I was invited to sit in an office before my accuser and the same grilling began. Two or three minutes later there was a roar of laughter from the adjacent office and a very good American friend of mine by the name of Jim, walked in on our conversation and announced,

"You've got the wrong guy. Captain Vellacott flies at 0.78. I know because a co-pilot had a good moan about it to me!"

Jim had overheard our conversation. He had been employed in Saudia for some 10 years and was well known and respected by the Saudis. There was a smile from my interrogator followed by a handshake and an almost unheard of apology.

Another month I worked with a pleasant young man who, unlike most of the Saudis, was completely black. He had been several years on the fleet and I eventually concluded that the reason he had not progressed to another more senior fleet was due to some kind of unspoken apartheid. He was an excellent pilot and far more knowledgeable about the aircraft and the operation than most of his compatriots.

I recollect him well, not only because it was most pleasant month but also for a specific incident. I think his first name was Abdul. Only his surname figures in my log book.

We were approaching one of the airfields, Arar, on the oil pipeline which runs along the northern edge of Saudi Arabia.

The wind was a very strong, South Westerly and the

cloud cover, unusually for Saudi Arabia, was thick with a low base. The only full instrument approach was to land East. The airfield was uncontrolled, that is to say there was no control tower. We had to use a procedure known as a 'Circling approach' which allows using an instrument approach to one runway followed by a visual procedural re-positioning for landing on a different runway, in this case the reciprocal. This is not to be confused with a visual circuit.

We descended with the wind quartering behind us to the approach minimums. The ground duly appeared when we were at about 800 feet above airfield height. I turned 45° to the right for about 20 seconds and then paralleled the runway keeping it firmly in sight. At the appropriate timed distance past the reciprocal runway threshold I turned left through 180° and called for gear down and full flap. Abdul obediently complied and while I attempted to manoeuvre onto the centre line he completed the landing checklist. I had completely underestimated the crosswind component. It quickly became evident that lining up on the runway was impossible as we had been blown well the north of it. I applied 'go-around' power and called for Abdul to raise the gear and select flaps to the go-around position.

The visibility under the cloud was good so I decided to have another go. Same procedure but this time flying downwind I went as far out from the runway as I could while still keeping it in sight. Belting over the sand dunes at 600 feet was an exhilarating experience. I glanced across at Abdul and in the gloom there was a glimpse of brilliant white teeth and the whites of his eyes. Abdul was enjoying himself as much as I was. This was aerial agriculture but not in a three tonne crop-sprayer at 90kts but a fifty tonne airliner at 180 kts. This time things went well and I completed the 180° turn positioning the machine well to the South allowing the cross wind to blow us onto the extended centre-line of the runway. Other than a near limiting cross wind we landed uneventfully.

13. Difficulties

Since 1981 the children had been going to a superb boarding school in South Africa. How this came about is a story all on its own, except to say that it was one third the cost of the equivalent schooling in the UK, the quality of the education was superb and included good family Christian ethics. It was also a non-apartheid establishment in the days when that curious aberration ruled the politics of South Africa. Distance was not much more than to the UK but in almost the opposite direction. The downside was that travel was complex.

On the home front things went from bad to worse. Wife, during the process of divorcing me and despite her Australian nationality, had taken up residence in the UK. With no knowledge that there was another suitor involved, I was finding that her handling of the children was deteriorating from careless to downright irresponsible.

One night the children arrived in Jeddah after a stay with their mother a day earlier than had been arranged and completely unannounced. By this time there were telephones with international access in all the ex-pat houses in the company compound in Jeddah so there was no excuse for the lack of communication.

Fortunately, not only was I at home but Andy, the Norwegian captain of a previous chapter was passenger on the same aircraft and he telephoned me on arrival to say the children were at the airport with him, asking why I was not there to collect them.

This incident resulted in the realisation that I was effectively on my own with the children. Shortly-to-be ex-wife could no longer be relied upon to care for them.

Arrangements in terms of exit/re-entry visas, tickets, school holidays and half term breaks required complex logistics and there was much trip swapping with colleagues and adjustments of days off with the company. The school were wonderful and the parents of other children, resident in South Africa were really kind, in some instances extremely so.

Despite assistance of this nature life was on something of a knife edge

The only sensible means of travel to South Africa was by using one of the twice weekly flights to Nairobi, Kenya and then there were plenty of connections on to Johannesburg.

One Wednesday I had a busy day's schedule lined up. The route was Jeddah, Abha, Bisha, Taif, Medina, Tabuk landing back at Jeddah around 5pm. The flight to Nairobi left at 8pm the same evening which allowed a spare day before collecting the children from the school at Mooi River, Natal on the Friday morning for their half term holiday. The downside was that if I didn't make that flight the next service was three days later on the Saturday evening which was useless for my purposes.

All went well through Abha and Bisha. Leaving Bisha with the co-pilot handling, after he called for the final stage of flap retraction, it became obvious that he was having some difficulty.

"Stabiliser trim not working captain, do you want to take control?"

"No, you can handle it. Carry on!" was my reply.

He glanced across in astonishment. Most captains on the fleet took over when there was the slightest problem but it seemed to me that manually winding the trim could be accomplished just as well by him as by me. He duly unstowed the manual handle on the trim wheel and began cranking away as the speed increased requiring more forward trim.

Once in the cruise I called the dispatcher in Jeddah on HF, told them what had happened and requested a diversion to Jeddah for maintenance rectification. For unexplained reasons this was refused and we were told to continue to destination Taif with the promise that a new unit would be sent by road for fitting on the ground there. I tried to protest but achieved nothing. My misgivings were personal, not operational. I knew the road journey from Jeddah to Taif would take a minimum of three hours. If the remainder of the day's schedule was to be flown it would be impossible, to catch the evening flight to Nairobi. It was not legal to continue after the next landing with an inoperative electric stabiliser trim motor.

The co-pilot did a superb job with the manual trim and we landed uneventfully at Taif. It was a full five hours later that the new electric trim motor was fitted and signed off in the technical log. I called Jeddah dispatch again on HF and asked if we were still required to complete the remaining three legs, Medina, Tabuk and back to Jeddah. I was desperately hoping the schedule would be cancelled and it would be a matter of a direct flight back to Jeddah. It was not to be.

We completed the day's schedule running very late and reducing the transit stops to the absolute minimum. We landed back in Jeddah on the left runway as the Nairobi flight departed on the right runway. The next suitable passenger flight to Nairobi was on the following Saturday night.

Despite being very tired after a six sector day there was no option but to work on an alternative means of getting to South Africa by Friday morning. The ghost of a plan formed.

By the extreme good graces of an ex-pat on duty in the flight operations centre I managed to get clearance to passenger to London on the last flight to Europe that evening. This was the wrong direction but there were still 36 hours remaining before I was due to collect the children and there was no viable alternative route.

Arriving at Heathrow early on the Thursday morning I went to the British Airways office and explained my dilemma. They gave me a staff discount ticket on their evening flight to Johannesburg via Nairobi which was unusually kind as there was only my company ID to prove who I was and I didn't have the required paperwork from Saudia.

There was a day in a Heathrow hotel and then the long, 12 hour flight to Johannesburg (via Nairobi) which arrived on schedule on the Friday morning. I hired a car and set off for the 5 hour trip to the school.

Realising I was running late I edged the car up to 140km/hr whereas the open road speed limit was 120km/hr. Traversing the Orange Free State there was a police radar trap and I fell right into it. Explaining what had happened I was let off with a severe warning. As soon as I was around the next corner it was back to 140km/hr. The South African police are clever. About five kilometres down the road there was another radar trap. Their colleagues had radioed ahead and this time there was no escape. With the prevailing regime in South Africa at the time I was fortunate not to be arrested. There was a subsequent heavy fine. The remainder of the trip was on and not above the approved speed limits.

The arrangement was to meet the children off the school transport at a shopping centre to the North of Durban. I arrived two hours late. The children were patiently sitting on a bench waiting for me. There was Naomi, 15 years old, Phillip, 13 and Bethany at a mere 11. After hugs and greetings I apologised for being late. Naomi said,

"That's okay, we knew you would come, you always do!" which brought tears to the eyes.

They were and still are wonderful children although; as I write these lines, with one over forty and the others not far off, they are hardly children any more. These days there are five grandchildren.

14. Last days with Saudia

My sojourn in the Kingdom of Saudi Arabia came to an abrupt and unexpected close.

Annual recurrent simulator training arrived and was carried out by a particularly volatile young Saudi training captain. I was having a good day and all the needles were in the right places and at the right times. As we went through all the mandatory procedures the instructor/checker became more and more irritated until he was shouting at everything I did. I stopped the proceedings and asked him to discontinue this tirade. I explained patiently that at forty years old, with a teenage family and many years of aviation experience behind me, to keep shouting was neither dignified nor necessary. If I was not handling things to his satisfaction he needed to tell me in a civilised fashion and I would attempt to improve my performance but failing that then I was obviously below standard and would resign gracefully.

He quietened down for a while but then it all began again. Even though we were in mid-flight I closed the thrust levers, set the parking brake, climbed out of my seat and walked out of the simulator. (It was the older type of simulator where you could still do this.... modern simulators are up on hydraulic jacks and to park and attach the walkway is a procedure all of its own). In some anger I scribbled a note resigning from Saudia and handed it to the instructor. He refused to accept it.

It was a Wednesday night when the debacle in the Simulator occurred and there was the Islamic weekend of Thursday and Friday to ruminate on the situation. There were also friends to talk things over with and try to obtain counsel. The general consensus, especially from the old hands was that I had irretrievably 'burned the bridges behind me'. There would be a de-briefing and suggestion that I go back in the simulator with a different instructor. However, the different instructor would be duty bound to his colleague with whom there had been the confrontation and I would be failed on some technicality.

On the Saturday morning there was a telephone call from the training office asking me to come down and discuss 'Wednesday's incident'. There was a civilised friendly de-briefing with two older Saudi Captains during which it was explained that some of the instructors had learned their behaviour from their TWA instructors. This was true. Some of the latter were indeed very irritable mainly because they didn't like being in Saudi Arabia and had been forced to take overseas contracts to keep their jobs in times of retrenchment back in the USA. Predictably, the session finished with the suggestion that I go back in the simulator with a different instructor and I would be cleared back to the line. I stuck with it and insisted that the resignation on the Wednesday was for real and final.

And so, I went to my home in the company compound and over the next ten days packed up my goods and chattels, worked through the long departure rigmarole associated with the company and the country and left Saudi Arabia for good.

In terms of aviation it had been a superb seven years with three different aircraft types, a multitude of fascinating routes and an amazing variety of characters met along the way. There had been awful problems but the two primary objectives, to pay for the private education of the children and to obtain an airliner command had been achieved. There were lovely friends amongst the ex-pats, a few of whom were to appear in my next employment and even some Saudis who I remember as fascinating characters and good friends.

SECTION V.

ATLANTIC AIRLINES

1. A job for life

Back in 1984, while working in Saudi Arabia there was an article in 'Flight International' about a brand new start-up airline. They were planning to run a daily schedule from London Gatwick to Newark, New Jersey (USA) with one Boeing 747. The owner was a flamboyant young man by the name of Richard Branson whose fortune had been made in the music industry. The name of the upstart airline was Virgin Atlantic. There is a clear recollection of saying to myself,

"That is the type of outfit I would never even think of working for!"

Arriving back in the UK after seven years in Saudi Arabia there was much to be sorted out. I was the sole parent of three teenage children. The family home had been sold as part of the impending divorce settlement so there was need of accommodation. Some funds had been saved but would only last at best for a few months so the primary requirement was work.

Type ratings on my UK licence for the Boeing 737 and Boeing 747 were obtained courtesy of a few days training with the now long defunct British Caledonian Airways at Gatwick airport. There was a suggestion from one of the instructors that Virgin Atlantic might be looking for Boeing 747 type rated pilots. There was also an advertisement in Flight International for a 737 Captain with Air Wales. A trip to Cardiff and an interview with Air Wales was quickly followed by a job offer. An interview with Virgin Atlantic Airways was also good but they were offering a co-pilot job. The response to my query reference promotion to captain was,

"Possibly after five years, maybe never!"

The bottom line was that there was no option. It would be totally impossible to care for three children and fly down to the Mediterranean every night with Air Wales. Virgin Atlantic offered a lifestyle far more compatible with the enforced status of single parent father.

It was a Providential choice but there was more to it than that. Shortly after joining I was to discover that his fledgling airline were hot on homework. They made detailed enquiries into a prospective applicant's background prior to interview. A recommendation came from Captain Bob Rowe, retired from BOAC/BA, and at that time, a current Captain with Virgin. Little did I realise in 1975 the significance of what had been to me an easy visual approach to Dar-es-Salaam.

I was to remain with Virgin Atlantic for the next 23 years leading right up to retirement and there is an eternal debt of gratitude to Captain Bob. Promotion to Captain myself came after only two years. Initially the job was very poorly paid but over time this gradually improved to industry standard. Above all, it was a lovely job in a friendly atmosphere and very happy memories far outweigh the few occasions when things were not so good. Air Wales seemed to disappear off the radar screen about 18 months later.

Accommodation also quickly sorted itself. I was not fussy. There was a suitable house in Worthing which had been on the market for a long time. Naïvely I offered the asking price which was accepted. The real plus was that a mortgage was arranged almost instantly and two weeks after viewing I moved in just in time for the children's return from

South Africa for their school holidays.

As soon as they went back to school I started work with Virgin Atlantic. It was not an auspicious beginning. The one Boeing 747 used a Sperry Flight Director[1] and the allocated two sessions in the simulator were a disaster. I was used to the Collins Flight Director which gave a totally different presentation. The company was incredibly patient and I was allowed a third session, this time with a different, very patient instructor by the name of Jim Smillie.

Smiling by name and smiling by nature, he even lived in a house called 'Smiles Cottage'. He quickly sorted the problem. Switching the flight director off and allowing me to fly on raw data things were quickly under control. On the line it was mandatory to use the flight director but I learned to look through it and ignore the indications until gradually, it began to make sense. Eventually, I was to recognise that the 'Sperry' presentation was/is far more precise than the Collins version but it was several months before I was completely at ease with it.

There were a total of twenty eight flight deck crew and somewhere in the region of one hundred cabin crew. The fleet had now expanded to two aircraft. Everybody knew everybody else. There were no 'standby' duties in the early days. If there was a problem or someone went sick we just phoned around until someone was found to fill the slot.

Work was straightforward being either Gatwick to New York (Newark) or Gatwick to Miami. I was completely familiar with Atlantic procedures from experience with both of my previous airline employers.

During the first summer there were two international events which could well have put paid to the fledgling airline. President Reagan, in his wisdom, bombed Colonel Gadhafi in the Libyan capital, Tripoli. Adding to the international mayhem was the Chernobyl nuclear disaster.

1 Flight Director. See glossary for expanded description

Despite fears all around as to the viability of the airline as passenger numbers fell across the board, Virgin not only survived but prospered.

At one stage there was a suggestion that one aircraft would have to be laid up for the winter. Even worse there was an attempt to become involved in the Islamic Haj. Together with an ex-Saudia colleague who joined the company at the same time we liaised in vociferous protestations. There were all sorts of difficulties with this kind of contract, not the least being the frequency with which, historically, financial promises were made but at the end of the day no-one paid up.

Deep at heart I think we both felt that to return to Saudi Arabia in any guise was the last straw.

In actual fact, loads to Miami, the second route, held up and we operated both routes successfully right through the winter.

On the home front things were difficult but manageable. The two rostering clerks very kindly gave me as much work as possible in the school term times resulting in less work in the school holidays. This was assisted by the differences in the South African academic year compared to the UK. I was happy to work hard when most of the UK were taking their annual holidays. Even so, when I worked a trip while the children were at home it was a case of dropping them off with my long-suffering parents and brothers who lived locally. Everybody was more than kind. On the way home after the all night flight from the USA the trip was reversed and I would be inundated with washing, cooking and all the chores demanded by teenage children not to mention the need to spend time with them.

Wife, absent from the home for the previous two years, achieved her desired divorce shortly after I started with Virgin. She obtained decrees nisi and absolute on the same day and married her most recent suitor 10 days later. She disappeared to Bahrain with her new husband and some years later they moved to the USA. We were to see or hear very little of them until two of the children got married in the year 2000.

A local Church in Worthing was also magnificent with all their help with the children and wonderful friends remain to this day from those years.

2. Progress

In aviation terms conditions with my new employer were superb. The flight deck crews were without exception mature enough to have nothing left to prove. The majority were retirees from other airlines, in particular British Airways. Most were in excess of fifty years of age. Their immense aviation experience more than made up for any shortcomings caused by advancing years.

One of them, almost Einsteinian in countenance with a shock of white hair looked much older than his actual age. He once ruefully described how on a day off in Newark some public spirited local asked him if he would like help crossing the road. He politely declined the assistance offered and was humble enough not to mention that the following night he would be in command of a transatlantic Boeing 747. For me to sit down to breakfast in Newark or Miami with a bunch of rational mature English flight deck crew was a cathartic contrast to the mayhem of trying to communicate with screaming ill-mannered Saudis. (The latter were far from all inclined that way but one remembers the bad times which generally were more in abundance than the good times!)

The year 1988 was a particularly good year. In late 1987 there had been an introduction to a single lady of a similar age to me. The introduction occurred as a result of a Vision which an older lady in the Church I was attending received. She was not given to match-making and gave me the lady's telephone number in some trepidation. Cutting a long story short, Diane and I were married in July of 1988. Diane is a lady of worth and we remain happily married in retirement as I pen these lines. To take on a second-hand husband and three teenage children is a forbidding task at the best of times and Diane coped magnificently. The love and companionship that has cemented over the years has been a great blessing for which I am more than thankful. On top of this, the problems caused by my constant absences were no longer and the children had an excellent step-mother as a role model not to mention the now rational family existence. Amongst many other plusses there was some adult female input into dress sense and general wellbeing of the girls who had suffered too long with a father who was brought up in a predominantly male household!

Re-promotion to Captain came with almost indecent suddenness. One day I was sitting by the pool at the crew hotel in Miami together with other crew amongst whom was Smiling Jim. Recently appointed to the post of chief training captain Jim said,

"We're making three of you up to Captain next week." He named me and two others. "We'll have you in the 'Sim' (Simulator) for a couple of sessions, do a bit of base training and you'll be out for line training."

This was exactly how it happened. There was none of the nausea associated with upgrade much beloved by established airlines and in particular my recent experience in Saudia. Invariably airline training departments get it all wrong. They heap the pressure on in a totally unrealistic fashion. Candidates' behaviour as a result becomes bizarre. For instance, you find non-drinkers drinking and confirmed inebriates become awkwardly teetotal. The accurate unpressurised assessment which comes with observation of normal operations as a co-pilot, an infallible pointer to future behaviour, is ignored. The end result is that potentially excellent captains fail the course and the odd complete disaster, in my humble opinion less than one per cent of experienced co-pilots, are made up to captain and their employers regret it ever after.

Less than two weeks after the poolside conversation, having completed the requisite Simulator and base training, there was a friendly parting remark from Smiling Jim,

"Do a couple of trips. When you're happy let me know and we'll put you up for a line check."

Command line training commenced. There were to be only two trips and both lived up to another unfailing rule of aviation. This runs something like, 'Anything and everything that can possibly go wrong will go wrong on command training'.

And so, for the first trip, it was off to Miami with Captain B. The latter, a great character whose background was many years in Cathay Pacific Airlines, was of medium height, darkish complexion, a thin face and possessed of a coarse sardonic nature. He seemed constantly to wear a mildly mocking smile with a hint of yellow tinge at the corner of his eyes which cooperated well with his naturally censorious nature.

Predominately, it was his voice that caught the attention. He spoke an octave and a half lower than most males of the species and the caustic comments seemed to emanate from the abdominal regions to emerge in a series of terse, cryptic remarks which, until you got to know him were quite intimidating. It was said that the one female rostering clerk, a bubbly but timid soul, would dissolve into tears at the mere sound of Captain B's voice. It would be completely below his dignity to admit it but somewhere, underneath the bluster, there was a heart of gold. He was later to be flight operations director in Virgin Atlantic for a number of years and was highly respected in that exalted status.

All went well until halfway to Miami on a Southerly route[1], we began to experience some really miserable turbulence. The cloud was of continuous strati-form type

1 Route. For the uninitiated in aviation see expanded explanation in the glossary.

and, as all aviators know, there can be unseen embedded thunderstorms in such conditions. Consequently, I was eyes glued to the weather radar as was Captain B. We were both adjusting tilt and gain and while large blobs seemed to appear on the monochrome screens just as we entered them, there was no advance warning. Captain B solved the problem with a cryptic suggestion in a deep base emanating from the abdominal regions,

"Suggest you try the other radar... Captain!"

The "Captain" was uttered with immeasurable sarcasm but there was a hint of ameliorating humour attached.

I moved the requisite switch. The screen filled with ugly blobs and it was then a simple matter of manoeuvring for the best passage around and between the thunderstorms using the autopilot heading selector. The weather radar fault was one that I had never encountered before and have not seen since. Radar sets normally either work or don't work. This one was working but was sending out such a weak signal that it was effectively useless. The two sets are entirely independent, the only common unit being the antenna. (Failure of the antenna results in total loss of the weather radar function.)

After twenty-four hours in Miami, the following evening, we set off on the return flight to Gatwick. The route was more normal this time, up the Eastern seaboard of the USA and passing over Newfoundland in the vicinity of Gander, to cross the Atlantic arriving over Southern Ireland and so on to Gatwick.

At about 150 miles before Gander, Captain B, playing the dutiful co-pilot, requested our Atlantic clearance from the Gander Oceanic control centre. This was granted as requested and the Captain began the mandatory laborious paperwork including plotting our cleared route on the chart. After a few minutes he was close to completing this duty when reports began to float in over the ether with regard to moderate turbulence on our cleared route.

Playing captain it was necessary for me to ask which of the Atlantic tracks were expected to be free of turbulence. Gander replied with the information that two of the most Northerly tracks were forecast to be smooth and there had been no pilot reports indicating otherwise. I knew and Captain B knew that this was probably not correct. The simple fact was that we had been cleared on one of the fastest time routes along with many other flights and turbulence reports were flowing in because so many aircraft were using these particular tracks. There were probably very few aircraft on the Northerly tracks thus reports were few also. However, I had to play the game and I could see Captain B looking furtively in my direction psyching himself up for the inevitable. He gave me an old fashioned look and with the edges of his eyes emanating a distinctly yellow tinge he said,

"I suppose the Captain would like a track change?"

Again, there was sarcastic emphasis on the 'Captain'.

"Yes", I replied, "I think we ought to make an effort to give the passengers a smooth ride."

Deep down, other than much paperwork for Captain B, I did not feel this was going to make any difference. Too many years on the Atlantic had taught me what was important and what was not important. However, to ignore the turbulence warnings while on command training was not a good idea.

With great difficulty due to the saturated clearance frequency, Captain B eventually managed to re-negotiate to one of the most Northerly tracks. This time the paperwork was serious. The computer flight plan had to be discarded and the new track written down long-hand extracting tracks and distances for each leg from a manual. Flight times and ETA's for each ten degrees of longitude had to be calculated and then finally, with an aggrieved sigh, he handed his calculations to me for checking.

To begin with the crossing was smooth and I was just beginning to congratulate myself on a good decision when there was a gentle shaking indicating possible trouble ahead. Shortly after this we hit serious rough weather. Captain B was not impressed. To add insult to injury he called up a flight on our original cleared track using the 'Atlantic chat frequency' and asked after their flight conditions,

"Smooth!" was the brief reply.

Captain B turned in my direction and eyed me venomously.

"Bad decision... CAPTAIN!"

Everything was not as bad as I had feared. Captain B wrote a more than generous report for the trip.

The next trip, a few days later was with Captain George. Another grand character, unflappable and later to become a fleet manager he emanated from the long defunct Laker Airways and more recently Kuwait Airways. The flight engineer, Peter, was an equally delightful older Yorkshireman recently retired from British Airways.

The route was Gatwick Newark and back, again with the usual overnight stop in Newark. The weather was forecast to be bad all over the Eastern Seaboard of the USA and I took plenty of extra fuel allowing time for holding and a diversion to Montreal which was forecast to be acceptable. It was mid-winter.

The Atlantic crossing was uneventful but things gradually began to deteriorate as we descended in the darkness towards Newark. There was some considerable holding before we were pulled off with radar vectors to make the approach to Newark's runway 22L. Passing overhead Teterborough airport at 3000 feet, about 9 miles out on the final approach, there was most unpleasant turbulence, not to mention heavy rain. Suddenly there was a brilliant flash as we received a lightning strike on the nose of the aircraft. Peter uttered an oath. George remembers to this day turning around and seeing a white faced Peter staring ahead, eyes wide and knuckles white as he gripped the thrust levers while handling the power for me. At about 1000 feet I took over the thrust levers and strove to hold a speed somewhere within twenty knots of that required for the approach while continuing to fly down the Instrument Landing system. The visibility below the cloud-base which was at about 500 feet was reasonable, despite the heavy rain but for a machine still weighing, even at this stage of the flight, two hundred and forty tons we were being thrown around like an oak leaf in an equinoctial gale.

The arrival was accurately positioned and in the flare George said more than firmly,

"Put it down!"

I had no intention of doing anything else as Newark's runway was of an un-generous length for a 747. I planted the machine untidily on the runway with a slightly insufficient correction for the crosswind. We were all glad to get to the hotel that night.

The return flight was uneventful.

The following morning there was a call from Smiling Jim,

"We're sending you off on your final check tomorrow, I take it you're ready?"

I indicated affirmatively. The final check, with yet another of our very few training captains, was uneventful and shortly after I was out as a real Captain again.

It was less than six months later that there was a call from Captain B. In his inimitable bass he grunted,

"We want you to be a training captain!"

Vanity at the thought of such unexpected promotion nearly made me say yes on the spot but fortunately reason prevailed

"Can I think about it for a few days?" I asked cautiously.

"No problem!" replied the impossibly deep voice,

"Let me know when you have made a decision."

Diane's observation was the most significant,

"Would you really be happy doing that and spending half your life in the Simulator?"

The honest answer was a resounding "No!" I would not be happy doing simulator training. All I had ever wanted to do was fly aeroplanes. Further advice from an old ex-BA captain clinched the matter,

"Go away and enjoy yourself for a few years and spare yourself all the hassle."

It was all good advice. There would have been better pay as a training captain but I was never to regret the decision.

It was about three years later that the incumbent chief pilot suggested over a meal in Tokyo that I had a responsibility to take up a training position. The airline was expanding rapidly and they had completely run out of suitable candidates to cope with the sheer quantity of training required. I reluctantly agreed and became a line trainer and eventually a check captain as well but I never took on the simulator training and again, have no regrets.

3. Rats in Russia

The airline inexorably expanded, two aeroplanes became four, then six, then eight. All were rather old and well used, some were very good machines, especially two from Singapore Airlines with up-rated engines. Others were just plain characterless, namely two from Qantas. Two were real odd ball aircraft with chequered histories each possessing its own distinct idiosyncratic behaviour. They were all 747-200 series machines except one which was a -100.

Similarly the route structure expanded and we found ourselves going to Orlando, Boston, Los Angeles, Tokyo and Moscow to name a few. A major commercial breakthrough was the successful negotiation of the use of London Heathrow and New York's Kennedy airports.

The Tokyo route brought some very different scenarios. The route was direct, across Siberia. The non-aeronautically minded reader would benefit from a look at a globe to understand the logic of this route. There was one serious drawback. The Russians, in approving Virgin to operate over their territory insisted that one flight per week transit Moscow in both directions.

Stories of Virgin Atlantic's operation through Moscow both delightful and (more often) not so delightful would fill a most entertaining book and maybe, someday, someone will write such a tome. I will restrict myself to just this chapter.

Because of the long flight times across Siberia it was necessary to position a crew to Moscow the day prior to the relevant Tokyo trip. It fell to my lot to perform the first such saga and indeed, saga it turned out to be. We turned up at Heathrow in civilian clothes and this was the first mistake. I was always amazed at Virgin crew off duty, especially the girls. Just how these pristine females in their glamorous red uniforms and sophisticated professional smiles could dress down such that they looked like a bunch of gap year students on the Kathmandu hippie trail I will never know. But on this particular day that is exactly how they looked. They were either overly made up or devoid of any enhancements. There were ripped Jeans, sloppy shoes and hangovers. Despite that, there was a good feel to the crew and there was an aura of adventure in the air.

We embarked on the flight and all was fine until disembarkation in Moscow. Nobody knew anything about us. There was no-one to meet the crew. No-one could speak English. Immigration could not understand that we were an airline crew who were operating a flight to Tokyo the next day. If we were a crew why were we not in uniform? Russians understand uniforms.

Eventually, the local British Airways manager, having heard of our plight magnanimously took pity on us. At least we had an interpreter. Even so, it took four hours to complete the arrival procedures.

Miraculously a bus appeared. We proceeded towards town on Moscow's equivalent of the M25. Approximately five lanes in each direction with no median strip it was utter mayhem.

Halfway to town it started to rain. I realised the bus had no windscreen wipers and the driver bore on with increasing lack of forward vision. Eventually, things became so bad he stopped. Even if there had been a hard shoulder (which there wasn't) it would have made no difference. He, along with all the other drivers, had stopped apparently at random, each exactly where they were. Our driver pulled a pair of wiper blades from under his seat, disembarked, fitted them, re-embarked and we were off again. All the surrounding vehicles had performed exactly the same procedure and all returned to the general mayhem. We were to learn that in the glorious Soviet Union, to leave windscreen wipers anywhere other than inside a locked vehicle was to have them stolen.

We pulled up at the grand 1950's style Salyut hotel which had a forbidding, prison style façade. The airport situation was repeated. Nobody knew anything about us. The receptionist's knowledge of the English language was almost non-existent. Airline crew wore uniforms and we were not in uniform so we couldn't be an airline crew. I recognised some Arabic being spoken by a young man loitering in the hotel lobby who turned out to be a Palestinian student. I could manage a little Arabic and he spoke Russian. We managed to get ourselves checked into the hotel, he translating my Arabic into Russian and vice versa. I was immensely proud of my linguistic skills until I heard our ageing flight engineer referring to

"The skipper's Eighth Army Arabic! "

Things began to improve especially when on sudden inspiration I produced some US dollars. From experience in the Middle East I should have known that if you are in possession of US dollars you actually don't need to be able to speak any language.

Despite that, when it came to the need to change money, we drew a blank. Crew allowances were in US dollars. We wanted roubles because we needed to eat. It was Sunday afternoon, there were no open banks and no-one would change any money. Eventually our sociable Palestinian acquaintance said he had a friend who would change some money. That was fine but then we found the restaurants in the hotel were all booked out with Eastern European tourists and there were no shops open. There was, however, an open bar serving dirt cheap local champagne and some un-appetising snacks.

One way and another we survived our first Moscow transit and the following morning it was a tired hungry crew who eventually boarded the aircraft arriving from London and after raiding the galleys in front of some astonished passengers, we set off for Tokyo.

Before leaving there had been another problem. We had all bought far too many roubles from our friend of a friend and didn't know what to do with them. I'm ashamed to say we sold them to the disembarking crew who brought the aircraft in from London and I've no doubt they sold them on to the next crew.

We learned to cope with Moscow but it was an art form gradually developed over many trips. After the first debacle positioning crew travelled in uniform. We took our own food, usually pork pies although I've never really understood why it had to be pork pies!

When I was young I spent hours delving into the glossy pages of a marvellous child's book of engineering wonders. There were many photos one of which was of a huge steam engine and the intriguing detail showed a diminutive engineer with simple oil can standing alongside one of the enormous wheels oiling some mechanical trivia. Metaphorically it was just such an oil can that I learned to take with me on all Moscow trips in the form of a wad of single US dollar bills. Every time there was an impasse a dollar bill oiled the wheels of the great Soviet machine and we would move forward. Others of my colleagues found that packets of Marlborough cigarettes provided similar lubrication. The mystique attached to the particular brand of cigarettes was never unravelled. The fact is that other brands lacked the same magic.

The aviation side of things was not without its difficulties and took some getting used to. All heights were in metres and this was before the days of glass cockpits where you push a button and the altimeter displays metres as well as feet. To further complicate matters altimetry was in QFE[1] where the altimeter is set to read zero at airfield height. This is in stark contrast to the international standard where QNH[2] (sea level) is used and confusion can be lethal.

1 2 QFE and QNH. See glossary.

Winter weather was extreme and was in stark contrast to the deserts of the Middle East which had been my bread and butter not so long before.

Moscow trips were very different but one other is worth recording. All the flight deck crew on this occasion were ex-Saudia so it was something of an unscheduled reunion. I was captain, my born-again atheist friend Mike, was my co-pilot and the engineer was a cheerful character by the name of Bill.

Having proceeded through the airport, been driven to the hotel and checked in with un-characteristic seamlessness (thanks to my rapidly diminishing wad of dollar bills), I suggested to Mike and Bill that we meet up later for pork pies and cheap champagne. Mike, always something of an adventurer quite apart from his leftish political leanings, stated firmly that he was not going to waste this, his first ever trip to the Soviet Union, eating pork pies and drinking cheap champagne in a hotel room. He wanted to eat 'local'.

Thus, at the appointed hour, against my better judgement we met in the lobby and proceeded to the hotel restaurant. Sure enough our way was blocked by the standard formidable female, the epitome of the values and virtues of The Socialist Republic.

"Rest-au-rant she is clos-ed," madam announced firmly her ample bosom heaving with finality.

"But there are people in there eating!" protested Mike.

"She is clos-ed, you haf to go eat in the bar."

Mike produced a dollar bill. Madam had a furtive glance but shook her head. Two dollars. Madam's eyes began to gleam but she was practised in the finer arts of haggling. At five dollars she relented and we were in.

The stark décor, uncomfortable chairs and pitiless glare of the naked high wattage light bulbs heightened the atmosphere of a prison refectory. The restaurant was packed and we were squashed in on an already over full table. It appeared that we had joined an East German tourist group.

There was no menu. Bowls of watery soup were expertly dropped in front of us, not hard enough to splash but sufficient to make us realise that we were unwelcome guests.

A few minutes later the soup bowls were swept away nearly full as it was so unpalatable that we each managed only two or three spoonfuls. Our companions on the same table made no secret of their disgust that we had not eaten the glorious Soviet food prepared by its loyal dedicated citizens. Main course arrived and it was stringy meat, watery boiled potatoes and over-cooked wilted cabbage. It would have been a source of complaint at a 1950's boarding school let alone a four star international hotel.

The restaurant began to empty. Vermin appeared, initially a few shy mice skirting nervously around the edges of the empty tables on the other side of the room. As dessert in the form of tasteless cake and glutinous cold lumpy custard was served, larger vermin appeared. The mice became bolder and started shinning up the legs of a table close by to feast on the un-cleared food. Mike accosted a waiter and pointed out our visitors. There was a shrug of the shoulders and total disinterest. We called it a day when rats, slightly less agile than their smaller cousins, also mounted tables to partake of the feast.

Mike was promoted back to Captain shortly after that trip. I met him one day as he was about to depart for Moscow.

"Got your pork pies Mike?"

"Yes", he said, ruefully "But did you not think that our little experience was interesting?"

I had to admit he was right.

Virgin Atlantic overcame the problem of Moscow transits about a year after we commenced the route. Apparently a large amount of money changed hands and the requirement for the Moscow transit was dropped. It was interesting to see that British Airways who had suffered this commercially very poor procedure for many years appeared to copy us and also bought their way out of it a short time later.

4. Lightning and Ladies

Lightning is an amazing sight from the air. It can flash above, below and all around the aircraft for considerable lengths of time in Tropical regions. It is not generally dangerous. The high voltage discharges which cause this phenomenon are cloud to cloud or cloud to ground. When an aircraft is struck the bolt of lightning has only found a split second temporary home and leaves to ground or another cloud. Machines have been damaged but to my knowledge it has never been proven to have caused a fatal aviation accident although in one or two bizarre catastrophes there have been suspicions.

There has been damage to aircraft. The worst I have ever heard of occurred to a Saudia Boeing 747 en-route Jeddah to New York. A friend of mine was the co-pilot and while I have forgotten the details there was serious disruption to the aircraft systems and they had to make an emergency landing in Shannon, Ireland. There are three separate brake systems on 747's and the only one left working was the last ditch reserve system.

One hot summer's day in the early 1990's I set off for Los Angeles from London Heathrow in a Classic 747-200. The co-pilot was a lady, not unknown to me as I had flown with her previously. We had a full load and the machine was close to maximum take-off weight. The flight time was in the region of ten hours and forty five minutes so we had a long duty ahead. Turning north after departure passing through 4000 feet there was heavy cumulus cloud in the vicinity. We had retracted the flaps and were settling into the climb when I saw a bolt of lightning heading in a sweeping curve in our direction from a nearby cloud. It was an unforgettable sight that I have seen neither before nor since. It hit the nose with a bang and I was thankful that I had observed its arrival otherwise there would have been a big question-mark as to the cause. The lady had not seen it and was anxiously scanning the engine instruments.

"Lightning strike" I said casually although I would not have been so relaxed if I hadn't actually seen it.

The flight engineer was scanning his panel and announced,

"All seems okay back here."

Shortly after, the cabin supervisor appeared in the flight deck doorway. He was a small likeable man who I knew quite well and in the fashion of the time his hair was spiked. He said in a slightly querulous voice,

"Is everything alright?"

The lady, by now recovering her composure said,

"Have you seen your hair?"

The response was without hesitation,

"And I thought you were blonde!"

The lady did a quick double-take before realising that she had not actually gone grey.

More seriously the supervisor said that a ball of lightning had gone down the entire length of the lower deck visible above the heads of the passengers and the two stewardesses seated right at the back of the aircraft said that it had exited the fuselage through the rear door area. I had heard of 'ball lightning' actually being visible in an aircraft cabin but had never experienced it and still haven't. I saw it only before it entered the aircraft.

A little more checking and we realised that the weather radar was not working. I switched over to the other set and that didn't work either. The lightning had obviously damaged the radar antenna. This left us with a problem. We were legal to continue to Los Angeles without a functioning weather radar system but would that be a wise thing to do? We were in good visibility on the climb and could manoeuvre around any threatening cloud. We scanned the weather charts for the entire route which was direct and fairly standard taking in Iceland, Greenland, Northern Canada, Hudson Bay, Edmonton and down to Los Angeles over the Rockies. There was no bad weather forecast so we decided to continue.

Ten and a half hours later we landed uneventfully at our scheduled destination. The flight had been straightforward and we had gained a little time and in consequence used slightly less fuel than expected.

Taxiing into the United Airlines terminal (United were our handling agents at the time) we realised that all the ground handling staff were stopping work to gaze at our aircraft, specifically the nose.

As we parked the ground mechanic came on the interphone from below,

"Say, what have you guys been up to on the way over from London?"

"Nothing special, why do you ask?"

"There's a mighty fine hole in the front of your airplane"!

When we disembarked we were naturally keen to have a look. Right in the centre of the radome which is a fibre glass moulding covering the radar antenna, was a jagged edged circular hole at least a foot in diameter. Obviously, the pressure bulkhead which is behind was unaffected.

The damage was un-repairable and the homebound flight had to be cancelled. The following day a new radome arrived by air from St Louis.

I have often speculated since whether the 747's performance would be enhanced if they built such a hole into the design. We gained time and consequently fuel so maybe Mr Boeing needs to take note!

5. New York Law

In the flush of success triggered by the right to use London Heathrow and New York's John F Kennedy airports, a measure of profligacy prevailed in terms of the standard of crew hotels overseas, especially at the new destinations. Reality soon prevailed and normality returned over the following months but until then there were some truly delightful establishments enjoyed on crew layovers. One of these was the Garden City Hotel about twenty miles East of New York's Kennedy airport, on Long Island. The hotel proudly proclaims that it was at this establishment that Lindberg spent the night before setting out on his epic solo Atlantic crossing in the late 1920's. While staying at this hotel on a normal 24 hour layover, I was to encounter US justice at the Nassau county court.

Breakfast was frequently a most pleasurable experience in the USA and since this was a trip on an old 'Classic' Boeing 747 there was the added companionship of a flight engineer as part of the crew. The 'Garden City', being very up-market, charged extortionately for in house meals so I took the First Officer and Engineer in the crew car to a local breakfast diner which had become a favourite. I parked in an almost empty car park behind a shopping centre and as the slots were largely unoccupied it seemed a good idea to leave the car facing out ready for an easy getaway after the meal. We settled into the full bacon and egg ritual which went down very well as the hour was 9am and with the time change from the UK the stomach was complaining that it was 2pm and it had not been fed.

After a handsome breakfast followed by a chat over numerous cups of good strong American coffee, the flight engineer and the First Officer announced that they would walk back to the hotel for the fresh air and exercise.

I returned to the car planning a shopping trip at the hardware shops several miles away. There was a piece of paper flapping in the breeze on the windshield held in place by the wiper blade. Examining the document it became clear that it was a parking ticket demanding $20 for the violation of local law as the car was parked facing out. I was aware that this was an offence when parking on the side of the street but a ticket for this misdemeanour in an ostensibly private off road car park seemed over diligence in the extreme.

Why it should be that I reacted as I did would be a useful subject for a budding psychoanalyst's doctorate thesis. The fact was that I was totally and completely enraged.

The address of the local courthouse was amongst the information printed on the ticket and it was to that establishment that I drove with fury increasing exponentially by the minute. I parked in front of the imposing edifice with an unnecessary screech of tyres needless to say with the car facing 'in', slammed the door and strode into reception. By this time I was mentally ready to declare war on the legal establishment of one of Her Majesties former colonies and throwing the parking ticket on the reception desk I let rip in full blooded righteous indignation at the large black female clerk sitting facing me.

It took about five minutes to inform the clerk that I was only in the country for 24 hours. The alleged infringement had occurred in a private car park and not on the street side. Was this any way to treat a foreign visitor who was engaged in the worthy trade of bringing foreign currency to the US treasury?

There were other sundry arguments long forgotten and dreamed up on the short drive thrown in as asides but seemingly important to my cause at the time. The large black clerk rolled her eyes during this performance but said nothing. When she realised the tirade had finally run its course she disappeared through a large oaken door behind her. She still hadn't uttered a word.

After a few minutes the presence re-appeared, rolled her eyes again and made a silent gesture indicating for me to follow. There was another oaken portal, more impressive than the first and Large Clerk held the door indicating that I should pass. There was an enormous oak panelled Perry Mason style courtroom and Large Clerk was pointing to the spacious dock indicating that I should go and stand in it. It suddenly dawned that I had overstepped the mark and might be in serious trouble. I began to regret the outburst of childish petulance and realised that the Rubicon had been crossed. It might have been wiser to pay the trivial $20 fine and swallow the pride.

There was a foreboding silence in the courtroom. It was empty except for a Caucasian Lady Judge of pyramidal proportions sitting on the bench. She was chewing gum, not in that bored action so typical of many Americans but slowly, deliberately, thoughtfully savouring each chew. Was this a carefully cultivated intimidating mannerism designed to cower malefactors into submission? The atmosphere was ominous. Madam Judge stared malevolently at the accused her only movement being the consistent up and down mechanics of her ample jaws.

I was lost for words as Madam continued to chew gum. After what seemed like an eternity during which nothing was said neither was any invitation made for me to speak I made a decision. "In for a penny, in for a pound" was the cliché that seemed appropriate.

The entire rhetoric was re-launched with a few extra embellishments to enhance my case. If the truth be told, I was feeling inwardly very small and increasingly foolish. Inevitably the not-so-clever postulations, despite their impassioned deliverance, drew to a close. There was a pregnant silence. Pyramidal Judge dispassionately viewed her prey in the manner of an entomologist about to dissect a hitherto unknown species. She was still chewing gum. I wondered if this preceded the instruction to "Take him down" or the US equivalent. Morale gradually sank so low I wondered how the company was going to find a replacement Captain to take the flight back to London that evening.

With extraordinary oral skill which must have taken years of practice, Pyramidal Judge pronounced her verdict with no hint of an interruption to the mechanics of gum chewing,

"Yah Gotta Pay!"

Sensing dismissal I gratefully withdrew. The malevolent eyes bored into my back as I hastily made for the door. The rest of the morning was spent obtaining and mailing a money order for $20 to Her Ladyship. I resisted the temptation to enclose a packet of chewing gum.

To give a piece of gratuitous advice. You can commit grand larceny, start a revolution or even assassinate a president but don't ever dicker with customs officers, immigration officials and now, since this incident I have added to the list, parking wardens.

6. Earthquakes

Many aspects of nature fascinate me, not the least being Geology, Seismology and Astronomy. I would like to prattle on for hours about these subjects but there has been plenty of professional material published and my knowledge is at best amateur. The fact is that we live on a very fragile planet which has an equally fragile shell subject to tectonic movement and the influence of planetary gravitational variations. It is common knowledge that the moon causes sea tides. What is not such common knowledge is that the land is also similarly affected but to a far lesser extent. I understand that earth tides are actually measurable. That is to say, the land surfaces fluctuate by an inch or so diurnally along with the sea tides which have infinitely greater displacements. When planets align there is greater gravitational pressure applied to their surfaces and weak points i.e. the tectonic boundaries are the most likely to be disturbed. This is not metaphysical but physical.

I have felt many earth tremors through the years, especially in Japan where they are almost daily events but also in Dubai and Kenya. The occurrence in Kenya was while I was working for BOAC. It was a Saturday night and the crew were billeted in the Pan Afric hotel in Nairobi. There was some difficulty sleeping especially as there was an exceptionally raucous band playing loud pop music in the club downstairs. Drifting off to sleep despite the noise, sometime in the small hours of Sunday morning I awoke to feel the bed rocking like being on board ship. I realised that we were in the throes of an earth tremor. The band faltered. I thought to myself,

"If the band stops I'm getting out!"

The band picked up and I went back to sleep.

The only strong earthquake I have endured occurred

in Los Angeles while working for Virgin. The city lies on a series of fault lines and my crew and I were on a forty eight hour layover in the suburb of Santa Monica. We were billeted in the Pacific Shore hotel, an establishment detested by the crew for its many shortcomings not least of which was a general lack of cleanliness. My room was on the top floor of this approximately eight storied building.

It came to be known as the 'Northridge' earthquake.

The following is copied direct from Wikipedia:-

The Northridge earthquake was a massive earthquake that occurred on January 17, 1994, at 04:31 Pacific Standard Time in Reseda, a neighbourhood in the city of Los Angeles, California, lasting for about 10–20 seconds. The earthquake had a "strong" moment magnitude of 6.7, but the ground acceleration was one of the highest ever instrumentally recorded in an urban area in North America, measuring 1.7 g (16.7 m/s2) with strong ground motion felt as far away as Las Vegas, Nevada, over 270 miles (435 km) from the epicenter. At least 33 deaths were attributed to the earthquake, with some estimates ranging much higher, and there were over 8,700 injured. In addition, the earthquake caused an estimated $20 billion in damage, making it one of the costliest natural disasters in U.S. history

Due to the time change from the UK, I was wide awake and sitting up at the room desk working on my diminutive early generation lap-top dressed in pyjamas. The room started to shake and I tried to recollect what one was supposed to do in an earthquake. The prevailing wisdom stated that one should get into a doorway. While trying to do just that, the shaking became so intense that all I could do was fall onto the bed and lie prone. The lights went out. It was like severe turbulence in an aircraft but this was not an aircraft, it was a hotel.

Wikipedia says the quake lasted 10-20 seconds. I thought the newspaper reports at the time stated 35 seconds. Anyway, it seemed to go on for an awfully long time. When the movement diminished I felt lucky to be alive.

With the hotel severely damaged, no lights except my personal torch (flashlight in American and a mandatory part of any pilots personal equipment) there was obviously a need to vacate the building. The mind seems to degenerate into utterly inconsequential trivia in the direst of circumstances. I thought to myself,

How should an Englishman appear in this situation?"

The immediate answer was,

"Fully dressed, of course!"

Five minutes later I emerged from the room in the darkness almost colliding with my female cabin supervisor, also fully dressed, emerging from the room opposite. I said something stupid like,

"Great minds think alike!" and together we negotiated our way to the emergency stairs at the end of the corridor.

The stairs were made of concrete and each storey had two separate flights. The bottom two steps of each flight had been demolished by the movement and needed care traversing.

We arrived in the car park outside the front of the hotel to find the rest of the crew already there. With two crews, some forty persons, there was much to-ing and fro-ing trying to check that all were present which was difficult due to the total blackout. Except for a very few they were generally in scanty night gear. It was cold. Not freezing but being January and the small hours, even in Santa Monica, it was not a night to be out in nighties or pyjamas.

The two cabin supervisors eventually announced that they had a full complement. Hotel security staff were keeping us well away from the building.

A man and a woman, complete with baggage emerged from the building some 20 minutes later, climbed into their car and drove off. We had no such provision. The only lighting was given by small fires in the neighbourhood which were apparently caused by broken gas mains self-igniting. Some of the cabin crew became distressed due to the cold. I asked for permission to return to my room to get blankets. This was refused. After an hour or so I insisted that something had to be done. I was told I could go to my room to get blankets with the proviso that I exit the building again as fast as possible.

Once in the room, by the light of the torch, I collected my anorak, blankets, sheets, as much as I could carry to provide the crew with some protection from the cold. There was a silly inspiration. I looked at the telephone and thought,

"I wonder...?"

I picked up the handset and miracle of miracles there was a dial tone!

I dialled international to our Gatwick headquarters,

"Good morning, Virgin Atlantic, how can I direct your call?"

"This is Trevor Vellacott calling from Los Angeles."

Instantly I was connected to the flight operations director. His first question was,

"How's the hotel?!"

I'm sure he meant "How is the crew?" In view of the fact that we all hated the hotel I had the greatest difficulty restraining the laughter.

"Damaged to the extent that we won't be staying here again. It will probably have to be demolished!"

"Is everybody alright?"

"Yes."

Specifically he then went on to ask about an ex-BA captain's son who was working as a steward on one of the two crews. Apparently his mother had already been on the phone enquiring as to her offspring's wellbeing. I was able to assure him that all were present, correct and uninjured.

Subsequently this proved to be not entirely correct.

Arriving back at the car park I found security extremely agitated at my long absence but the crew were most appreciative of the attempt at getting them some warmth. I handed out blankets and clothing mentioning that I had been in contact with Gatwick. The male supervisor on the other crew sidled up,

"We have a problem. I made a mistake. We are actually two persons down"

My heart sank,

"Who is missing?"

"Richard ___ and ___", he gave me one other male name.

Richard was the ex BA captain's son.

We re-negotiated with security for the supervisor to go and check the rooms of the two missing persons. He re-appeared a few minutes later with one of the missing stewards in tow. It was not Richard. Apparently this one had subjected himself to some heavy socialising before retiring and had slept right through the magnitude 6.7 earthquake! To my infinite relief, Richard appeared sometime later. He had gone out to Venice Beach for the evening and when the earthquake struck he had decided to stay where he was.

At about 7am with dawn lighting up the scenes of devastation around us, we were allowed back into the ground floor of the hotel but were warned to stay in the lobby or the bar.

California earthquake building codes are excellent. Many of the ground floor windows of the hotel had shattered but those on the upper levels were intact. Presumably, the windows most likely to cause damage or injury in an earthquake were built and fitted to a very high specification.

Conversations were bizarre.

A pretty young stewardess, an East-ender with a cockney accent was sitting on a bar stool. Scantily clad in a nightie, sipping a drink, she described how when the earthquake struck she had lost control of her natural functions. Decorum dictates that I omit the exact transcription but it was as much delightful as it was graphic!

The captain on the other crew was holding forth to his two co-pilots about our poor pay and conditions! Having just survived a major earthquake without loss of life or limb it was difficult to understand the sense of priority.

Later, access to rooms was allowed following which we assembled downstairs to try to locate some breakfast. Some genius located a restaurant not far from the hotel which had obtained electrical power. We gratefully tucked in to a standard generous American breakfast in an eating establishment which despite the chaos had decided to open its doors.

Later we walked north to the Santa Monica shopping area. There was much devastation. Most of the shop fronts were out and there were piles of rubble on the streets. There were a few completely collapsed buildings but as far as we could see there were no fatalities in our immediate neighbourhood.

One of my co-pilots was a delightful well-mannered young man whose name was Phil. He was a trainee who had just joined the airline. I think he hailed from the recently defunct Dan Air. Phil ventured across the rubble into one of the shops. He was just curious. I was horrified. I yelled after him,

"Get out of there, Phil, they shoot looters in this part of the world!"

Phil beat a hasty retreat and re-joined us. As I write Phil is a long established and well respected captain with the airline.

Things gradually sorted themselves out. We were moved to a hotel close to the airport which being further south was less affected by the earthquake. The inbound flight nearly had to divert but at the last minute was allowed to land at Los Angeles. My crew was due to take the flight back to London the same evening. There were aftershocks, some quite severe, so there was to be no sleep. Consulting with the rest of my crew we agreed to operate after the statutory minimum rest in the new hotel and so we set off back to London the same evening.

7. Weird, Wonderful and Winter weather

Weather! Ice, snow, St Elmo's fire, thunderstorms, fog, hurricanes, tornadoes, noctilucent clouds and so on, the list is endless. Thunderstorms have already been mentioned and it would be easy to write much more about the various weather phenomena. This chapter mentions briefly some of the curiosities encountered.

St Elmo's fire used to be a fairly common occurrence on older aircraft without adequate bonding. Nowadays it is rarely seen. Bonding is the linking of all conductive components of an aircraft such that they have a common earth. St Elmo's fire, if it is observed, usually occurs in the vicinity of thunderstorm activity in strati-form cloud. Normally squelched VHF radios emit violent static. HF radio communication is impossible. Electrical discharges, appearing as mini lightning flashes, streak across windscreens. The flight-deck is bathed in an eerie bluish tinge. To the uninitiated it can be quite scary but it holds no real danger.

Noctilucent clouds are extremely rare. They are beautiful, almost ethereal very high altitude clouds that occur at dawn and are illuminated by the rising sun. Some say they are at an altitude of 250,000 feet or thereabouts. The top of normal terrestrial cloud is rarely above 50,000 feet. There was one fantastic display homebound over the Atlantic that I witnessed in the late 1990's or early 2000's. The Atlantic VHF chat frequency was alive with awe at the sight. This phenomenon is so rare that a recent occurrence was considered worthy of reporting in the UK national press.

Not meteorological but a regular night-time phenomenon in Northerly latitudes is the Aurora Borealis with its sister in the Southern Hemisphere, the Aurora Australis, which I have never seen. The displays are varied, colourful and ghostly. Sometimes they will be visible for several hours on a night flight.

A couple of icing encounters.

We had departed Tokyo, destination London, in a Classic 747. Entering wet dense cloud at 4000 feet there was heavy icing and the aircraft engine and airframe anti-icing systems were only partially effective. The system kept the leading edges of the engine cowlings and the wings free of ice but the four engine pylons collected more and more until, when we emerged into clear air climbing through 28,000 feet, we had a gigantic streamlined block of ice on the leading edge of all four pylons. (Pylons are the struts jutting forward and downwards from the underside of the wings on which the engines are mounted). I have never seen this before or since and have speculated that the particular aircraft on that day had a problem with the anti-icing systems although it is most strange that all the pylons were affected. The ice took some four hours to dissipate which must have been caused by engine heat creeping up the pylons as with an outside air temperature of less than minus 60°C it certainly wasn't due to warmer air temperature!

The concept of reverse power on a jet aircraft is so crude it could have been devised by King Canute although the actual mechanisms are refined and complex. Blocker doors extend into the normally rearward flow of the jet efflux (and/or fan air) and deflect it in a semi forward direction. After landing it assists slowing the machine at high speed. The mechanism is usually reduced to reverse idle at about 60kts on the landing roll and is cancelled completely at taxi speed.

Landing late one evening at New York's John F Kennedy airport following an earlier snowstorm we found that in the inimitable fashion of the JFK port authority, the runways had been cleared of snow and gritted but the taxiways were sheet ice. I wanted to shut down the numbers two and three engines and taxi using the outers[1] but this was firmly resisted by my Co-pilot and the Flight Engineer as 'Not recommended procedure!' In Saudia this practice was common after landing to prevent high brake temperatures caused by holding the excessive residual thrust[2] using the brakes. It is not good to have disagreement on the flight deck even though I could have overridden their recommendations so all four engines remained running.

Coming up behind another 747, which was stationary on the taxiway, our machine was unstoppable. We were travelling at about two knots. The anti-skid units were working to perfection on the sheet ice but that didn't help our case! I pulled back all four reverse levers to reverse idle. Other than a spectacular cloud of powdered snow kicked up by the outboard engines there was no noticeable halt to our inexorable attraction to the tail of the machine in front. We must have been on a slight downslope and at a weight of approximately two hundred and forty tons there was some considerable inertia. With little left between us and a humiliating, expensive and dangerous ground accident I pulled all four levers back to a serious amount of reverse power. The aircraft shook like a terrier emerging from water and the external visibility reduced to zero with a self-generated snow storm. The INS ground speed also reduced to zero. We had stopped! I do not think Mr Boeing would have approved of this treatment of one of his creations.

1 On the 747 inners rather than outers are shut down due brake source considerations.

2 Residual Thrust. See glossary.

8. Flight Engineers

The year 1994 brought a radical change. Virgin Atlantic introduced 747-400's and Airbus A340's. Both of these types were pilot only aircraft. The flight engineer position was eliminated.

It is an appropriate place in this volume to make a few comments about flight engineers, if nothing else, as a tribute and an epitaph remembering many grand characters who had been colleagues and companions for many thousands of flying hours.

Flight engineers seriously arrived on the aviation scene during World War II. Aircraft were becoming larger and heavier and consequentially used larger, increasingly complex and more powerful engines. Each engine typically on a larger piston powered machine would have three primary controls, throttle lever controlling engine boost, propeller pitch or constant speed control for adjusting the propeller pitch and fuel flow to adjust the air/fuel mixture at differing altitudes. On top of this were all the ancillary engine controls such as boost pumps, magneto switches, anti-icing etc. Air conditioning, pressurisation, hydraulics and electrical systems were also increasing in complexity and the primary control and management of all these systems became too complex for the pilot to handle as well as fly the aircraft.

So, typically, behind the pilot and co-pilot sat the flight engineer. He had a large panel of switches, circuit breakers and indicators which he used to control the various functions of the machine and in most parts of the world he gradually became integrated into the whole operation. Even after the advent of jet transports with their much simpler engine controls the flight engineer position remained for many years in long haul aircraft design and it was not until the advent of modern computerisation that the position began to be eliminated as functions were automated. In the USA there was a tendency to use pilots in the flight engineer's position and these were generally junior to the Captain and Co-pilot. They operated the systems while awaiting the time when their seniority would allow them to transit to the co-pilot's seat. Elsewhere the flight engineer was more commonly a man with considerable ground aircraft engineering experience and in possession of the ability and desire to use his talents in flight rather than remain a ground mechanic.

Generally, the latter were considered to be the salt of the earth. They were a 'third man' both airborne and when off duty on the ground at outstations. This provided a superb balance both operationally and socially. They operated the systems and watched the flying side of the operation with critical eyes unaffected by the tunnel vision which could afflict both pilots in a particular situation. They were very adept at warning a pilot that he was about to do something utterly stupid. Without any hint of sarcasm they could even make what was a gross censure sound like a compliment and were thus a major contribution to safety. They were also generally great characters and there were very few bad flight engineers and equally very few who were indifferent in their standard of operation.

A few flight engineers and flight engineer stories most of which are first hand but some hearsay.

There was Sir Lancelot, not his real name of course, who sang old time hymns sporadically, while in the cruise. On a very long Australia trip with BOAC and Sir Lance as the Flight Engineer on the daylight five and a half hour sector from Brisbane to Perth he was in full vocal flow.

Leaving the aircraft in Perth where it was taken on by another crew for the next leg to Colombo the flight deck crew were allotted a separate car from the cabin crew to take them to the hotel. Sure enough, Sir L. embarked on

"Onward Christian Soldiers", in sonorous tenor, not quite Pavarotti but a good emulation. He suddenly stopped in mid verse, tapped the driver on the shoulder and asked loudly in his best and deepest aristocratic voice,

"Driver, tell me where I can find a house of ill repute?"

You ask an Australian a question and he answers in full and we had 10 minutes of the merits of the few red light districts of Perth and a suggestion that if Sir L. would like to be taken to Kalgoorlie that was the best place for the type of entertainment he might have in mind.

Kalgoorlie was at least five hours drive away. This actually had nothing to do with Sir L's real desires but was designed to put me in my place. I had listened to the various sacred renderings with interest and had wondered if Sir L shared the same Christian faith as me. Sir L was advising in his own way that he didn't and this was his way of letting me know in no uncertain terms.

There were several doggie stories and this one relates to an incident on a transit stop in Teheran, again in BOAC. It is probable that the perpetrator kept the matter under wraps for many years.

It was the Flight Engineer who went outside in all weathers and checked the exterior of the machine before departure. This is a vital function in all types of aviation. Filler caps, covers and panels, tyre condition and inflation, obvious damage to the exterior and control surfaces of the aircraft, not to mention ice accumulation, freight securing, the list was endless and performed before each departure.

On the walk around on this particular flight he noticed a melancholy canine encaged in the rear cargo hold. This condition was hardly surprising. Alone in a pressurised cargo hold for hours on end and being given a biscuit and bowl of water at each transit, provided someone remembered, was not a pleasant existence for the family pet. The Engineer took pity on the dog, let it out of the cage and fondled it lovingly trying to make it feel less abandoned.

Unfortunately a local feline appeared out of the darkness no doubt engaged in a personal vermin hunt which was probably not difficult in the environs of the old Meherabad airport. The dog's ears pricked up. Melancholia and all self-control vanished instantly. Away into the night it went in hot pursuit. For the next ten minutes or so the Engineer sought desperately to locate the animal without success.

Departure time was approaching. He shut up the now empty dog cage, returned to the flight deck and said absolutely nothing to anyone. No doubt telexes encircled the globe for months trying to determine the fate of the missing pooch and presumably compensation or insurance eventually paid up. In all probability the crossbred descendants of the canine are still at large in the urban areas of Teheran to this day.

Another doggie story on a more sombre note relates to the sad tale of a luckless but delightful flight engineer by the name of Dennis. This occurrence was in Virgin Atlantic.

Dennis arrived at London Gatwick airport after a flight from the USA and, as frequently occurred in the early days of Virgin Atlantic airlines, customs met the aircraft. On this occasion they had brought along their drug expert in the form of a very excitable Beagle. Dennis loved dogs.

The beagle and handler appeared on the upper deck of the 747 just as the flight deck crew emerged from their workspace and the delighted Dennis gave the dog some loving attention and a pat on the head. The crew disembarked and bussed over to the customs shed. They lined up in front of the benches and were told to open suitcases for inspection. The dog, which had been brought in by his handler made a beeline for Dennis. Initially it licked his shoes and then, confirming his pleasure, sat down next to him and looked adoringly up into his face.

This was all customs needed. Convinced they had finally caught up with Pablo Escobar, or some South American drug baron of equal repute, Dennis was marched off and strip searched in the most intimate way leaving him distraught, confused and seriously embarrassed.

After hearing of this incident if ever customs appeared with an inquisitive canine it became my habit to surreptitiously advise the crew to ignore the beast. Should it start to show any personal interest a discreet meaningful kick would be sure to alleviate any unwelcome attention.

One day, with Virgin, we set off from Gatwick on a standard trans-Atlantic trip. The captain was George, mentioned previously, I was the co-pilot and an older man, Bob was the flight engineer. It was very early days with the airline when the destination was almost invariably Newark.

George and I were swapping experiences while crossing the Atlantic and Bob, while showing no particular interest had obviously been listening. In particular, I had been talking about agricultural aviation. Newark, being the regular destination was bread and butter to the crew and this was a case of familiarity breeding contempt. The runway was 04L, the cloud base was about 1000 feet and the Instrument Landing System was unserviceable.

A VOR approach ensued and I was the handling pilot. A VOR approach gives directional guidance but unlike the instrument landing system there is no descent profile guidance. On older aircraft it was necessary for the crew to work this out. With a little simple maths and forethought it was no problem albeit the precision of the ILS is absent and the approach limits are consequently much higher. To top off the whole situation, Richard, prior to him becoming Sir Richard, the owner, founder of the airline himself was in the flight deck jump seat and had been most amenable company along the way.

Lack of planning and an unexpected tailwind on the approach resulted in the aircraft being too high and when breaking out of the low cloud cover it was obviously impossible to make a landing. There is nothing more dangerous in aviation than an unstable approach with a heavy aircraft and George and I simultaneously realised a go around with all the extra hassle involved was the only option. In the middle of this manoeuvre which Richard watched with stunned silence there was a mutter from Bob behind,

"Agricultural pilots!"

This incident was my fault due to simple bad planning. I inwardly smarted with embarrassment for several weeks until I heard that a training captain, whom I held in very high regard, had managed to get too high on an approach and suffered the indignity of a go around for exactly the same reasons.

This same Bob and I were working together on another trip after I had been promoted to captain with Virgin. He had a young family and was always bringing home bags full of groceries from the USA. At the time the price differential compared to the UK was significant and made this a very worthwhile exercise.

Proceeding Eastbound across the Atlantic in the middle of the night there was a loud 'pop', almost a mini explosion from the direction of the flight engineer's panel which instantly rang alarm bells in the minds of the three flight deck crew. The sound was electrical in nature and similar to that normally associated with an electrical short or circuit breaker popping.

Nothing seemed to be amiss with the instruments and the dreaded electrical burning smell which I only ever once experienced in flight was happily absent. Eventually the crew, unable to determine the cause settled back into their routine but remained slightly edgy as unidentified sounds on aircraft leave an uncomfortable feeling that something is amiss.

About an hour later Bob went to retrieve an item from his briefcase and all was explained. Slightly red faced he tapped me on the shoulder and pointed to the reason for the anguish.

A family size packet of potato chips had exploded in his briefcase due to the differential pressure at altitude and this had been the reason for the 'pop'.

One final story about Bob. A new co-pilot had arrived from BA and in the manner of airline seniority he was flying co-pilot for me even though he had been a senior captain in the previous existence. Before the days of computer generated take off calculations it was the co-pilot's duty to compile the take-off data card. This quite complicated exercise involved extracting data from tables resulting in speeds and limitations for each take off associated with the atmospheric conditions, aircraft loading and a mass of other parameters.

The co-pilot, a small man and slightly irascible by nature, passed the completed card to Bob for checking. This was normal procedure. Bob examined it. As a statement rather than a censure he said,

"V1's wrong".

V1 is the decision speed after which, should there be a malfunction the take-off must be continued regardless as there will probably not be enough runway left to abort the take-off. This is a most important speed and it is vital to get it correct although there can be anomalies which allow a leeway of two or three knots.

The co-pilot insisted that it was right. Bob, who had undergone a minor surgical operation on his face which left him with a permanent non-erasable smile, insisted that it was wrong. Co-pilot took the smile as a personal affront and was clearly becoming enraged. He obviously felt that his professional integrity was being questioned. With his countenance going a deep shade of purple intervention became necessary before the outbreak of open warfare.

"How many knots are we talking about?" I asked,

"One knot," was the flat reply from Bob.

"I think we can live with either figure but I would suggest using the lower of the two."

One knot while accelerating rapidly through 150 mph is not a big issue and peace reigned.

There was one serious and extremely rare example of a not so good flight engineer. Take off to the West at London Gatwick in an old Boeing 747-200. The company procedures at the time called for the flight engineer to set take-off thrust when called for by the handling pilot. The engineer was then supposed to set the engines to about one third of the required thrust, wait for them to stabilise lest one was slower to run up than the others and then set the calculated thrust.

Cleared for take-off by ATC (Air Traffic Control) and all checks complete, I called for the flight engineer to set take-off power. The machine weighing in the region of 340 tonnes began to roll veering dramatically to the right. I applied hard left tiller which controls the nose-wheel steering and hard left rudder although this would have little effect at such slow speed. The aircraft continued in the direction of the side of the runway and the swing was completely uncontrollable.

Seriously in danger of going onto the grass I relapsed to crop spraying days and used some left brake which stopped the swing and brought the aircraft back to the desired heading down the runway.

Aircraft have differential braking, that is to say the left brake pedal[1] will attempt to stop the left landing gear wheels

1 The rudder bar on aircraft is on the floor and operated by the pilot's feet. Pushing the left side gives left rudder and the machine will yaw left and vice versa the right. Atop the rudder pedals are the brake pedals operated by the ball of the foot and the left trucks will be braked if the left pedal is pushed and vice versa the right.

and vice versa the right side. Unfortunately braking is not exactly an enhancement when trying to get an aircraft off the ground on a limiting runway, however, on this occasion there was adequate runway length for the weight of the aircraft and the surface conditions. The asymmetric power had rapidly resolved itself and I continued with the take-off.

It was not difficult to assess the reasons for the swing. The relatively new engineer who had only just been released after line training had simply failed to allow the engines to stabilise and demonstrably the left outer engine had gone to full power without delay and the right outer had been slow to accelerate. About 10 minutes later, settling in to the climb after acceleration and flap retraction, I turned around and said to the Flight Engineer,

"What on earth happened there?"

Profuse apologies followed and I decided not to report the incident as the lesson had been learned. I was sad to hear that the man was sacked about a month later and could only conclude that there was a general poor performance that continued after the one incident that I had witnessed.

Stories about flight engineers are legend and many have been recorded elsewhere. It was with great sadness and a sense of grievous loss that their services were to pass into history with the advent of pilot only aircraft. I was one of the first in the airline to leave the Classic 747 fleet and qualify on the new type which only required two pilots as operating crew. Flight engineers continued for a number of years in many aircraft but have now largely disappeared especially since the terrorism of 9/11 which caused a contraction in the industry when many of the older aircraft types were retired.

9. Medical misfortunes

Life in aviation has been filled with curious events, interesting people, fascinating phenomena and many, many incidents, ranging from the bizarre to the distinctly colourful.

There have been numerous medical problems affecting both crew and passengers. Time, space and energy permit only brief mention of a few.

I was sitting on my own in a Delhi hotel in BOAC days, sometime in the mid 1970's, enjoying breakfast and generally minding my own business. A middle aged lady, obviously British, asked if she could join me. She had figured I was BOAC crew (not difficult!) and announced that she was from cabin crew management at Heathrow. She had flown in the night before and her curious assignment was to locate a stewardess who had gone missing a week previously.

The story had a touch of mystery. The stewardess, feeling ill, had opted to stay in her room rather than go out for an evening with her crew. The following morning her room was found to be empty and nobody knew what had happened to her.

The manageress had already commenced investigations and had established some basic but vital information which previously no one had been prepared to impart. Apparently a doctor had been called and on his advice the girl had been taken to an isolation hospital. Just where this hospital was and the nature of the suspected disease were unknown. My unscheduled breakfast companion was obviously desirous of company in her searches in the formidable sprawling environs of Delhi. After breakfast we set off together in a taxi.

Cutting a long and intriguing story short, we eventually found the girl, in a nondescript hospital which lacked even basic air-conditioning. She was sitting on a bed in a multiple ward, fully dressed, surprisingly chirpy in the circumstances, wondering whether anyone would ever think to determine her whereabouts and effect a rescue. The suspected disease was diphtheria and it had become obvious that she was not thus afflicted.

We were unable to secure her release as the doctor was not on hand but it was a very relieved soul we left behind, assuring her that now she had been located, release and return to London was imminent.

In Virgin Atlantic days, sometime in the 1990's I recollect sitting in a Newark (New Jersey) hospital casualty room at 3am on a Sunday morning with the cabin supervisor and one of our female cabin crew. The latter had undergone cosmetic surgery on a previous trip in Johannesburg and it had gone badly wrong.

Her problem was insignificant compared to what we witnessed that night. I suppose I have led a very sheltered life. There were stretcher cases resulting from gang warfare, folk coming in with knife wounds and blood pouring from battered heads, nurses and doctors calmly and casually dealing with what looked like what one must see in a frontline wartime field hospital. It was approaching dawn by the time a doctor could be spared to check out our comparatively trivial misfortune.

On another occasion we were heading back across the Atlantic from the USA. The health of a passenger had steadily deteriorated from departure. The cabin supervisor had been very reluctant to take him on board at all, however, his family begged us to allow him to fly saying he had a minor stomach upset. Eventually, professional advice on board insisted he needed hospitalisation immediately. We landed unscheduled at Shannon in pre-dawn darkness in wild weather. The patient was offloaded and was taken to the local hospital in an ambulance. The family, who then continued to London, finally spilled the beans. The man was suffering from terminal cancer, had been to the USA for a final 'fling' and had no medical insurance.

Similarly, there was a sick child on another flight. We had come from Florida and were passing New York en-route London. A young GP, who was a passenger, insisted that the child had appendicitis and should be hospitalised immediately. The cabin supervisor was not happy with the diagnosis. Further medical advice was sought.

An elderly anaesthetist eventually, reluctantly, made himself known. (Hippocratic oath and all that I suppose?) The cabin supervisor, anaesthetist and I held a mini conference on the flight deck. The old man thought the child had wind! It was up to me to play devil's advocate. These days with satellite communications and a twenty-four hour doctor/nurse ground advice service available these impossible situations no longer occur. I decided that with two hours to go prior to actually commencing the Atlantic crossing from Newfoundland and with several good airfields with hospitals en-route, we could carry on for a while and watch developments.

Approaching Newfoundland the child went to sleep. She awoke as we landed at Gatwick with no symptoms. It probably was wind! A diversion into New York would have been incredibly expensive and with the possibility of running out of duty time, passengers and crew accommodation for the night etc., let alone the on-going disruption to the airline. I was most thankful for the diagnosis. I subsequently wrote a personal thank-you letter to the anaesthetist and we exchanged friendly correspondence.

There was another medical incident that did not end happily. An elderly man suffered cardiac and respiratory arrest over Frobisher Bay, Baffin Island. This isolated settlement is located close to the Arctic Circle in North

Eastern Canada. It was winter, around 2am local time and the conditions and surface temperature at Frobisher which is not a suitable airport for a Boeing 747 anyway, were most uninviting. The nearest sensible airport was Goose Bay, Labrador, an hour to the South. Amazingly we had two paramedics on board who were passengers. They did a sterling job and the patient was still alive when we landed and offloaded him at Goose Bay. It has been my practice to follow up these situations and subsequently I learned that, sadly, he passed away three days later.

10. 747-400

In February 1994, shortly after the Los Angeles earthquake it was off to Seattle for a 747-400 course.

While still basically a 747, the flight deck was radically different. The flight engineer position was no longer. All the ancillary controls and switches were located on a large overhead panel within reach of both pilots. The multitudinous pilot instruments on classic 747's had been replaced by two main CRT screens (later upgraded to LCD), a Primary Flight Display and a Navigation Display. These were duplicated for both pilots and there were two other screens in the centre displaying engine instruments and much other supplementary information. The mode control panel on the glare shield contained all the auto pilot controls and additional switches for many other subsidiary functions. This general configuration is the norm on most modern airliners.

The computer based ground school course was a little too rapid followed by a minimal amount of simulator time. Simulators had improved and were designated 'Zero Time'. That is to say, when I turned up at Gatwick for my first flight in this brand new aircraft I had not even sat in the pilot's seat of a real 747-400.

There was me in the captain's seat, a Boeing instructor pilot in the co-pilot's seat and Richard, another Virgin captain also converting to the type, in the jump seat along for a look see. Behind us were four hundred and ninety five fare paying passengers and a full cabin crew.

On the crew bus to the aircraft I had asked the Boeing instructor pilot a couple of questions which it seemed to me to be reasonable under the circumstances.

"Are you familiar with airline operations?"

"Yeah, Yeah, Yeah!" was the confident reply.

"Are you familiar with operating procedures on the North Atlantic?"

Again, the response was a confident affirmative.

We were to find otherwise.

After some forty minutes performing pre-flight procedures Mr Boeing was looking distinctly confused. He was supposed to be loading the Flight Management system which is the brains of the aircraft. He was unable to get the system to accept our Atlantic entry point. Finally he was forced to confess that he was stumped. Richard, always quiet and appearing slow on the uptake (he was far from it) eventually found the solution. I will not attempt to explain the detail but it was very simple.

We finally became airborne and Richard found himself obtaining the necessary Atlantic clearance and subsequently doing the HF radio work. Mr Boeing, while generally familiar with the aircraft, was possessed of some grave shortcomings. I was extremely thankful to have the extra man in the jump seat.

The next trip was with a Virgin training captain who had been sent to Lufthansa for a while to learn the type and things were straightforward.

The third trip, again Orlando, the sole route for the new aircraft at this stage, was my final check flight on the type. It was a good trip. Another Boeing instructor pilot was assigned and he was of a different calibre to the earlier disaster.

Of Latino appearance, he was short with a droopy moustache and spoke with a Mexican accent. I cannot remember his first name but it had to be Lopez and one assumed he lived in a whitewashed adobe hut on the US Mexican border, ate burritos, owned a donkey and had hundreds of children.

We worked well together and he was a quiet patient instructor and asked me to do all the Atlantic procedures admitting that he was not familiar with them. The crossing was uneventful.

Approaching Orlando, the local air traffic control who never really seemed to understand the inertia of large aircraft, had masterfully placed us so high that to make an approach was really marginal. Realising his mistake the controller's voice came over the VHF,

"Virgin, I -ah, I seem to have got you bit high there... can you make the approach?"

Lopez glanced across questioningly with his twinkling brown eyes and droopy moustache. I nodded 'yes' in reply.

"Tower... he says to say... he can make it!"

Being uncomfortable with all the magical automatics I reverted to basics, disconnected everything and flew the approach manually arriving fully configured and at the correct speed at 1000 feet on the final approach which was a company requirement. It was a wonderful machine in the sense that disconnecting automatics and flying manually the aircraft handled almost exactly the same as a Boeing 747 classic with which I was more than familiar. Lopez was very pleased and I was signed off, fully qualified on the return sector.

As the years went by the fleet expanded to thirteen aircraft. The job remained most enjoyable with this superb new equipment. The route structure similarly expanded and we found ourselves flying to some of the Caribbean Islands, San Francisco, Johannesburg and many other destinations. The new Airbus fleet tended to operate all the Far East trips although I was to fly a few Hong Kong trips on the Boeing.

Category three (blind landing equipment) was excellent and for the first time in my life this was viable and reliable. There were still visibility limits but only to the extent that they would not permit a landing if visibility was so poor that taxiing would be impossible. It was a fascinating experience to engage all three autopilots (which checked each other) and except for configuring flaps, gear and speed the machine would fly itself accurately down the approach, closely monitored by the crew of course. Sometimes we would only have the barest glimpse of the runway lighting system before the machine performed a near perfect landing. The procedure was so mesmerising that it was easy to forget to engage reverse power after landing. Also, when one attempted to turn off the runway using nose-wheel steering the aircraft would simply refuse to deviate from the centre line until the auto-pilot was disengaged. The many diversions due to fog on the older types were a thing of the past.

As time went on further equipment was retrofitted to the -400 fleet. GPS became the primary navigation aid and Satellite communication was installed and activated. No longer was one isolated from base with the only communication being very poor and sometimes unusable HF. Eventually the congested North Atlantic air traffic system benefitted from the advanced communication systems. These days one types in one's requested track on a data link. Shortly after the cleared track is printed out, emanating from the oceanic controller.

11. Early days with the -400

Some amusing events occurred with the new fleet. Only about two months after receiving the first -400 I was bound to Orlando (where else in those days!) with earthquake Phil. He had just joined the fleet and was my trainee co-pilot. There were just the two of us on the flight deck and as usual the aircraft was full.

Heading down the East coast of the USA we were in the vicinity of Jacksonville, when air traffic control announced that Orlando airport was closed due to thunderstorms. Being overhead Jacksonville where the weather was good we ascertained that we were in possession of the correct approach charts and then descended and landed to wait for the weather at destination to improve.

These Orlando trips with only two flight deck crew were very tight for flight time limitations so if there was any significant delay we would have to stop overnight with all the hassle of finding accommodation for passengers and crew not to mention the chaos caused at destination with a full load waiting to go back to London.

Jacksonville appeared to be a sleepy rural airport and we really did seem to be out in the 'sticks'. A disinterested handling agent appeared on the flight deck followed by a small bulky bucolic looking character who announced that he was the re-fueller. We asked the agent if he could contact our base and extract some paperwork, namely a fight plan for the onward sector. The re-fueller asked how much fuel we wanted. A quick assessment and I said,

"Forty Tonnes, please."

"What's that is in pounds, sir?" asked the bucolic. A quick flick with the calculator,

"Eighty-eight thousand pounds."

By the look of amazement on his face I don't think he'd

ever put anything like that amount of fuel in an aircraft before.

"That's a lot of gas sir, we'll have to go and find another bowser!" He disappeared.

Leaving Phil in charge of the flight deck I fought my way back along the upper deck trying desperately not to engage with the passengers. We were really going to have to make this a fast turnaround or we would run out of hours. Down the stairs and out of the door I could see bucolic and his sidekick had managed to open the refuelling panel under the port wing. However, they were standing looking at it scratching their heads. I went over.

"We're having trouble sir, never seen anything like this before!"

In training there had been a day spent on ground handling. Re-fuelling was covered in the space of about ten minutes and in normal circumstances I would never have expected to have to recall this vital information. At most major international airports re-fuellers are competent to handle the equipment.

Mounting the staging they had placed under the panel I examined the large number of switches and dials. It seemed fairly logical and I determined that most of the panel was associated with manual refuelling where one could load specific amounts of fuel into individual tanks but in one corner was a specific set of switches and dials for automatic refuelling. I moved some thumb wheels to 40,000kgs and moved a switch. Lo-and-behold the fuel required indicator obediently indicated my request. With some satisfaction I suggested bucolic try again. The fuel still refused to go on board. This was getting serious.

Making haste back to the flight deck I found earthquake Phil with manuals scattered everywhere trying to do a take-off data card from raw data as there were no specific charts for Jacksonville. Recognising that the take-off card was a very trivial problem especially with a good long runway available I said,

"Forget the take-off card, we've got to find out how to re-fuel this thing!"

We turned out the document stowage with no success at all. One important looking manual that said 'Re-fuel manual' was a source of temporary delight but all it contained were manual dip stick readings. I said to Phil,

"I'm going to have to find a phone and call base." (This was prior to sat-com being installed).

Back down the upper deck, again parrying the questions of curious passengers, out of the door to find bucolic and his sidekick with big smiles,

"Sorry sir, the problem was with our bowser. We forgot to open the valve!"

Air traffic advised that the thunderstorms at destination had cleared and we shot off to Orlando like a scalded cat. The transit had been exactly one hour so it was not too dis-honourable. After landing at destination, it took us another full hour to sort out and fill in all the paperwork associated with the Jacksonville transit.

How I missed the flight engineer. He would have seen to all the ground handling, completed the technical log and other paperwork and I would have sat like Lord Muck on the flight deck and supervised the operation over a cup of tea!

As a postscript I was to discover that I had missed the obvious. The lid of the re-fuelling panel folds down forwards. On the inside of this are clearly printed refuelling instructions in plain man's English. If I had only turned around!

Another incident, again into Orlando concerned the operation of the magical Flight Management System and Primary Flight Displays.

On this occasion I was working with a young man called Nick. Like Phil he is now much older and a well-respected captain.

Orlando has a VOR placed at about eight miles from

the airfield. The reason for this anomaly is that the new Orlando international airport is actually what used to be the McKoy air-force base and the VOR is placed at a civil airport eight miles away. The instruction came through,

"Virgin Fifteen, proceed direct to the field."

"Just how do we do that?" I said to myself. With the location of the VOR not at the airport it was no use heading for it which would have been the normal procedure. We were still some twenty miles out and couldn't yet see the airport due to poor visibility and some low cloud.

Inspiration! I typed the ICAO[1] designator for Orlando (KMCO) on the top of the Flight Management system 'Legs' page and inserted it. I should not have done that! The anticipated display was a direct course to destination. Instead the screens went virtually blank. We had basic flight instruments left and fortunately airspeed but the flap extension speeds had disappeared and the Navigation display vanished completely. The instrument landing system had also vanished from the screen.

Thankfully there were all those years flying the 'classic' 747. I flew manually; Nick managed to tune the instrument landing system also manually, although on this advanced machine it had to be typed in using the Flight Management computer. I called for the flaps based on memory of 'classic' 747 limiting speeds. As we landed everything resurrected itself and we were left scratching our heads.

I should have reported this but being more than a little embarrassed and convinced I had committed some heinous crime I kept quiet. Nick did likewise. Some six months later a bulletin came out from Boeing.

"On no account place an ICAO identifier at the top of the legs page until the FMS program has been upgraded."

It was a genuine 'glitch' and not my fault at all!

1 ICAO International Civil Aviation Organisation

12. Bomb on board

Cabin supervisors are an interesting breed, come in both male and female varieties, are generally superb at their job and on a large aircraft they carry a huge amount of responsibility. Various airlines assign them various titles. Sometimes these are adjusted to even grander, almost royal status depending upon the power of the cabin crew management in the particular airline.

In the case of Virgin for many years it was simply Inflight Supervisor or IFS for short. Almost invariably they were friendly and helpful in their interactions with the Flight Deck which was the ultimate authority on the aircraft. Similarly, Captains could rely on their cabin supervisor to deal with all the problems associated with junior cabin crew and above all passengers. Their primary function was, of course, safety but the daily grind of handling and feeding large numbers of the general public in an extremely cramped and confined space for long hours was the bread and butter of their profession.

Typically on a Boeing 747 there were either two or three flight deck crew and up to 18 cabin crew. The cabin crew were under the control of the Supervisor who had two subordinate second-in-commands controlling their respective sections of the cabin.

Which is all by the way!

Yet another Orlando trip. At the pre-flight briefing I had surmised that the IFS for this particular trip was a no-nonsense lady who gave no quarter to passengers or crew alike.

About two and a half hours into the flight she arrived on the flight deck when the machine was well out over the Atlantic and announced with zero emotion, almost an accusation,

"There's a bomb in a rear toilet!"

Initially I was completely nonplussed. In the co-pilot's seat was a trainee and there was no other pilot on board. Instinctively I turned around to speak to the flight engineer.

Flight engineers for the previous twenty years or so had handled all things unusual such as floods in the cabin, broken cabin equipment and even oven fires so this was definitely his department. Of course, this was a 747-400. There was no cheery, profane engineer sitting in the third seat. There was just a blank panel with a few circuit breakers and a data feeder.

Thoughts racing I said to the IFS,

"Where in the toilet is the bomb?"

"In the pan!" She replied witheringly. She didn't actually say

"Of course" or "You silly boy" but the suggestion was unmistakable.

"What does it look like?" Again, a withering reply with a touch of increasing impatience,

"It is about this long," she held her two forefingers about ten inches apart,

"It is black, and...," waving her hands expressively "Has a battery and lots of wires and things!"

"Okay, I'd better come and have a look."

Turning to the co-pilot I said,

"I'm going back to check this out. You have control."

Looking as completely out of his depth, exactly as I felt but for different reasons, the trainee co-pilot acknowledged.

Climbing out of my seat I headed back down the cabin to the stairway located at the rear of the upper deck. There were some sixty passengers on the upper deck and the single aisle was easily negotiated but downstairs things were different.

The IFS seemed suddenly to have disappeared which in itself was most unusual. When there is a cabin problem it is normal for the supervisor to accompany the flight deck crew member assigned to investigate right to the location of the problem. She had probably decided that the safest place on the aircraft was as far away from the bomb as possible which was naïve in the extreme. Any bomb exploding and we would all be dead! Thankfully she had not told the rest of the cabin crew what was going on.

There was a meal service in progress and about three trolleys had to be negotiated en-route to the back of the aircraft each of which required some expert manoeuvring by the cabin crew. They in turn gave enquiring glances as to my presence so far back in the cabin. I gave a reassuring smile but said nothing especially as in each case there were passengers within earshot.

Arriving at the rear of the machine I noted a carbon copy of 'Andy Capp' sitting on the door Five Left slide housing with a lighted cigarette dangling out of the corner of his mouth. He was out of order on two counts. Passengers, in the days when smoking was permitted on aircraft, were only allowed to practise their habit while seated in their allocated seat in the smoking section. In addition, sitting on the slide housing was prohibited as it was not stressed for such use. He was sitting on a large red notice which said, 'Do Not Sit'. Such misdemeanours were trivial in the circumstances and I viewed the various toilets trying to decide in the absence of further information just where to start. There were some eight toilets at the rear of the aircraft.

There was an attention getting clearing of a throat behind me. Andy Capp had a voice. In the peculiar manner of inveterate smokers, mouth unmoving and cigarette remaining expertly poised in the corner of his mouth he said,

"Yer lookin fer the bomb mate?"

Such were the Supervisor's and Andy Capp's lack of emotion the whole situation was become something of a farce. Were bombs on aircraft everyday events that somehow had escaped my notice over the years?

"Yes, as a matter of fact I am!"

"In there!" Andy pointed to one of the cubicles.

I pushed open the folding door of the offending unit and examined the contents of the bowl. The object was precisely as the Supervisor had described. Black, about 10 inches long, plastic tubular case about 2 inches in diameter. The case had obviously broken and there was a torch battery, a printed circuit board with diodes, resistors and transistors and 'lots of wires and things' which all looked very scary. Peering into the malodourous bowl I examined every detail. A spark of optimism coursed through the brain. The brief experience of handling gelignite working underground twenty six years before at Hill 50 had not been wasted. There was no sign of explosive or a detonator. However, what on earth was this object doing in a 747 rear toilet unless it was some kind of a sick joke?

Examining more closely I noticed a diminutive fan and a tiny capsule looking like a short piece of candle stick. All became instantly clear. I backed out of the toilet. Andy Capp obviously expecting a cataclysmic announcement briefly removed the cigarette from the corner of his mouth and stood up. I pushed open the door of the adjacent toilet and sure enough, attached to the bottom of the mirror was a long black object, about 10 inches long, two inches in diameter but not broken.

Virgin, especially in the early days brought much unconventionality to the historically staid trade that commercial aviation had become. There were many innovations, some were excellent and revolutionary and quickly copied by other airlines. Some were good but didn't last and there were a few disasters which were dropped almost as soon as they were started. This was in the latter category. Some bright spark in the catering management had presumably purchased a job lot of cheap air fresheners which were battery powered and emitted a pleasing deodoriser at pre-programmed intervals. These had been stuck with ineffective adhesive on the toilet mirrors of the 747-400. The inevitable had occurred. This one had dropped off the mirror and smashed into the bowl disembowelling itself in the process. I removed the offending device and gave it to one of the cabin crew to dispose of.

Telephoning the flight deck I assured the, by now, very anxious co-pilot that all was well and slowly returned towards the front of the aircraft.

At the top of the stairs stood the supervisor, bristling belligerence with folded arms, legs apart blocking further progress,

"Well?" she demanded,

"Air freshener", I said flatly. The thought flashed through my mind that I should have added "You silly girl!" but common sense and the avoidance of World War three prevailed and I discarded such lunatic thoughts.

"They're in all the toilets stuck on the mirrors. This one came unstuck. You might write this up in your flight report and suggest they are all removed before there's serious trouble and someone diverts thinking it's a real bomb."

"Oh!" Slightly crestfallen the IFS resumed her duties and it appeared, at least in her eyes, that I was temporarily forgiven for whatever it is about males that some females frequently find so unforgiveable.

13. Ferry Flying

In the normal course of an airline pilot's life he will sooner or later ferry empty aircraft from A to B. Depending on the regulating authority there may or may not be a requirement for one or more cabin crew. With Saudia there was no requirement for a cabin crew member and on the very occasional ferry flight my colleagues learned to keep me away from the galley. Gerry's attempts in Australia to instruct me in the finer arts of food preparation were never a success. Actually, I think he learned his trade in the British Navy and snippets of information that came my way at a later date suggested that he spent more time under lock and key for drunken disorderliness than in the ship's galley. As a result he probably wasn't the best instructor.

It seemed that such was my inherent deficit in this area that I was even incapable of heating pre-prepared meals without reducing a potentially excellent meal to an unpalatable mess.

Virgin Atlantic, on the other hand, benefitted from 'Big Brother' in the form of the Civil Aviation Authority. We carried a cabin crew member for all ferry flights for 'safety reasons' which simply involved arming and disarming an automatic door slide. On longer ferry flights there was the added advantage of having a tea-maker, cook and general factotum.

Heavy maintenance was carried out by a variety of different organisations in various parts of the world and inevitably this involved ferry flying. The organisations were in Manchester (UK), Dublin, Amsterdam, and further afield, Manila (Philippines) and Auckland (New Zealand). There was also much shuttling of aircraft between Heathrow and Gatwick for commercial reasons and I was to operate a large number of these flights. Most ferrying was uneventful.

There were a few exceptions.

There was a Dublin maintenance flight on a classic 747. The flight engineer was a lovely mature character by the name of John. We deadheaded over to Dublin on another airline and waited patiently for about three hours until the aircraft was buttoned up and signed off. It was on an extended check and had been in the Aer Lingus hanger for some three weeks.

There can be serious oversights after heavy maintenance and I was particularly careful with the pre-flight checks and asked my colleagues to exercise similar vigilance.

Eventually we started the engines and having satisfied ourselves that all was in order taxied out to the runway. Having been cleared for take-off I turned around to have a glance at John's panel which is a normal procedure as the Flight Engineer is effectively un-monitored. Things didn't look right,

"John, I don't normally see all those amber lights?"

"Sorry, Captain!" There was unusual deference as in Virgin we were invariably on first name terms.

John moved some switches and the amber lights disappeared. In our rigorous checking to make sure everything was normal, John had forgotten to switch the fuel boost pumps on. I have no idea what would have happened if we had attempted a take–off with the boost pumps off. The tanks gravity feed to a certain extent but with the low take-off weight, low fuel load and consequent rapid acceleration followed by high rate of rotation we could have suffered one or more engine flame outs on departure.

A few minutes later as we cruised over the Irish Sea in the direction of London, John pointedly cleared his throat,

"Er, are you going to report that, er, incident, Captain?"

Again the uncomfortable deference.

Turning round, I said gently, "What are a few boost pumps between thee and me?"

I didn't even have to think and had already forgotten about it. John was an excellent flight engineer and everybody is entitled to make a mistake which is why crew monitor each other so rigorously. Besides this, John was the flight engineer on a difficult flight just after I had first checked out as a captain with Virgin. We had to shut down an engine in mid-Atlantic. With his and the co-pilot's excellent work on that occasion, it was immensely pleasing to be able to bestow a little payback.

A facet of most long haul airliners is the need to preserve engine life by using reduced power for take-off. The need for a full power take off is rare. There are some complex calculations pre-departure (nowadays all computerised) to determine the required power to take the machine safely into the air.

There was a Gatwick Heathrow ferry with one of the ex- Singapore Airlines classic 747's with the uprated Pratt & Witney JT9D-7Q engines. For these trips we used to have a standard fuel load of thirty tonnes and by definition there was no payload. All this is to say that the machine was extremely light. The co-pilot and I tossed a coin to decide who was going to handle the sector and I was pleased to win as being a training captain I was short of handling practice.

Carrying out the pre-flight checks I realised with some dismay that due to the very strong surface wind at Gatwick the performance manual declared that a full power take-off was mandatory. It was the co-pilot's duty to do the calculations and I was hoping he would miss the relevant clause in the manual. He was far too diligent and completing the data card he announced almost gleefully,

"Book says a full power take-off is mandatory!"

A few minutes later, cleared for departure and lining up on the runway I called for the flight engineer to set take-off power. A brief pause at about one third power to stabilise the engines and he pushed the four thrust levers almost fully forward and we were away. The machine leapt forward like a rampant stag and we were pressed back into the seats with the massive acceleration. In no time at all the co-pilot called,

"V1" and "Rotate" simultaneously.

I eased back on the control column and we went rocketing skywards. The operations manual called for an orderly reduction in power at 1500 feet but with a blocked altitude at 3000 feet this would be too late to avoid a violation.

To keep the forward acceleration under control the angle of climb was outrageous and the vertical speed indicator was effectively pegged out at some impossible figure. At only 800 feet above the ground I pulled all four thrust levers back to about halfway up the quadrant, pushed the nose firmly down bringing things under control such that we levelled off at the 3000 feet requirement. The control tower passed us over to the departure frequency with a cryptic, uncalled for comment,

"Showing off today, are we, Virgin?"

The co-pilot neatly parried the insult. Instead of explaining the real reason he said,

"Yes, fun wasn't it!"

And so we made our way to Heathrow.

On another occasion I was called from standby to take a 747-400 from Gatwick to Heathrow. Arriving at the airport I went to our crew office on the ground floor of the ugly edifice that makes up the Gatwick terminal complex to find a hand written note pinned to the door. The barely legible instruction said,

"Closed due flooding," and gave directions to an office on the fourth floor.

Arriving at the suggested room I found it unlocked. Within were a table, a chair and a telephone. Normally in these situations there is a bustling office and much activity.

There was not a soul in sight. After some ten minutes I began to feel a little unwanted. The phone worked. Via the airport operator I managed to locate a friendly voice who seemed to know what was going on,

"Aircraft is in the remote parking area, co-pilot's going to be late, stewardess with you shortly and paperwork's on the way!"

Shortly after, a clerk arrived with the paperwork and a shy nervous stewardess also arrived. The clerk disappeared.

"Never done a ferry flight before," said the little girl, her voice quavering with anxiety.

"No problem, all you have to do is arm[1] door Two Left when we are ready to go and dis-arm it when we arrive. If you have time to make us a cup of tea as well that would be excellent."

She began to relax although I suppose it was all so different to a normal departure she had a right to be apprehensive. The aircraft was needed at Heathrow for a commercial flight that afternoon.

"We need to go," I said, "The co-pilot can catch up with us later."

"I suppose so," said the girl, but I think she really wanted to go home.

We went through to airside and found a crew bus. I asked the driver to take us to the remote parking area. There was only one 747-400 in Virgin colours in the area. The bus dropped us by the aircraft and left. There were steps up to door Two Left but the area was deserted. The girl followed me nervously up the stairs and we went up to the upper deck. I sat in my seat and began the pre-flight preparations. The girl sat on the edge of the jump seat.

"Why don't you go back and make us both a cup of tea?" I said, trying to get her to relax. At that moment a

1 Doors are armed before flight such that if opened on the ground the escape slide will automatically deploy.

re-fueller stuck his head around the flight deck door,

"Ow much yer want, guv?"

Some things are irresistible. Turning to the girl who was still on the flight deck I said,

"Where would you like to go; Sydney, Seychelles or Western Samoa?"

I was going to embellish as in a 747-400 with no payload and full fuel we could potentially have gone almost anywhere in the world. The damage was done. She shot out of the flight deck like a startled rabbit. I felt foolish and wondered what to do. To her it was manifestly not a joke at all.

"What's 'er problem guv?" said the concerned re-fueller.

The situation was saved by the arrival of the first officer who met the girl fleeing down the stairs. They knew each other which made things much easier. He assured the girl that I was really joking and the short flight to Heathrow was relaxed and uneventful.

Standby duty is a problem, especially if you live at the limit of the distance permitted by the company for getting to work on time in the event of a call out. Most crew seem to stretch this rule to the maximum. If there is a panic call out, the suitcase needs to be packed ready for any length of trip and all climates. It is not much use packing for East Coast USA with thermal underwear for mid-winter and then spending the next two weeks in Calcutta. Likewise there is a problem with what activities one indulges in when on standby. There was the lovely BOAC flight engineer's story which exemplifies potential problems.

The man was carrying out some serious renovations in his lounge while on standby. (It is a weakness of many flight crew to become involved in outrageous DIY). He mixed up a barrow load of cement and wheeled it into the lounge; shovel upright in the mix in true builder's fashion. The phone rang,

"Rostering here, we need you for a trip…!"

The engineer abandoned the DIY, rapidly donned the uniform and shot off in the direction of London Heathrow.

Three weeks later he arrived home. The house was deserted. There was no sign of his wife and family. In the kitchen he found a note on the table dated the day of his departure,

"Gone to Mum's with the kids. Give me a call when you get home!"

He went into the lounge to find the barrow load of cement still there, shovel sticking out exactly as he had left it, but of course, all rock solid.

And so it was that I, having recently moved house, was renovating the kitchen together with the kind assistance of one of my brothers.

The phone rang. It was an unusual request

"Crewing here. Got a trip for you. Deadhead on KLM flight ___ from Heathrow to Amsterdam, departure time ___. When you get there take aircraft G-VXLG (a 747-400) for a test flight. Carry out five full flap retractions and extensions. If everything works bring the aircraft back to Heathrow. If there are any problems take it back to KLM at Amsterdam and await further instructions from us."

All went as planned until we arrived at Amsterdam's Schipol airport. There were only three of us, myself, a co-pilot and a stewardess. No-one met us. It took serious negotiations at the KLM information desk before someone recognised who we were and what we were there for. Eventually transport arrived and we were taken over to the KLM maintenance area,

"Where have you been, we've been waiting for you? The aircraft was signed off two hours ago!"

Situations normal! They went on to explain the flap problem which was obscure and intermittently recurring. They were confident that it had finally been fixed.

We departed heading over the coast towards the middle

of the North Sea. Having negotiated clearance for our manoeuvres at a suitable altitude we gradually slowed through the flap extension speeds, increasing the increment as rapidly as speed reduction allowed and at 20° of flap it was 'gear down' and then flap 30° which is full flap. Reversing the procedure we retracted the flaps and raised the gear. Through the assigned five procedures everything worked perfectly but the whole process took some forty five minutes. The co-pilot had performed a splendid job co-ordinating our idiosyncratic passage with air traffic control. I noticed that by now we were getting towards Stavanger, Norway.

"Well, I guess we'd better head for Heathrow", I said.

The stewardess had been sitting in the jump seat watching all the activity,

"We're fully catered. Do you want to eat?"

Another facet of aviation is that crew are always hungry. I glanced at the co-pilot. His eyes suggested he was no exception to this rule.

"Okay, how long will it take?"

"I figured you'd both be hungry and put the meals in the oven immediately after departure, they're ready now".

It was a comparatively short flight time back to Heathrow. The aircraft was not scheduled out that night. It is not good to eat too fast. We slowed down to minimum 'clean' speed, about 220kts. Minimum clean speed is the slowest safe speed flyable with the flaps retracted.

There was a leisurely feed. A call over the ether from a puzzled ground controller, who presumably had been watching our snail's pace progress on radar,

"Why so slow tonight Virgin?"

"We're eating!"

"Oh, and why not indeed? Enjoy!"

The day was not over.

We landed at Heathrow at about 10pm and were

directed to a remote parking area. Chatting with the company on the number two VHF radio they advised that a crew bus was on the way to collect us but they were having problems locating a driver for the motorised steps.

We shut the aircraft down and waited. Twenty minutes later we reminded them that we were still waiting.

"Doing all we can but still unable to find a driver for the stairs!"

I could see the bus waiting outside and wondered how long before he lost patience and drove off. I said to the stewardess,

"How are you with ladders?" A trace of anxiety flickered across her face and she glanced downwards,

"No, no, no, not your stockings! I'm talking about fire engines, window cleaners, loft ladders, that sort of thing!"

"Well, I do occasionally use a loft ladder."

The co-pilot glanced at me suspiciously,

"You can't be thinking of using the inertia reels?"

"No, no, no, I wouldn't even dream of inflicting that on you!"

The inertia reels were designed to enable emergency egress from the flight deck in the event of a crash landing where all other exits were blocked. There were four of them. You were supposed to open the hatch in the roof, grab a handle and leap into space whereupon the descent to the ground would theoretically be relatively under control. The device had been used very rarely in the entire history of the Boeing 747. I for one, thankfully, had no such experience.

I explained what I really had in mind and there was general assent.

The three of us descended to the lower deck. In the left aisle of the J class section I pulled back the carpet and raised the hatch leading to the electronics and equipment compartment. Boeing, in their wisdom provide convenient service lights in these areas and the switches are thoughtfully located. So we descended into the depths with adequate lighting. I opened the exterior pressure hatch in the floor of the E&E bay, a plug type device about 30 inches square and together we lowered the extending ladder down the rear of the nose-gear leg.

"Will you be alright with this", I asked the girl?

She was game for anything and so we exited the aircraft in most unconventional style. The bus took us to the terminal and we went home.

The following morning it was back to renovating the kitchen.

One day I was in the airline head office. This in itself was an unusual event and the reason for the visit is beyond recall. Many long haul air-crew can avoid their head office for years unless they have the misfortune to be invited for tea and biscuits with management which usually means disciplinary action over some misdemeanour, trivial or otherwise. Just before going home I put my head around the door of the chief pilot's office purely for the purposes of exchanging greetings and was gratified to be invited in with a measure of welcome.

The chat was brief and general and I was just about to leave when it occurred to me that this might be a good time to ask about a current rumour. Apparently Alitalia had cancelled a requirement for no less than five Boeing 747-400's and Virgin had swept up the entire order. In addition it was rumoured that Air New Zealand had the contract to fit these machines out with seating and passenger entertainment systems and there would be some ferrying between Seattle, Auckland and the UK.

The response was immediate and pleasing. The rumours were entirely correct. Being in the glorious position of number three on the company pilot seniority list, should I wish to operate one of the delivery flights it was mine for the taking. I asked if I would be able to take my wife and again the response was yes. Pushing the luck even further I negotiated leave such that Diane and I could spend a week or two in those beautiful islands to visit friends and have a holiday.

So, a few weeks later we found ourselves en-route to Seattle in the North West corner of the USA. I warned the lady that it was necessary to take a smart outfit as on the previous two occasions when I had been with a team collecting an aircraft from Boeing the manufacturer threw a good party the night before the delivery. About three days after we arrived the aircraft was declared fit for service and the next day was designated as departure day. There was no talk of a party.

Unusually I was the senior representative of Virgin present and was invited to sit down at a large round table with some very serious looking Boeing management and their lawyers.

Sandwiches were laid on and I was handed pieces of paper to sign most of which seem to have astronomical sums of money written at the bottom but even so, in my limited knowledge of these things, the numbers were well below the figures I would have expected for the purchase of a brand new Boeing 747-400. I made a respectful enquiry as to the real price of this aircraft. There were nervous glances around the table and one of the peaky faced lawyers mutters a nine figure number which was many millions more than the amount I was seeing on the pieces of paper.

Subsequent private rumination suggested that Virgin managed a huge discount as these aircraft were designated for the Mediterranean operator and were considerably different to our normal specification even to the extent that passenger signs were inscribed in Italian. The reason for the lack of a party needed little further speculation and I could only admire the airline management for their commercial perspicacity which was the reason why we still survived as a pint sized airline in a world of mega-carriers.

We made our way over to the aircraft dragging suitcases as this was a private delivery operation and the usual paraphernalia of an airline departure was curiously absent.

We were eight persons. Myself plus wife, another Captain, two Co-pilots, two stewards and a ground engineer whose function I forget. Hugh, the other Captain agreed to be in command for the first half of the flight and I would then take over for the second half and arrival into Auckland. I carried out a careful walk around the aircraft while Hugh was preparing the flight deck. As on previous similar occasions I was delighted by the pristine condition of the machine, especially the wheel wells which would very quickly become soiled and grubby when the aircraft entered service.

All aboard and closed up and Boeing performed their usual act of deep mistrust of airline pilots by towing the aircraft on to the runway at Paine Field. Whether for insurance purposes or because they simply do not trust those who actually fly their creations it appears that, *de rigueur*, with a new aircraft, Boeing will not allow airline crew to taxi the few hundred metres to the departure point.

Checks completed and clearances obtained, Hugh stabilised the engines at 50% N1 and then pressed a 'TOGA' button. The four GE90 engines smoothly accelerated to take off power.

The machine was comparatively light with only two passengers and no freight on an aircraft capable of carrying five hundred. There were only a few seats on the upper deck. We carried an unusually large load of fuel. We surged forward and were quickly airborne heading South West into the rapidly darkening skies of a Friday evening.

There was a long night ahead with a planned flight time of 13 hours. Sometime in the middle before I took over from Hugh, noticing Diane was awake, we did a tour of the aircraft. A 747 with no seats on the lower deck is an eerie sight. 'Haunted ballroom' is the phrase that springs to mind. It could be compared to a long empty low ceilinged barn with the two galley/utility areas standing out as ugly interruptions in the middle of the cabin. It was dark outside, there were no seats or furnishing downstairs but the cabin lights were all on.

One of the stewards had bought a bicycle in Seattle to take home to the UK via Auckland! He was cycling slowly around the lower deck as if this was the most normal activity in the world in mid-Pacific at 39,000 feet.

About half way across the ocean we crossed the Equator and I took over from Hugh together with the relief co-pilot. Later, crossing the International date-line, the twenty four hours that constituted Saturday evaporated in less than a micro second and it became Sunday morning. We start to talk to New Zealand's Oceanic control.

There was a suspicion of fog at Auckland's Mangere airport and I asked the co-pilot to obtain weather reports for suitable alternates. Being off our normal airline routes the company operations at Gatwick allotted significant extra fuel for our departure so there was no problem except that the suggested alternate of Sydney was not where we wanted to go. With some aeronautical knowledge of New Zealand, albeit well out of date, I requested weather for Wellington and Christchurch, the former not really suitable for a 747-400 and the latter very much further South. The options were, Auckland number one, Christchurch number two and Sydney number three. The complication was that Christchurch was not a cast iron alternate due a hint of fog also. There was not enough fuel to have a go at Christchurch and then go on to Sydney. For reasons that I fail to remember, use of the Cat III blind landing equipment was not an option, either because Mangere was not suitably equipped or because the new aircraft had not yet been signed off for Cat III. We discussed all of this with Auckland and I visualised the discussions in oceanic control…

"Stone the crows, what else are these Pommies going to ask?!"

As we approached Auckland and commenced descent the weather was clear. We landed and taxied over to the international arrivals area. I couldn't help recollecting the first time I arrived at this airport just after its opening some 27 years before.

There was a hitch with immigration in true Antipodean style. It concerned Diane. For the rest of us as crew and also the ground engineer, even though we were not in uniform, there was no problem but the lady was a passenger, albeit un-ticketed. We were solemnly informed that the law stated that no passenger was permitted to land in New Zealand unless coming from a port recognised by the government of New Zealand. Paine Field, Seattle was not a recognised international airport.

Eventually the immigration officer, who was not pleased anyway at being hauled out of bed for a single arrival at 3am on a Sunday morning, was persuaded to record that we were arriving from Seattle Tacoma airport and the matter was resolved. He headed for home muttering about 'Pommie' irregularities.

And so, after a night in a hotel to recover from the humungous jet lag, we hired a car and headed off for the South Island. There was a glorious holiday in the New Zealand winter.

Two weeks later we returned to Auckland to take one of the aircraft back to the UK. There was already a problem. The aircraft was delayed and I was required back on the line for some training duties. The suggestion was that I would have to fly back as a passenger on a commercial flight. Worse was the amount of 'stuff' Diane and I had procured in New Zealand.

When you have your own private 747 for global transportation it is amazing what you can acquire especially with the exchange rate prevailing at the time. Most of it would have to be left behind. The crewing department at base insisted on calling me at 3.30am each morning. Complaints about the 12 hour time difference went totally unheeded which was one of the delights of working for an airline like Virgin. Eventually all ended well as the company relented and we waited a further week until the machine was ready.

Two co-pilots and two stewardesses had been flown out passenger from London and had also been waiting a week so we were definitely ready to go home. Other than minor problems with some recalcitrant communications equipment the return flight was uneventful and we spent a night in Los Angeles with the aircraft en route. The following morning, with no passenger load but the holds filled with a substantial cargo of grapes, we set course for London.

14. Airbus A340

The Bible says that man lives to threescore years and ten or by reason of strength to fourscore years! If you examine global statistics, average longevity falls well short of this. In so called 'First World' countries the statistics go the other way. However, despite his ingenuity man cannot determine his lifespan neither can he get off this planet to which he is assigned for the duration. Somewhere else in the Bible it says, 'God looks down upon the circle of the earth and laughs!' This was written well before the concept of the earth as an oblate spheroid was even dreamt of by the scientists of antiquity.

Which is all by way of saying, suddenly, middle age was marching inexorably towards old age and I was sixty!

International legislation declared that it was not permissible to be the captain of a civil airliner over the age of sixty.

With as much ceremony as is attached to the weekly chore of putting out the trash I was de-moted to co-pilot. One day I came home to Heathrow flying in the right hand seat of a Boeing 747-400 as training captain with a trainee captain in the left seat. The next trip I went out in the same seat as a co-pilot, under training. The company, in the unimaginative way of most companies, saw that on paper I was a trainee co-pilot on his first trip and sent along an experienced First Officer as 'cover'! (You would have to be in the trade to understand the full indignity of this). The training captain, who I think had once been my trainee, seeing this ultimate humiliation, had the extra man taken off the trip.

For the next eighteen months I flew as co-pilot. Captains were more than pleasant and life was fine. The only problem was that I was steadily losing interest and getting lazy. Commanders were going to make all the decisions so the thinking processes declined.

There had been rumours for many years that the age limit would change. Just after my sixty-second birthday the reality came. This created a conundrum for the company. They were overstaffed with Boeing captains and understaffed with Airbus captains. I am not party to the full politics but I think somewhere I heard that basically they wanted the four of us de-moted captains on the Boeing fleet to stay there as co-pilots. Nevertheless, there was an official invitation to convert to the Airbus A340 as a captain and never being able to resist a challenge off I went.

Twenty eight years of Boeings was imprinted on the brain and it was by the Grace of God and magnanimity of the training department that I finally checked out as an A340 Captain. Never a fast learner and at sixty two years of age it was something of a miracle to have actually absorbed the totally different technology and successfully completed the course. Having said that, of the four of us, two seemed to sail through, I only just made it and one remained a co-pilot.

Although, by the time retirement arrived I was becoming comfortable in the machine, there remain some disturbing questions. Why has Airbus made such a complicated aircraft? Has Boeing gone in the same direction? The most recent Boeing I have flown is the 747-400 which is 1980's technology. I know nothing of Boeing's latest offerings.

To my simple brain, if the pilot applies back pressure on the control column of any aeroplane in level flight, the pitch should change upwards and a climb should commence. Similarly, if you apply forward pressure the opposite should occur. With an Airbus this is not the case. You apply backward pressure on the control column, in itself a diminutive side stick and the fact that you have performed this action is communicated to five separate computers.

The computers then hold a board meeting to decide if they will permit you to go up. All of this takes a micro second and the effects are instantaneous but the problem potentially is; what if the inputs to the computers are wrong, or worse, there is a common as yet undetermined glitch? Suppose they will not permit you to climb when you really do need to go up (like you are about to hit some trees at the end of the runway which is actually a known early event recorded on film).

There were other facets with which I was most unhappy. Both Airbus and my employer recommended use of auto thrust for all landings. I was to find that this facility lacked the finesse to sort out the rate of descent in the flare especially in gusty conditions. My practice quickly regressed to use of manual thrust for all approaches except those involving low visibility.

There were alarming anomalies in the systems. One afternoon I taxied out for a departure from Heathrow with an aircraft that had a history of fuel control computer problems. Half way to the holding point a series of warning messages appeared which while not prohibiting our departure made it unwise to continue. Back to the ramp and the engineers started work. An hour later they were still scratching their heads. A shift change sorted the problem. The engineer assigned from the new shift said,

"I've met this one before. You are having messages indicating a problem with number two fuel control computer. In actual fact the problem is number one fuel control computer which takes number two down with it!"

The whole genesis of aviation systems is duplication. To have one system take the other down with it is not good.

I say all these things with too little time on the aircraft to be overly critical. The two and a half years were really insufficient to even begin to understand the machine in the way I understood Boeings. There is no question the Airbus is a good aeroplane, appreciated by pilots and airlines alike, especially airline accountants! I am not sure the trend to over automation is good in any aircraft. The erosion of basic flying skills is a very serious spin off which is slowly being acknowledged.

There was one amusing incident on the Airbus worthy of recording.

It was a late night departure out of John F Kennedy for London. The ground engineer greeted us in the terminal and shook my hand. This was unusual protocol and suggested trouble.

"Er, Captain, we have a problem with your aircraft…!"

He went on to describe the nature of the difficulty. Everything on the Airbus is computerised and this time it was the toilets that were playing up. The computer was saying the effluent collector tanks were full even though physical indications were that they were empty. As such, only two toilets were functioning on the entire aircraft with a full load of some three hundred passengers checked in. The engineer was very keen for us to take the flight. It was the last service to London that evening and nobody, least of all the ground staff, wanted the chaos of a cancellation. I consulted with the cabin supervisor. She was happy to take the flight provided the passengers were told prior to boarding such that they should use the terminal toilets bearing in mind the limited facilities on board.

As a flippant aside, before the engineer went back to work I said,

"When I have a problem with the drains back home I just stick a broom handle up the pipe and that usually fixes it!"

About fifteen minutes later while we were seated in the flight deck doing pre-start checks, there was a horrendous smell from behind and the engineer re-appeared. His white overalls were streaked with effluent and blue fluid. He said sadly,

"That didn't work either captain!"

I didn't dream that he would take my suggestion seriously.

And so we departed. Being a night flight most passengers slept all the way and there was no problem. There was justification for my established practice of telling passengers the truth even if not the whole truth!

It all came to an end. My third from last flight was a nine day Sydney via Hong Kong. The crew, knowing of my imminent departure, made it a very pleasant experience. As a result I didn't tell the crew on the last two trips, a Delhi followed by a Shanghai, that I was going home for good.

Much has been written in these pages. Many incidents have been highlighted but the truth is that most aviating is a straightforward experience for passengers and crew alike. The book is written with an ulterior motive and I would beg the reader to spend a few minutes reading the epilogue.

EPILOGUE

So... what exactly is IT all about? By IT, I mean Life itself, the Universe, God, the devil, birth, death and so on.

Plato, Aristotle, Galileo, Isaac Newton, Neils Bohr, Albert Einstein, Stephen Hawking and countless others of lesser or greater repute through the ages have delved into the mysteries of the universe and come up with some answers.

Isaac Newton with the laws of motion and much else had some good scientific answers but he didn't need to know the 'Why' as he was a devout believer in The Lord God Almighty. Neils Bohr discovered much about the astonishing world of Quantum mechanics. Similarly Einstein put together the mind boggling theory of relativity. He was a believer in a Creator but regrettably never encountered a personal God...he just seems to have realized that the perfect order of the universe could not have occurred by accident.

Stephen Hawking[1] seems to have delved further into formulating 'The Theory of Everything'. His astonishing statement at the end of 'A brief History of Time'... "If we knew the answer to that we would know the mind of God!" betrays at least an acknowledgement that there might be more to life than physics. Apparently he has recently backtracked on this statement! String Theory is much in vogue these days. There is the possibility of eleven dimensions or more.

---

1 I was informed by the cabin crew towards the end of a flight from Los Angeles to London that the esteemed professor was on board. After landing I went downstairs to say hello before he disembarked but it was a curiously one sided conversation as they had taken away his computer which is his only means of communication!

It seems, the more we discover the more there is to discover. I would suggest that the multi-billion €uro "Large Hadron Collider" assembled at taxpayer's expense on the Franco Swiss border, will just reveal new mysteries.

One matter that is left completely blank in the realms of scientific discovery is the so called 'Spirit World'. True Believers in Almighty God have experienced this as have those who so unwisely delve into the realms of the occult. There are very few atheists in this world... plenty of agnostics as well as plenty who have simply not bothered to think about these things.

Those through the ages who have maligned or persecuted Believers simply for the sake of it are the most interesting. Why does real Christian Faith engender such hatred in so many? But then, who am I to talk? It is a wonderful and mysterious privilege to have encountered the true Love of God.

My friend Mike, fairly well known in the Aviation world, was the only true professing atheist I have ever met. Many years ago I made the mistake of trying to prove to him that God exists. This I manifestly failed to achieve. Since then I have never tried this again with him or anybody else but I can have a stab at proving the existence of the devil. Why does the human race feel the need to beat the brains out of its fellow humans individually and collectively sometimes on a grand scale at regular intervals in the paltry 6000 years of recorded human history?

The 'Theory of Everything' (which does exist) will neither be discovered nor revealed on this planet until at least the imminent end of the current human dispensation if at all. The reason for this is delightfully simple.

At the beginning of the Holy Bible there is the story of Adam and Eve and the Garden of Eden, the fall of man from God's grace and favour, and subsequent expulsion from the paradise that was the Garden. Worse was the loss of direct communication and intimate association with the Creator. Man was excommunicated for disobedience and "Cherubim with flaming swords were placed at the entrance to the garden lest man partake of the Tree of Life, become like one of us and live forever".

It is my contention that the Tree of Life is the 'Theory of Everything'. Only two trees in the Garden of Eden were named, the Tree of the Knowledge of Good and Evil, partaking of the fruit of which instigated the downfall of mankind, and the other the Tree of Life.

For years after my conversion I attempted to communicate my faith to those who were interested using intellectual discussion. This amounted to an unspectacular uphill struggle. I seemed to achieve little if anything at all. Some twenty years ago an older man suggested a different approach.

"Just tell folk what happened to you!"

That is the primary purpose of this book although I hope the reader will find the aviation recollections entertaining as a by-product.

Many have suggested, in some cases extremely forthrightly, that my talents would have been better employed in Missionary Aviation. There have been openings and I have been connected with these superb organizations over the years. The first approach was back in the late 1960's. A pioneering mission in Borneo was looking for a pilot to fly its one aircraft. Things went well with my application until there was a flat statement. We will need you to be first a missionary and secondly a pilot. Rightly or wrongly I felt that my heart was really towards aviation as a primary profession and that I would have made a very poor missionary.

Finally, I am not an evangelist. My wife Diane is and has proved over the years that she has a definite calling in this respect. However, by definition, I am a witness to my belief. Many times I have suggested to colleagues and others who are interested,

"Read one of the biographies of Jesus."

My favorite is John's gospel but there are three others, Matthew, Mark and Luke. It is surely very little loss to perform this small exercise. If in consequence there arises a spark of interest, it is no great difficulty to say to the Almighty, as I said some forty five years ago,

"If *You're* really there, what's *IT* all about?"

It doesn't matter if you are King Solomon, Richard Dawkins, Mother Theresa or Stephen Hawking; we all meet the same end. Repeating what I felt the need to say to one retired colleague shortly before he passed away,

"Eternity goes on for an awfully long time!"

Thus says the Lord…

"Let not the wise man glory in his wisdom,

Let not the mighty man glory in his might,

Let not the rich man glory in his riches;

But let him who glories, glory in this,

That he understands and knows ME,

That I am the Lord who practices

Steadfast love, justice and righteousness

In the earth;

For in these things I delight, says The Lord."

(Jeremiah 9v23)

GLOSSARY

DME. Distance Measuring Equipment. A ground transmitter that sends a signal which the aircraft equipment translates into distance from the transmitter. Australia seems to have developed this device for civil use long before the rest of the world. Eventually it became paired with VOR's and instrument landing systems internationally.

Downburst. Meteorological effect that can be encountered close to the ground in the vicinity of a thunderstorm. Thunderstorms, by definition involve rapid vertical movement of air both up and down. A rapid movement downwards, close to the ground has been termed a 'downburst' and is in effect a very serious form of windshear which can be lethal to an aircraft in the take-off or landing phase.

Elevator trim. Aircraft require trimming about all three axes; that is longitudinal (pitch), lateral (roll) and in azimuth (yaw). This is to avoid the pilot having to apply constant pressure on the controls. Large machines would be virtually un-flyable without elevator trim. The latter requires constant re-adjustment and this is usually accomplished by altering the angle of incidence of the stabiliser. From the flight deck this is often actuated by a thumb operated button on the control column. Airbus have made elevator trim automatic.

ETA. Estimated time of arrival.

Flight Director. Raw data instrument presentations are massively enhanced by the super-imposition of a flight director. The amount of pitch or bank required to maintain the correct flight path appears on the primary flight instrument in terms of following 'V' bars (Collins) or cross wires (Sperry).

HF. High Frequency communications radio. Long range radio using a characteristic of the ionosphere which allows the signal to bounce back to earth giving over the horizon communications.

Indicated air speed (IAS). The speed indicated on the airspeed indicator which, other than minor corrections is the pressure measured by the pitot head. This is a tube pointing forward into the airstream and at very low altitudes (e.g. crop spraying) it is giving an approximation of true airspeed. At high altitudes and varying air temperatures it is providing very useful aeronautical information with regard to stall/onset of buffet speed but it shows a considerably lower speed than the true speed of the aircraft through the air. True airspeed is computed and displayed on a different instrument although above about 28000 feet Mach number is used which shows a percentage of the speed of sound.

INS. Inertial Navigation system. This was a spin off from the US space programme. In essence precision gyros are fitted with accelerometers which detect any movement. Movements are then computed and presented to the pilot in terms of latitude and longitude. The present position of the aircraft before flight must be inserted by the pilot to enable the device to have an initial reference. The supreme advantage of this equipment is its total independence from external signals, e.g ground or satellite based radios.

ITCZ. Inter tropic convergence zone. This is an area of thunderstorms, predominately over land masses that, fluctuate North and South in the vicinity of the equator. They can be in line form and difficult to circumvent without a major route excursion.

Knots. (Kts) Nautical miles per hour. Measure of speed used for aviation and marine navigation. To be precise one nautical mile is the distance subtended by one minute of latitude on the surface of the earth. One nautical mile (nm) is about 15% more than a statute mile.

Leg and leg about. In most airlines the standard method of operating aircraft is for the Captain and co-pilot to alternate their duties. The captain retains overall authority but generally will share the flying with his co-pilot. So, for each sector or leg from A to B one man operates the aircraft using a combination of manual and automatic methods depending on the phase of flight and the other will operate all the ancillary equipment, gear, flaps, radios etc. as required by his colleague. For the next sector or leg the duties are reversed. There are variations on this for specific reasons such as a newly checked out captain will do all the flying for a probationary period. A captain can at any time choose to take control himself for reasons such as marginal weather or if the aircraft has a technical problem.

Lower 41. A cramped compartment under the flight deck of the Boeing 707 which gives some access to the nose wheel gear operating mechanism and some of the aircraft electronics. It was called 'lower 41' as this was the lower half of the aircraft fuselage and 41 inches aft of the aircraft datum which was defined as the forward pressure bulkhead. The position of any point in the fuselage could be defined by its distance in inches aft of this datum point. The corresponding much larger compartment on the Boeing 747 is also known (erroneously) by the same name which was inherited from the 707.

NDB Non Directional radio beacon transmits unidirectional signal for navigational purposes.

QFE Altimeter Pressure setting such that the altimeter will read zero at airfield height.

QNH Altimeter pressure setting such that the altimeter reads height above sea level.

Residual Thrust. Jet propulsion is in essence very simple. Air is taken into the front of the engine, compressed by a compressor, fuel is injected and ignited and the greatly enlarged mass of the burning fuel/air is ejected rearwards (through a turbine which drives the compressor) providing the thrust which drives the aircraft forwards. Electric ignition is used initially but after start-up the combustion is self-sustaining and the electric ignition is switched off. One of the inescapable by-products is residual thrust. The minimum self-sustaining rpm of the engine is such that a small amount of thrust is present at the lowest idle power setting. While taxiing, this can cause heating of brakes on earlier types with steel brakes, excessive and expensive brake wear if the brakes are repeatedly applied at taxy speeds with more modern carbon brakes and can be a great source of embarrassment when manoeuvring on slippery or icy taxiways.

Routes. Because of the distortion caused by wall maps which generally use the Mercator projection there are often questions from passengers with regard to the route an aircraft takes flying from A to B. To understand direct routes it is necessary to look at a globe. Despite this there are often variations caused by political boundaries, meteorological conditions and in particular flight planning for favourable winds. The latter can result in extraordinary route variations. E.g., the direct route Jeddah (Saudi Arabia) to and from New York, USA, in my experience, has varied from the most Northerly where we passed overhead Stornaway in the Outer Hebrides to the most Southerly, where we passed overhead Casablanca, Morocco.

Tropopause. Temperature decreases with altitude at approximately 2°C per thousand feet up to the Tropopause whereupon it stabilises and remains approximately the same until well above current aircraft operating altitudes. The tropopause varies in height being typically lower at the poles and higher at the Equator.

VHF. Very High Frequency radio. Short range line of sight communication.

VOR. Visual Omni Radio range. Ground radio signal from which the aircraft equipment interprets and displays which radial through 360° that the aircraft is flying from/to as a direction from the transmitting station. Line of sight only so not long range.

Windshear. Rapid variation of wind-speed which can be dangerous to aircraft especially when operating close to the ground, i.e. take-off and landing phases of flight.

Zero Fuel weight. A structural maximum weight designated by the aircraft manufacturer being the sum total of the payload and the aircraft prepared for service weight. The latter includes everything on board including crew and catering but not fuel.